Managing industrial relations

Consulting Editor
Professor George Thomason

Managing industrial relations

Mick Marchington

McGRAW-HILL Book Company (UK) Limited

London · New York · St Louis · San Francisco · Auckland · Bogotá
Guatemala · Hamburg · Johannesburg · Lisbon · Madrid · Mexico
Montreal · New Delhi · Panama · Paris · San Juan · São Paulo
Singapore · Sydney · Tokyo · Toronto

Published by
McGRAW-HILL Book Company (UK) Limited
MAIDENHEAD · BERKSHIRE · ENGLAND

British Library Cataloguing in Publication Data
Marchington, Mick.
  Managing industrial relations.
  1. Industrial relations.
  I. Title.
  658.3′15   HD6971
  ISBN 0-07-084580-8

Library of Congress Cataloging in Publication Data
Marchington, Mick.
  Managing industrial relations.
  Bibliography: p.
  Includes index.
  1. Industrial relations. 2. Industrial management.
  I. Title.
  HD6971.M3278   658.3′15   82-15319
  ISBN 0-07-084580-8   AACR2

1 2 3 4 5 AP 85432

Printed and bound in Great Britain at the Alden Press, Oxford

Contents

Preface

Industrial relations is a subject that always seems capable of attracting a great deal of attention whether it appears on the news, in the papers, on courses, or just in general conversation. The number of books written on industrial relations has grown over the years but there are still numerous gaps in the market, particularly for publications geared towards the intelligent manager who has not sufficient time to undertake an in-depth study but wants some further information or analysis on the subject. Such a person, it seems to me, has to make one of two choices—assuming, of course, they decide that further reading is worth while.

First of all, they can turn towards the more 'practical' texts such as those written by Whitehead (1977), Hunt (1977), or Hawkins (1979). The main purpose of these books is, to quote Hawkins, 'to assist managers—especially those who are apprehensive of industrial relations—to grapple with at least some of the problems they are likely to encounter from day to day' (1979, p. 11). Those by Hunt and Whitehead are even more practically orientated—the former geared towards an analysis based on a long period of experience in personnel management in the motor industry and the latter a very straightforward book in the Teach Yourself series. Neither of these make enough use of the available relevant work emanating from industrial relations academics, preferring to concentrate on the 'practical realities' as they see them.

On the other hand, interested managers can turn to the more 'academic' texts as those by Jackson (1977) and the rewritten and updated version of Clegg (1979). From previous experience, despite some useful chapters in both of these, the sheer volume and, at times, the complexities of academic argument have tended to put managers off searching for the relevant material. Again, Jackson, despite his attempts to 'demystify' industrial relations, often seems to confuse and alienate the management student of the subject. Similarly, many of the books on more 'detailed' subjects—such as the work on shop stewards by Batstone et al. (1977)—are often ignored because of their sociological language and mass of information, and this causes the student to overlook the rich insights that books such as these are able to offer. In a similar vein, books such as the ones by Beynon (1973) and by Nichols and Beynon (1977) tend to be mistrusted because of the perceived 'political' undertones, although, these too can contribute significantly in helping managers to understand issues because they are written from a different perspective.

What would appear to be needed by the average line manager is a book that synthesizes the best from the academic and the practical work and presents it in a readable yet analytical form. This is most necessary from the angle of the academic work since a more practical approach is needed in relatively plain language. Another priority would appear to be a publication that provides line managers with more background knowledge relevant to their own jobs—one that will assist them to make decisions (by whatever means) based on more appropriate information and guide them as to possible sources for gathering this for themselves in the future. And finally—and perhaps most important of all—one that challenges them to examine their own attitudes and behaviour and to see the way in which this might influence their approach to industrial relations. In other words, to apply some form of gentle criticism for a failure to treat industrial relations rigorously enough, and an exhortation to adopt a systematic approach to the subject.

This book, therefore, addresses itself to two fundamental questions. Firstly, in what way does industrial relations impinge upon the job of the line manager who, after all, has major priorities in achieving production objectives rather than in developing employee relations? And, secondly, what does the line manager need to know and do in order to fulfil these aspects of the job? The remainder of the book is organized around these particular issues.

More specifically, the text proceeds as follows. The first three chapters set the scene by outlining the way in which industrial relations has evolved into its present-day state.

In *Chapter 1*, we introduce the subject by the use of a case study examining an issue that arose in a company in which the author was undertaking a detailed research investigation. This takes the form of a series of interviews with people from the factory—with management from different functions, a foreman, two shop stewards, and a man off the shop floor whom I literally bumped into! The aim of this case study is to bring out some of the widely differing perceptions that were held of this issue and the differing objectives, opportunities, and constraints that the issue had for each person. In addition, it will enable us to explore some of the underlying concepts of industrial relations that will guide us through the rest of the study. The second half of the chapter provides a brief run-down of industrial relations over the course of the last 15 years and describes the way in which this is influencing the job of the line manager. While acknowledging that there may be a potential conflict between the industrial relations demands on the manager's time and that of the production/consumer demands, it is suggested that a longer-term approach to industrial relations is required by the line manager, one in which he is willing not only to examine his own attitudes and biases, but also *really* to try to understand the position of other actors in the workplace. To focus, that is, on integrative and long-term approaches to bargaining, as Walton and McKersie (1965) term it, rather than on the fire-fighting skills or short-term negotiating tactics that may result in no more than Pyrrhic victories.

Chapter 2 considers the development and nature of trade unionism in Great Britain. Without going into too much historical detail, we attempt to analyse the significance of the past and describe some of the consequences of this development, particularly as these may influence workplace industrial relations. Although it may not always have been in the direction that management would like, trade unions have adapted considerably over the past century, and, it is argued, it is better that individual managers know more about this evolution so as to enable them to work with unions in a more effective manner.

In *Chapter 3* we look at the management approaches to industrial relations, noting the distinction between pluralistic and unitary frames of reference originally applied by Fox back in 1966. Three fundamental differences are observed between these two frames of reference: that is, in their willingness to accept the role of unionism, in their desire to maintain traditional managerial prerogatives in relations with employees, and in their understanding of, and approach to, conflict resolution. It is suggested that the pluralistic approach offers the more appropriate way forward for the line manager, although it is noticeable how easily managers can shift between the two, adopting some kind of, what might be termed, 'pragmatic pluralism'.

The next three chapters analyse the role played by the other actors in the workplace industrial relations system and attempt to suggest ways in which the line manager might be able to understand and improve these interpersonal relations.

Chapter 4 looks at the position of employee/union member and assesses the significance of employment and union membership for this group of people. In particular, the chapter is directed at a consideration of different approaches to employee motivation, to 'loyalty', and to union commitment. The concept of 'loyalty'—or dual loyalties, split loyalties, or 'disloyalty'—is especially significant in industrial relations and it is often suggested that managers tend to equate opposition with disloyalty. But, loyalty works from both angles in the employment relationship, and many employees feel that it is the management, rather than themselves, who is disloyal, uncooperative, and inefficient.

In *Chapter 5*, the analysis moves on to consider the role of the key workplace union representative—the shop steward—so as to bring our appreciation of this role up to date. Some basic information is provided concerning the duties that the steward undertakes and recent research findings are used to outline the different types of steward that exist, the ways in which they come to occupy their position, and the relations with their constituents. Some attention is paid to the increasing significance of steward organizations in the workplace. We conclude by suggesting some ways in which managers may learn to work *with* the shop steward.

Since the steward is often seen by foremen as a direct competitor for influence on the shop floor, we shift our analysis to the latter in *Chapter 6*. A brief historical review helps us to place the position of the foreman in perspective and enables us to identify a number of problems that seem to have been confronting such a person for a number of years. If anything, the position of the foreman is becoming even more uncertain and ambiguous as we enter the eighties, and we suggest that management—as a whole—needs to be aware of just where the foreman is going to fit into future organizational design.

In *Chapters 7, 8, 9,* and *10,* we turn to an analysis of power—and the way in which conflict may be generated at work—and then to a description of several different mechanisms for channelling or institutionalizing that conflict on the one hand, or trying to promote consensus on the other. In *Chapter 7*, the analysis of power causes us to focus on the nature of that concept, and on the so-called negative or positive manifestations of that power by unions and their members. More specifically, union power is analysed in terms of four separate elements—namely, capacity, realization, testing, and outcomes—in an attempt to explain why it is that certain groups of workers appear to be more successful in their use of power, or more willing to use it, than others. In addition, it must not be forgotten that some of the most powerful groups in society never need to 'flex their muscles' since their demands are readily met without any attempt to confront them. In the case of unions and workgroups, management has not been slow in devising strategies to either lessen the likelihood of action or reduce the chances of unions succeeding should they decide to take any form of industrial action; we conclude the chapter by looking at some of these strategies.

Chapter 8 provides an assessment of procedures as a potential mechanism for institutionalizing discontent and smoothing the process of change. The primary emphasis in this chapter is with grievance and disputes procedures, on the value they may hold for managers, and on a brief interpretation of their design. This idea is continued in *Chapter 9* when we look at the impact of the law on workplace industrial relations, focusing in particular upon dismissal and discipline, and on health and safety. Advice is given on the basic ground-rules of handling disciplinary issues and on the kind of issues that may confront the line manager. This chapter is not intended as a substitute for either a regularly updated employment case law book or the use of experts in a personnel department; rather, it is intended as a supplement to these so as to enable line managers to operate fairly and within the law. The use of agreed procedures is seen as a vital element of good industrial relations.

In *Chapter 10*, we look at attempts to promote consensus or structure expectations through the use of employee involvement. Rather than restrict ourselves to a description of the variety of available forms of participation, we concentrate on the different meanings that participation has to the different actors in the workplace, and on the problems and opportunities it may present for the line manager. Since joint consultation has undergone some kind of resurgence during the seventies, we base our discussion around this institution. In particular, we stress that management commitment to consultation extends far beyond the confines of a monthly meeting, and the success of consultation may be judged on the shop floor by day-to-day management activity and adherence to a participative approach.

The importance of placing industrial relations within its overall situation is dealt with in *Chapter 11*. That is, that certain environmental factors or contingencies may have a considerable influence upon workplace industrial relations, especially in the way in which they may be perceived by managers—and consequently their approach to decision making—or they may affect employee attitudes to work. The framework that is developed in this chapter should help the individual line manager to place industrial relations in his own establishment in a clearer perspective. Finally, in *Chapter 12*, we tie up a few loose ends, and take another look at the case study.

Three final points need to be made before we enter the main body of the book. Firstly, the use of the word 'employee' refers to people on the shop floor in the main, and is used solely as a means of distinguishing between managers, foremen, shop stewards, and the 'ordinary' employee; it is not meant to imply that these other people are *not* employees—at least, it is better in this respect than the use of the word 'worker' to describe these people! Secondly, the pronoun 'he' is used regularly to refer to the line manager during the book; again, this is not meant to be sexist and, whenever possible, I have used the collective word although this has not always been appropriate. Finally, it is to be hoped that this book stimulates the reader to think a little bit more deeply about industrial relations and apply some of the ideas to his own place of work. Because of this, the whole thrust of the book is geared towards a long-term conception of 'good industrial relations' rather than the currently fashionable 'macho' management techniques adopted in certain workplaces. It is the belief of the author—and many other writers and industrialists, as well as union leaders—that cooperative approaches offer the only realistic solution to minimizing problems in industry, and for developing the trust that is essential for good employee relations at work. This book is written with such a perspective in mind.

Acknowledgements

It is always difficult to acknowledge specific contributions in a book such as this, especially those that help in the formulation of ideas. Many managers have talked to me, been interviewed and observed by me, and discussed issues with me during day-release classes over the years; as such, they have all played a part in this book. Geoff Broad, John Purcell, and, in particular, my colleague at Preston, Roger Armstrong, have all made helpful criticisms of the first draft of this book. Barry Fitzpatrick read and commented upon Chapter 9 with a legal eye. George Thomason provided some very useful and appropriate advice and Dorothy Fincham (of McGraw Hill) spurred me on. Nora Griffin and Julie Cummins did most of the typing of the book with occasional help from dictionaries and other staff in the Polytechnic. The best support, however, came from Lorrie Grice who took paper cuttings, read some of the manuscript, encouraged me, and, above all else, ensured I was at my desk for a full day's work. If, after all this help, any errors remain, I accept full responsibility.

MICK MARCHINGTON
Preston
July 1981

1. Managing workplace industrial relations

Twenty years ago, it would probably have been neither appropriate nor necessary to write a book on industrial relations for the line manager. Over this period, however, there have been a large number of changes that have elevated the industrial relations aspects of his job to a crucial level. As we shall see below, many of the recommendations of the Donovan Commission— which reported in 1968—have been taken on board by companies, and the line manager faces a variety of pressures from senior management, personnel departments, and shop stewards that were barely visible back in the sixties. Consequently, two fundamental questions need to be posed:

1. What impact has industrial relations had upon the role of the line manager?
2. What does he need to know, and do, in order to manage the industrial relations aspects of his job effectively?

The remainder of the book is organized around these two separate but interrelated questions.

The aim of this first chapter is to set the scene and derive some broad ideas about industrial relations at workplace level. We shall do this by describing an issue that arose in a company in which the author was involved in a comprehensive research project for a period of two years. We shall examine the issue by drawing upon the case notes of interviews with a number of people at the factory, and then using these to outline some of the key concepts of industrial relations. The second half of the chapter will then focus exclusively upon the line manager; we shall describe the dominant approach to industrial relations over the last 10 years and assess how this affects the actual job done by the line manager. With this in mind, we can conclude by suggesting a number of things of which the line manager needs to be aware in order to manage workplace industrial relations.

Industrial relations in action

As in many cases, it is rarely a single incident that *causes* unrest on the shop floor; rather, this incident may seek to bring more deep-rooted fears to the surface or provide an issue around which support can be mobilized. This particular incident that led to a walk-out in one department—and that later came to be called a 'demonstration' rather than a strike—is no exception.

The company—with the pseudonym Kitchenco—operates in the kitchen furniture market and is located in the West Midlands. It employs (1976 figures, which is when the issue arose) approximately 700 people, of which nearly 500 work on the shop floor. It is part of a larger holding company that allows a considerable amount of autonomy to each of the subsidiaries in their industrial relations. At the time, the market was highly variable, competition was intense, and there was pressure from consumers to reduce delivery dates; This final factor posed serious problems for line management as it attempted to maximize production in the face of machine breakdowns, lack of piece parts, and shop floor pressure for job security and consistent earnings. To say the least, its working days were hectic!

Two separate issues brought the matter to a head in one department. Due to a sudden demand for orders, management had to switch production from one predetermined plan to another; this was not an unusual occurrence. It became obvious that certain parts would need to 'bought-in' from outside, rather than assembled on the premises, in order to satisfy this demand. Again, in previous meetings with the joint shop stewards committee, this practice was not opposed provided there was prior consultation with the stewards; this was generally done by senior line managers although, on this occasion, a failure to conform with procedural nicety led to a strong shop floor response. On its own, this would probably not have resulted in a walk-out although, when combined with the second issue, it appeared to the shop floor that management were only concerned with production matters and not with their concerns or fears.

The second issue was a recurrent problem with heaters. Management had been made aware of breakdowns in the heating equipment that, during winter, were particularly serious in those parts of the factory that had large doors to enable fork-lift trucks to come in and out. For several days in succession, the heating equipment alongside these doors had failed during the morning; the maintenance section had mended them temporarily while a search was made to discover whether an alternative system would overcome these problems. Eventually, and largely due to the first issue explained above, the members of this department—over 100 in all—had 'downed tools' and gone home. As it happened, the men and women were back at work 24 hours later.

In order to see this incident from a number of angles, we shall deal with the case notes that I put together from interviews with the following people on the day of the stoppage:

1. The production manager.
2. A foreman in the department involved.
3. The personnel manager.
4. A steward in the department involved.
5. The senior steward.
6. A shop floor employee from another department.

The production manager

The production manager saw the issue of the bought-in parts as a very unlucky occurrence. It was not that management did not intend to consult but, rather, that the truck arrived at least one day before it had been expected. The heating issue was regarded as an 'old perennial' and one that could not be solved without a complete overhaul or purchase of new machinery; this was something that, he felt, maintenance could have put more effort into. He felt that he had problems not only with production but also with the calibre of his foremen and the stewards. In particular, he emphasized the lack of foresight of the foreman in the department involved and of the failure of the steward to 'control' his members. He used his powers of persuasion to organize a meeting with the stewards later in the day and spent the rest of his time collecting information relevant to the case. He was concerned that the stewards might escalate the issue and break down the trust he felt had been achieved in the factory; he was also concerned that, in order to get the men and women back to work, he would end up being even more tied to prior consultation than he was before.

The foreman

The foreman did not have much sympathy for the shop floor over either of these issues; he felt that it should have been prepared to carry on working despite the cold and that it was much too 'mollycoddled' by the personnel department and legislation on health and safety. Concerning the 'buying-in' of materials, while he could appreciate its fears over job security, he did not think its action was likely to do any good whatsoever. He also felt that there was a lack of support for the walk-out—he had spoken to one or two people as they left—and that the stewards had been carried away with the euphoria of a mass meeting. In many ways, he had 'opted-out' of a number of his responsibilities, particularly in passing issues straight through to manage-ment. His attitude was that, since he did not have any authority any more, it was a waste of time trying to deal with them on the shop floor. He was very resentful of the access the steward had to, and the rapport he had with, senior management.

The personnel manager

The personnel manager was highly critical of both the line management and the stewards for letting the issue get to this point. Having devised systems for dealing with grievances—such as the heating issue—and introduced a consultative and steward–management committee system, he was annoyed that neither party appeared to use them. In particular, he was critical of the foremen and managers in view of the training they had received. He felt the steward in the department concerned was a bit of a troublemaker but his relations with the senior steward were such that he hoped to persuade him to deal with the issue. He felt it was important to stress the sovereignty of procedures and that this was the best line of attack to get the men and women back to work. He was upset that this strike was the first for four years—he thought industrial relations had improved.

The departmental steward
Two things were clear from an analysis of the departmental steward's case notes. Firstly, as far as he was concerned, management had now lost all credibility; particularly, since it had made promises concerning prior consultation at the previous stewards meeting and then, just two days later and having denied a delivery was imminent, it had bought in parts. The heating issue just showed that it was only concerned about production, and employee relations counted for nothing. Secondly, he had never known feelings run so high on the section—'the men were really *heated* about this!'—and he felt that he had little option to keep them at work even if he had wanted to. They felt let down by management after all they had done to try and keep production up.

The senior steward (same union)
The senior steward's whole response was overwhelmingly procedural; that is, that despite any good reason for taking action, a walk-out was not the best way to get the issue resolved. He felt that the stewards—as a body—would now find it harder to persuade management to follow procedures now that the stewards themselves had acted on impulse. He had called in the full-time official to see if he could deal with the issue more quickly. Despite the fact that all the members were in the same union, there was not much love lost between the various departments. For one thing, action or lack of production in one department soon affected the others. Secondly, employees in the two major departments—mills and assembly—had been in separate unions until 1971 and, even now, it was difficult to overcome the hostility between the different sections of the membership. Nevertheless, he did feel that an important principle was at stake and that, now management were aware of the intensity of feeling in the factory, a return to work would help them in their forthcoming discussions with management.

Employee from another department
These notes came from a fairly brief chat with someone whom I had met during the earlier part of my research. This employee was highly critical of the

other section for walking out and could see no reason for their so doing. So far as he was concerned, the issue revolved around the heating problem and it was seen as a response to a lack of heating on that particular day *alone*. Consequently, he felt the action was unjustified. In addition to the fact that he was 'against any strikes altogether', his knowledge of the particular issue was very sketchy indeed. If anything, he was the most 'hawkish' person I talked to that day.

At the meeting on the afternoon of the 'demonstration', the management and stewards worked out a formula for a return to work. Management convinced the stewards of the 'need' for the bought-in work in view of pressing order commitments. It also agreed to give as much prior consultation as possible on any future occasion; in practice, this resulted in being little more than information disclosure a few days in advance of a delivery. For their part, the stewards persuaded management to overhaul the heaters, bring in extra equipment when appropriate, and to install a new door system wherever this was possible. The atmosphere was tense for the next few weeks but then things returned very much to normal; there were no more stoppages during my period there. The uneasy alliance between the different departments continued and a subsequent analysis of questionnaires—in response to another sub-ject—showed clear-cut differences between members in their attitudes to work and commitment to unionism.

Key characteristics of industrial relations
Industrial relations is centred around the institution of collective bargaining and, as can be seen from the interview material, this emerged in a number of ways during the incident at Kitchenco. Bargaining can take place at a number of different *levels*; between line management and stewards is probably the major one for the purpose of this book, but it is also important to consider the way in which bargaining at national level may dictate terms and conditions in certain industries and leave very little room for additions at establishment and workplace level. Personnel managers and full-time officers often have a degree of contact that extends beyond a formal relationship around the bargaining table and each may try to persuade the other through informal chats or other mechanisms; so too may convenors in their relations with senior line management or personnel. At a lower level, a high degree of informal bargaining may take place as a matter of course between foremen and stewards, particularly in the context of piecework systems.

However, it is too restrictive to conceive of industrial relations in terms of pay or the effort-reward bargain alone. The *scope* of collective bargaining can involve, as we saw above, discussion over working conditions, work allocation, or job security issues. In addition to such substantive issues, managers and stewards (or full-time officials) will usually be involved in negotiating matters of procedural concern; that is, devising grievance and disputes machinery, disciplinary procedures, or those to cover health and safety, redundancy, or the introduction of new technology. Again, in the absence of industry-wide or company agreements, these may be negotiated at workplace level. While it is usual for most of these agreements to be written down or codified, it is not always the case (Marsh, 1981, p. 47).

Finally, collective bargaining can be analysed in terms of the *degree* of joint regulation that it provides. This could be seen as a continuum with total employer control or insistence upon managerial prerogatives at one extreme, and total employee or union control at the other. Management, for example, may refuse to disclose information or bargain about plant location or investment policies. Conversely, there will be occasions on the shop floor where employees maintain job control through custom and practice, or where unions regulate entry to a trade through the apprenticeship system.

If collective bargaining is a key characteristic of industrial relations, it follows that such bargaining will take place between different *parties*. In simple terms, we can conceive of a union side and a management side. However, such a notion is wide of the mark for at least two reasons. First of all, neither 'side' is consistently unified and much bargaining, and also disagreement, takes place *within* either party as well as *between* them. Within management, for example, we have identified the possibility of conflicting objectives between different functions and between different levels. It is common to see the objectives of a sales department conflicting with those of a production function. Similarly, the demands placed upon line management in terms of adherence to procedure agreements may cause conflict between it and the personnel function. Generally, however, the overriding objective of companies to secure adequate profitability will help to integrate these differing sub-objectives. On the union side, this is less easy. As we saw above, conflicts can also exist between departments—and the membership in each of these—and between different levels in the steward hierarchy. Even greater differences may become manifest between different trade groups, or between the leadership and the rank and file, and this is something we shall examine in detail in Chapter 2. Suffice it to say at this stage that manifest conflict within the union movement has often led to change and a response from the leadership to take account of the dynamics of unionism, particularly at workplace level.

But, the simple notion of two parties also falls down due to the neglect of a role for *third-party governmental intervention*. This can take a number of forms; for example, legislation in employee relations has developed considerably since the sixties and in Chapter 9 we deal with this in detail. Furthermore, the role of the Government in pay restraint or regulation has been primarily interventionist since the Second World War, whether it be through some formal mechanism or through imposition of strict cash limits for local and central government. Of course, the Government also has a dual role as a major employer. However, for the private sector, the role of third-party intervention has probably been seen at its most favourable through the agencies of 'independent' or tripartite bodies such as the Advisory, Conciliation, and Arbitration Service (ACAS) set up in 1975.

A third key characteristic of industrial relations that deserves attention, alongside the institution of collective bargaining and analysis of the parties to it, is that of *conflict and cooperation*. It would seem that, for many people, industrial relations is all about conflict since this is often the only time it comes to their attention through exposure on the television, radio, or newspapers. Consequently, there is a danger that the general public develop a distorted view of industrial relations, one that does little to help our competitive position at home or abroad or may lead to pressure for legislation that would be neither appropriate nor necessary for much of industry, and may indeed serve to be counterproductive in attempts to improve both productivity and industrial relations.

Of course, it would be equally naive to assume that industry is always based upon cooperation. As we saw in the case study, conflict is to some extent inherent in industrial relations; it may become manifest through a strike, for example, or it may be contained or institutionalized through the joint development of procedures. Just as it is wrong to assume that conflict is *necessarily* bad, it is equally wrong to automatically equate a lack of conflict with cooperation, good industrial relations, and high productivity. Conflict may become manifest as a strategy for either side, just as may cooperation, and—as we saw above—industrial action may be taken (that is, conflict may become manifest) after years of industrial peace (when conflict was either latent or channelled into alternative areas).

Finally, and this was probably the clearest factor to emerge from the case study, we must take into account the perceptions of issues, and the meanings they have for the participants when we examine industrial relations. In this case, the line manager saw the 'demonstration' in terms of personalities whereas the personnel manager conceived of it by way of procedures. The foreman felt it was yet one more example of management weakness and shop floor strength: the stewards saw it in terms of principles—one of a failure of management commitment, the other in terms of maintaining unity and procedures. For the employee from another department, it was just stupid. Clearly, the interpretation that these different individuals put on those events influenced the way in which they ordered their reactions to them, and what may seem illogical to one party may be perfectly rational when seen from the standpoint of another. This kind of approach, which is usually labelled action theory, will underpin much of the rest of the argument.

To reiterate the terms of reference within which we shall operate, we shall study throughout the whole book the institution of collective bargaining—both between the parties and within them—in order to appreciate the likelihood of conflict or cooperation in industrial relations, emphasizing in particular the importance of the perceptions of key actors involved in the process.

Post-Donovan industrial relations

In all probability, the most significant impact upon plant-level and workplace industrial relations over the last 20 years has come from the Donovan Commission, and the subsequent activities that have occurred to alter relationships operating in the plant and the position of labour law. The Commission was set up in 1965 due to a concern that the industry-wide system of industrial relations, which had operated effectively in this country for a number of years, was no longer capable of coping with pressures occurring at workplace level. This was being expressed in a number of ways:

1. A failure to deal with grievances and disputes quickly enough.
2. An increase in unofficial strikes.
3. 'Chaotic' pay structures and earnings drift.
4. Restrictive practices, a growth in overtime, inefficiency, and a reluctance to change.
5. A general decline in discipline on the shop floor.

What it was felt was needed, therefore, was an examination of the system and some new initiatives.

The Commission's major finding is well known; that is, that Britain has two systems of industrial relations: one formal and the other informal. As mentioned above, 'the formal system assumes industry-wide organisations capable of imposing their decisions on their members. The informal system rests on the wide autonomy of managers in individual companies and factories, and the power of industrial work groups' (1968, p. 36).

The report then went on to indicate the details of these differences in terms of the scope of bargaining at both levels and the formality of agreements committed to paper. It continued, 'the formal and informal systems are in conflict. The informal system undermines the regulative effect of industry-wide agreements. . . . Nevertheless, the assumptions of the formal system still exert a powerful influence over men's minds and prevent the informal system from developing into an effective and orderly method of regulation'. It considered that there was no way in which the informal system could be forced to comply with the formal since 'reality cannot be forced to comply with pretences' (1968, p. 36).

Recommendations placed the onus on boards of directors to review industrial relations within their undertakings and to develop orderly and effective agreements at the level of the company or establishments. This, it was felt, would take into account the realities of workplace industrial relations and lead to the development of agreements that 'suit the circumstances' of each organization (1968, p. 262). Factory agreements would cover *substantive* items such as pay, overtime, productivity, health and safety, and job evaluation, and also *procedural* items such as facilities for shop stewards and for redundancy, grievances, and disciplinary matters.

As Purcell has argued, these changes were mainly concerned with the structural elements of what the Commission saw as good industrial relations; there were also processes that accompanied these reforms and these rested on three basic assumptions; firstly, that there would need to be a centralization of power and authority within both management and union organizations. Secondly, and alongside this, there must be some acceptance by those governed by these new institutions that the rules that they produce are 'appropriate, relevant and workable'. On both sides, this can be open to question. Finally, the negotiators would need to achieve a new working relationship with each other developed around 'a set of shared understandings based on discretion and trust' (1981, pp. 29–30).

In other words, the reform of industrial relations required not only structural alterations but also some change in attitudes by both parties.

On the management side, a number of changes were suggested. Firstly, and at an attitudinal level, it was expected to accept trade unions formally as partners in the workplace rather than allow *de facto* rights to stewards as was the case in many industries. Secondly, it placed the onus upon it to enter into advance planning on a much greater scale than had previously been the norm. The most fundamental notion that Donovan and others appeared to wish managers to hold was that industrial relations required foresight, planning, and top-level involvement, at least in giving support to changes in it; above all else then Donovan promulgated the necessity of having an industrial relations strategy. Finally, and developing out of this, it required management to take the initiative in reforming industrial relations; to quote Flanders' famous phrase that management 'can only regain control by sharing it' and that 'the responsibility for the reconstruction of workplace relations must fall primarily on the mangement of individual companies ... it is an exercise in planning—by consent ... so as to produce order and consistency within the workplace' (1970, pp. 172 and 208).

Many companies have adopted the Donovan proposals and developed a coherent industrial relations policy. For example, Gill describes the formulation of policy at the CWS (1974, p. 22), Hawkins gives an example of a series of policy statements for a hypothetical local authority (1979, pp. 236–43), and Friedman and Meredeen explain Ford's policy of forward planning and a strongly proactive management strategy (1980, p. 346).

There are a number of reasons for having such a policy; firstly, as a means of ensuring *consistency* between operations and different establishments. Secondly, it enables line management to know exactly where it stands in industrial relations in order to remove uncertainty, and it provides guidelines to assist it in its activities. Thirdly, if published, it enables employees (other than management) to know the position of their employer on a variety of matters. Indeed, the intervention of the law in the fields of dismissal and health and safety has also increased the necessity for this. Fourthly, it causes management to plan ahead in industrial relations and encourages it to be 'prospective, proactive and creative' in its conduct rather than 'restrospective, reactive and defensive' (Shields, 1979, p. 13). Finally, and perhaps most optimistically, it should enable industrial relations objectives to tie in with general business objectives and allow for the importance of industrial relations to be identified as a crucial variable in managing the organization. Interestingly enough, a recent survey noted that, even though managements were generally more 'systematically' alive to employee relations nowadays, the use made of policies and new machinery is 'patchy and there is only intermittent evidence that, at bottom, Boards of Directors have moved far from the traditional view that employee relations are a factor to be taken into account only as and when the need arises' (Marsh, 1981, p. 35).

Before moving on to examine the position of the line manager confronted by these possible changes, it might be worth summarizing what would be the key elements of an industrial relations policy. It would be wrong to prescribe a 'model' policy since differing organizational demands should lead to emphasis on certain aspects to the neglect of others; rather the checklist below might be most usefully seen as a stimulus to ask these sort of questions of one's own organization.

---

1. *What is the role of trade unionism in the company?* e.g., union recognition, which unions, degree of recognition, steward activity, facilities, training, constituencies, and union membership—encouragement (?) of closed shops.

2. *Organization and structure of collective bargaining?* e.g., flexibility allowed by external agreements, incomes policy, and so on, scope of collective bargaining, degree of joint regulation, appropriate levels at which to bargain, role of custom and practice, design of payment systems, bonus, overtime arrangments, and health and safety factors.

3. *Role of management in general?* e.g., part played by personnel departments, need for specialists, discretion for line management, role of supervision in industrial relations, and management 'philosophy'.

4. *Procedure agreements/legal enactments?* e.g., importance of procedures for discipline, grievance, disputes, redundancy, willingness (?) to abide by the law, knowledge of the law, counselling, appeals, and so on.

5. *Participation and consultation?* e.g., objectives of these arrangements, aims, aspirations, scope of consultation, level most appropriate for consultation, and board membership.

6. *Training and development?* e.g., management development, specific training in industrial relations, and role of joint management–steward training.

It must be remembered that policy should not be drafted 'on high' and implemented without a considerable amount of discussion and involvement. Clearly, a policy can never start from a clean sheet since there will be existing policies and practices that need to be taken into account, clarified, and, if no longer appropriate, amended. It may well be that a policy does no more than 'articulate and justify well-established attitudes and operating methods'. If it contains *'aspirations, objectives and strategies which are alien to the existing framework of custom and practice, it is unlikely to be observed by those managers to whom it applies'* (Hawkins, 1979, p. 229—my emphasis).

The role of the line manager

Up to this point, the emphasis has been on the degree to which management might seek to be proactive in industrial relations, to take the initiative, and to establish procedures for governing on the shop floor. The commitment to greater forward planning is something that is enshrined in any policy and is probably one with which most managers would agree; to plan ahead is important, they would argue, but industrial relations on the shop floor (and, to a much lesser extent, in the office) moves far too quickly to allow this to take place. Rather, the essential requirement for the 'good' manager is an ability to think quickly, to be flexible, to judge when to move and when not, and, most important of all, to get production out of the door. Employee relations is important in so far as it can affect production, but the latter has to take priority; because of this, there may be some conflict between himself and the personnel department.

A large number of studies have been undertaken on managers' jobs in an attempt to classify and categorize the nature of managerial work. Most of these have used diaries and have been geared towards improving training courses (Stewart, 1965, 1967a, 1967b, 1976). Other researchers have used participant observation to enable classification or to improve understanding of the manager's job (Mintzberg, 1973; Marchington, 1980).

Whichever the method adopted, a very similar picture emerges; that is, one of superficiality caused primarily by the open-ended nature of the manager's job, the heavy workload, and the large number of conflicting demands on his time (Mintzberg, 1973, p. 5). Mintzberg summarizes the job neatly as one 'characterized by brevity, variety and fragmentation. The vast majority (of contacts) are of brief duration, of the order of seconds for foremen and minutes for chief executives. A great variety of activities are performed, but with no obvious patterns. The trivial is interspersed with the consequential so that the manager must shift moods quickly and frequently. There is great fragmentation of work and interruptions are commonplace' (1973, p. 171). Marples sees more order in the day and conceives of the manager's job pictured as 'a stranded rope made of fibres of different lengths—each fibre coming to the surface one or more times in observable "episodes" and representing a single "issue"' (1967, p. 287). Despite assertions to the contrary, this style is not disliked; there tends to be a gravitation towards the 'active' aspects of the job, and the manager may well show a preference for brevity and interruption in his work (Mintzberg, 1973, pp. 35 and 171). Indeed, it has also been suggested that top management likes exciting as well as profitable companies (Winkler, 1974, p. 200) and that this may lead to a dislike of forward planning, paperwork, and working on one's own.

To the outsider, the manager's job often appears hectic and disorganized although, for the manager himself, there is no reason to suppose it lacks any inherent logic. Batstone and his colleagues, in their study of shop stewards in the engineering industry, recorded that the manager's day was characterized by 'continual uncertainty and the need for rapid adjustment to crisis. . . . Snap decisions have to be made . . . the situation is highly mobile . . . acting on the basis of "hunch" and "gut-feeling"' (1977, p. 157). Other studies have also indicated a similar situation in a variety of industries as diverse as engineering, chemicals, electrical switchgear, and furniture manufacture. In other words, activity on the shop floor may not be particularly conducive to central direction or forward planning. Indeed, as Brown remarks 'the rules that actually prevailed (on the shop floor) had little or no resemblance to those that had originally been laid down by management (at higher levels) or by formal agreement'. (1973, p. 85.)

One does not have to look far to see why this should be so. The line manager is essentially caught between two conflicting pressures; those of the product market on the one hand—which accords a priority to the consumer, to production, and to profit—and those of the labour force on the other—with the consequent emphasis upon fairness, consistency, and pressure for involvement in or, at least, accountability for decision making. Owen expresses this concept diagramatically and sees the manager caught very much between two fires, each pushing him in opposite directions (1979, pp. 5–9).

The more he attempts to satisfy one, the more he is *likely* to experience difficulties or pressures from the other. Optimistically, however, Owen does not see this as an insurmountable problem but, rather, as a challenge for which the manager needs to use his skills and develop his ability (1979, p. 12). Nor is this kind of problem peculiar to any one kind of organization; whether big or small, the manager's job has primarily to be related to efficiency whether this be profit or cost orientated and he has to manage his resources to achieve this as best he can.

Since production values, expressed through the pressure of immediate and measurable targets, are generally the predominant concern, it is industrial relations that is often sub-optimized or satisfied (Purcell, 1979, p. 1040). Directives from personnel departments may not have quite the same force or immediacy as those emanating from the customer or the production director. After all, it would be argued, it does not matter how 'good' our industrial relations are if we have no market in which to sell goods or we do not meet deadlines. Because of this, rule breaking can even be accommodated on pragmatic grounds. Indeed, as Purcell argues, 'even if industrial relations have been formalised and structured it has proved to be difficult to maintain the system, especially in the face of pressures from the product market, for example, to meet delivery deadlines. Compromise and "making-do", getting agreement even if it means breaking the rules laid down often predominate' (1979, p. 1038).

Is it worth while, then, actually formulating and publishing an industrial relations policy in view of the nature of the line manager's job? Some would argue that it is not since rule breaking and informality are inevitable on the shop floor. At least four reasons are put forward in support of this: firstly, it is impossible to apply any rule consistently and to the letter since the characteristics of each case may be peculiar to that particular one. Secondly, it is useful for the line manager to have some flexibility in order to 'trade' with the shop floor. Management (or supervision) may apply a rule leniently in exchange for cooperation on production or 'rush' jobs (Terry, 1977; p. 81). Thirdly, and developing on from this, the flexibility to condone leniency also allows the manager the ability to *withdraw* that privilege should he fail to get the cooperation he wants. And, finally, management may not consider it to be worth the effort and possible disruption to change these practices unless they get totally out of hand (Terry, 1977, p. 88).

In reported cases in which an industrial relations policy was introduced or there was some move towards the establishment of centralized in-plant bargaining, line management has complained of its loss of freedom and authority, and has initially viewed the policy with resentment and suspicion (Gill, 1974, p. 24). This is particularly the case if there is a feeling that the policy has been drawn up by personnel departments keen to enhance their own status at the expense of line management. The latter may feel—despite assertions to the contrary—that a policy is being introduced 'because of the inability of line management to deal with industrial relations matters. This implication may be reinforced when line management have been constantly informed that specialist 'advice' is necessary on matters which were once their sole prerogative' (Gill, 1974, p. 24). Indeed, an industrial relations policy that appears neat and well-formulated, embodies the basic principles of good management practice, and ensures uniformity and consistency may appear very differently when viewed from the position of the line manager than it does from the level of senior management or personnel.[1]

However, rather than argue that industrial relations policy or strategy has no role to play because of this inevitable informality, this had led some writers to proclaim that there is an even greater need for control mechanisms and for central direction (Purcell, 1979, p. 1038). Perhaps too much has been expected from the formulation of policy objectives or from their commitment to paper. The prescription of a set of rules that is so tight as to cover every eventuality would tend to stifle rather than enhance cooperation between the parties. If an industrial relations policy is seen as an overall attempt to lay down broad

1. Of course, these are not the only problems that may be experienced through the introduction of an industrial relations policy or strategy. The policy may be so general as to be meaningless, it may not be possible to define business objectives let alone those of industrial relations, and management may not wish to publish its strategic thinking to other audiences (see, for example, Hawkins, 1979, pp. 228–245; Gill, 1974, pp. 22–35; Gill and Concannon, 1977, pp. 13–20; Anthony, 1977, p. 20).

guidelines primarily operating at the level of strategic decision making within the organization, then there is no reason to suppose that it should determine the intricacies of shop floor behaviour; of course, it could not do this. But, by giving line management more idea about the *directions* in which its organization is moving, about *objectives* in relation to trade union recognition and the role of unionism in general, about *sources* of information of specialist issues, and about general *standards* in relation to discipline, health and safety, procedures, and productivity, it can be of considerable benefit. And the fact that the process of discussing the formulation of policy leads management to plan ahead, to consider its current position, and to evaluate strategies for the future can only be beneficial for the development of good industrial relations. By so doing, it can produce a shift from a defensive posture to an active initiating posture. More particularly, it necessitates an end to 'fire-fighting' and a move towards 'fire prevention' (Gill, 1974, p. 28).

Indeed, one test of the effectiveness of a policy is the extent to which it provides managers who are responsible for the conduct of industrial relations with a framework of general principles that they regard as helpful and within which they are able to act decisively on day-to-day problems. In other words, formality and informality need not be mutually exclusive; both can operate at different levels of the organization and fulfil different purposes.

The needs of the line manager

So, what does the line manager need to know, and do, in order to help him in his management of workplace industrial relations? We can identify issues that need to be explored in at least six different areas:

1. *Prior planning* is an essential attribute of industrial relations just as much as it is one of other functions of management. The opportunity for such planning may be dependent upon the type of industry and markets within which the manager operates and, as suggested above, fire-fighting will continue to be a crucial part of his job. What can be done, however, is to reduce this to a minimum and to plan in advance to try and prevent, or at least predict, the explosion of issues.

2. It is important to make use, wherever possible, of what has been termed *'integrative bargaining'* (Walton and McKersie (1965). Bargaining is not just about beating the other party over the head, or achieving a total submission, even though this may be successful for either party in the short term. Stewards or union officials need to satisfy their constituents and it has not been unknown for management to help the other party if it feels a valuable negotiating relationship is in danger. Industrial relations has to be judged on a longer time perspective and, even though one may win the battle in the short run, this may seriously affect the opportunities for cooperation over time. In fact, the tactics or strategies for negotiating have not been dealt with in this book for precisely this reason; that is, that more

emphasis needs to be placed on longer-term issues, on background knowledge that can help to put industrial relations into perspective, and on the need for *preparation* prior to face-to-face negotiation. For the manager who wants a list of 'tactics' to be used around the negotiating table, Atkinson's book (1977) should prove worth while.

3. Knowledge about one's own *company* is essential: its objectives with regard to industrial relations and its traditions in the field of employee relations. Many managers may know what their procedure agreements actually say in terms of details for dealing with issues but not about the philosophy behind them or the potential advantages that they may gain from using them. It is crucial to know the role and status of the personnel department within the organization and to appreciate the relationship between personnel and themselves.

4. One should know more about the *unions* with whom one will be dealing, and the degree of autonomy that is formally given to stewards within that union. In Chapter 2, we outline some of the basics of the union movement and give details about some of the major unions. To have specified constitutions of particular unions would not be appropriate since most of these would have been irrelevant to any one manager and have made extremely turgid reading. The traditions of unions, and the way in which they have developed or evolved, still exert a considerable influence over their contemporary organization in a large number of cases.

5. It is important to know where to *look for information or advice*, not just with regard to unions but also concerning procedures, legal enactments, and so on. The line manager has not got the time nor the inclination to become an expert in these matters and it is more important that, having built upon the appreciation of industrial relations offered in this book, he should know where to look or who to go to for relevant advice. Clearly, personnel departments ought to play a key role here in both providing information and acting as a sounding board for proposals. Again, however, the exact role depends upon the position occupied by personnel within the organization. Outside agencies such as ACAS and the Health and Safety Executive, as well as part-time courses at local educational establishments, can offer help as can a judicious selection of journals, books, and magazines on employee relations.

6. Finally, and this has already been mentioned above, the manager has got to be willing to *examine his own attitudes* to industrial relations. He needs to see why he interprets events in a particular way and whether he has rejected alternatives by virtue of what may be a limited perspective. It is much easier to see the way in which another party's attitudes may influence their actions but less easy to see one's own. It is one of the intentions of this book to cause the manager to focus in on himself as well as learning about other participants in workplace industrial relations.

Indeed, it is the link between knowledge and attitudes that is so crucial to industrial relations; in training courses, it is apparent how easily managerial prescriptions for dealing with issues have been severely handicapped by a lack of knowledge of industrial relations or have been taken on board with little thought. On the 'closed shop', for example, it is quite common to find that those managers who are most vehemently against it have had little or no experience of working with unions; conversely those who can see advantages, *for themselves as managers*, have generally experienced working in a closed-shop situation. To some extent, knowledge has a powerful influence upon attitudes; on the other hand, attitudes cause us to organize our knowledge, accepting certain pieces of information while rejecting others. But, this is moving us into a more philosophical level of debate and away from the practicalities of industrial relations; let us start our examination of these by considering the role of trade unions and this is the subject of Chapter 2.

Conclusions

Each of the subsequent chapters begins by posing a number of questions or outlining a number of issues that are especially pertinent to the management of workplace industrial relations. In order to provide a flavour of the remainder of the book, it seems appropriate to draw up a list of the types of question that we shall attempt to answer below:

1. How is it that British trade unions have developed into their present form? Are there too many unions? How can management best work with the union movement and foster good industrial relations?
2. How do management approaches to industrial relations influence its character on the shop floor? In particular, can management attitudes actually hinder the process of achieving good industrial relations?
3. How can the manager motivate people at work? Is it realistic to expect employees to be 'loyal' to their companies? What do people on the shop floor feel about their own membership of unions?
4. What is the nature of the link between shop stewards and their members? How have stewards' organizations developed? How can management best work with the shop steward?
5. What kind of role is there for foremen to occupy in present-day industrial relations? How can the supervisor come to terms with the increasing influence of the shop steward?
6. Have trade unions really got too much power today? Do certain unions have more power than others? Why? What has management done to counteract union power?
7. How extensive is industrial action in this country? What effect, if any, have procedure agreements had in institutionalizing and channelling conflict at work? What are the basics of procedure agreements?
8. What impact has the law had on industrial relations? In particular, has the

legislation on unfair dismissal tilted the balance towards the employee and made it impossible to dismiss someone? What effect has the health and safety legislation had upon the workplace?

9. Does worker participation still hold an appeal for the various interest groups in industry? What do they each expect from it? How can managers develop a participative policy?

10. What influence do external factors—such as the product market, technology, and size of firm—have upon workplace industrial relations? Is it realistic to advocate a universal policy or does strategy have to be devised to suit the unique situation of each company?

2. Understanding the unions

For the line manager, there are a number of aspects of trade unionism that are difficult to appreciate. In effect, at least three charges are regularly directed at the movement; first of all, that there are far too many unions in Britain today. Secondly, that trade unions are far from democratic institutions and are bedevilled with internal conflict. And, thirdly, that trade unions are opposed to change and, consequently, hinder the efficiency of British industry. Since each of these charges is related to a potential problem for managers, simple solutions are often advanced, particularly to the issue of multi-unionism. It is the aim of this chapter to put these issues into perspective by first outlining the emergence and subsequent development of unionism in this country, and then addressing ourselves to these problems (and so-called solutions) with this in mind.

Concern about the nature of unionism is neither new nor confined exclusively to managements or governments. As Pelling reports, *The Times* ran a series of articles in 1902 on 'The Crisis of British Industry' in which it was argued that 'trade unionism and the restrictive practices it encouraged were responsible for the weakened competitive position of British industry compared with American and German (1971, p. 125). Furthermore, as might be expected, trade union leaders and sympathizers have also questioned the purpose of unions in present-day society. In rejecting simple solutions to the question of 'what are trade unions for?', Flanders reminds us categorically that their 'first and overriding responsibility . . . is to the welfare of their own members. That is their primary commitment; not to a firm, not to an industry, not to the nation' (1970, p. 40). This is not to say that they should not take into account issues of national, industrial, or company importance, but that these should be secondary to those felt to be relevant to the membership as a whole, and should be developed by the unions and not as defined by others in their alleged 'true' or 'best' interests.

Before moving on to describe the development of unionism, one other point needs to be made although it will not be discussed in detail. The link between the trade unions and the Labour Party is more easily appreciated if we remember the crucial role played by the unions in the formation and subsequent growth of the Party. Trade unions were well developed before the Labour Party grew in strength; consequently, it has often been suggested that British trade unions favour *industrial*, rather than *political*, means as is the case in some other countries. Moreover, the degree of influence of the unions over the Labour Party—and vice versa—is highly complex and likely to shift from year to year. Both are, however, also keen to ensure their independence from one another as well as maintaining the links.

Early developments

The precise origins of trade unionism in this country is a matter for some debate; some would argue that the movement has its roots back in the craft guilds of the Middle Ages in which combinations of masters and journeymen came together for the purpose of protecting standards, restricting and regulating entry to the trade, and for fixing the prices of the product and the rate paid to journeymen. However, such combinations had no right to withdraw their labour and, comprising both supervisor and supervised, were somewhat different from the craft societies that developed much later in printing, for example (Pelling, 1971, pp. 17–22). Pelling goes on to note the way in which printers presented a wage claim in 1785, which was couched in very respectful terms, expressed gratitude for the consideration of an earlier application, and stressed the fact that their *request* was in no way 'subversive of decent and respectful behaviour' (1971, p. 23).

Either way, the development of unionism in the early part of the nineteenth century was restricted very much to the *craft* trades and it is from these groups that much of the legacy from the past emanates. Craftsmen were used to a large degree of unilateral regulation of their work, particularly over the way in which it was organized and the quality or standards expected from it. By combining together, this enabled them to extend this job control to other areas as well; notably, in regulating the number and quality of new entrants to the trade through the apprenticeship system. Lee notes that 'in particular the craft societies were not prepared to see the labour market flooded with new entrants in order to cope with short-run deficiencies in the supply of skill, a policy which would exacerbate even the gentlest of future recessions' (1979, p. 38). Moreover, by presenting a united front to the employer, it enabled craftsmen to ensure that skilled work could not be undertaken by someone offering their labour at a lower price than agreed in the district. Secrets of the trade were carefully guarded and new entrants were socialized into the expected norms of the job, often by elaborate initiation ceremonies and the daily vigilance of established customs by the more senior members. As well as printers, there were combinations of tailors, millwrights, carpenters, and joiners to name but a few. Each one of these was organized around a specific craft and made no attempt to incorporate either members of other crafts or the less skilled members of the working population. Neither was there much of a move towards any form of national organization within any *one* trade and, as Pelling describes, 'most combinations were of a much smaller and more localised type. There were innumerable clubs each with usually not more than a few dozen members yet each pursuing an existence which was either completely independent of or only very loosely linked to other clubs in the same trade' (1971, p. 33). They were based, to a large extent, on public houses or 'houses of call' (Musson, 1972, p. 17). Since a high proportion of their members were usually in employment—even during recessions—it was possible to charge high subscriptions and this gave the clubs some element of financial stability. Moreover, it enabled them to pay high benefits to their unemployed or sick members in order to ensure that they did not attempt to work for lower rates of pay. In other words, the (relatively) strong position of skilled workers allowed them, with collective organization, to preserve and enhance their status.

By the 1830s, there was some evidence of a move towards national integration (Musson, 1972, p. 17) although it was not really until the 'new model unions' of the 1850s that this was effectively achieved. Through this, unions (still craft orientated) began to present a more respectable front to the world by progressively abandoning the image of small secret societies and replacing them by centralized administration, printed rule-books, and so on (Pelling, 1971, p. 51). They still retained strong local organization (Musson, 1972, p. 32) and the new model involved 'no significant relaxation of the vertical boundaries of union organization: other crafts were often viewed suspiciously, as potential rivals in demarcation conflicts; the lower skilled were a possible threat to the craftsmen's job monopoly' (Hyman, 1975, pp. 45–46). These two factors—strong local autonomy and clear lines of demarcation—are still very apparent in craft unions, or those with strong craft traditions such as the AUEW.

The fact that early developments were highly restricted to craft trades and closed to the general mass of other workers meant that the latter had to look elsewhere in order to build organizations for themselves. The traditions and successes of the *general* unions are very different from those of the craft unions described above. The latter were not only unwilling to accept unskilled members into their organization (which is understandable enough since they did not want to weaken their power base) but also were not particularly helpful in terms of guidance for the general workers. A number of false starts were made because of this. For example, in 1829, John Doherty—a young Irishman—formed the Grand General Union of Operative Spinners of Great Britain and Ireland. A year later, he founded the National Association for the Protection of Labour. The guiding principle behind this form of unionism was that it was open to workers in any grade or craft from any industry; as such, it was totally different from existing forms of craft organization. However, its openness was also a source of weakness in that it was extremely susceptible to any recession; the Grand General broke up within two years of its inception when it attempted to support a strike of Lancashire Spinners and failed to maintain solidarity among the membership and, after the secretary of the NAPL absconded with most of the funds, it too disappeared in 1832 (Pelling, 1971, pp. 36–38).

The next serious attempt at a national general union was by Robert Owen in 1834 with the Grand National Consolidated Trades Union, which had the grand long-term aims of rationalizing the structure of combinations, providing a centralized control for movements in wages, and coordinating assistance for strikes. This, too, failed within the year although it is reputed to have built up a membership of anything between 16 000 and half a million (Pelling 1971, pp. 39–42; Musson, 1972, p. 33). It failed primarily because of the problems of coordination and due to the lack of power of its members; being unskilled, for the most part, they were the most likely to be unemployed, they were unlikely to be able to afford high subscriptions, and, possessing few skills, susceptible to employer domination.

General unionism took off properly in the late 1880s and early 1890s; these 'new' unions were formed at national level by leaders who were not usually from the same occupation—and, in some cases, a different class—and who were more tied to the social and revolutionary fervour of the time. They were organized around the London area, primarily, on such diverse groups as match girls, gasworkers, and dockers and the primary characteristics of the new unionism were that they would:

1. Recruit practically anybody.
2. Charge low subscriptions.
3. Adopt aggressive strike tactics.
4. Organize nationally.
5. Have more explicit political links.

As we mentioned above, it was out of the general unions that the Labour Party developed (Pelling, 1971, pp. 93–102). In addition, these unions grew in size during the early part of the twentieth century and, throughout the twenties, a series of amalgamations reduced their numbers. For example, one of these led to the formation of the TGWU in 1922 from a series of unions covering industries as diverse as docks, transport, building, and flour-milling. One of these unions—the Worker's Union—had grown in size from 4500 in 1910 to 143 000 in 1914 to almost half a million by the end of the First World War (Lovell, 1977, p. 46). Despite the tradition of 'open' recruitment and the massive growth of the general unions, Farnham and Pimlott suggest that the 'new' unions became more exclusive, with their power dependent on their ability to recruit in certain key industries and large works such as gas and the docks (1979, p. 25).

Despite this, however, the *general* unions are still seen as catering very much for the lower skilled; again, factors in the development of these unions are still apparent today. In the TGWU, for example, there are strong trade groups in certain industries (such as the docks) that coexist sometimes less than peacefully with other parts of the membership. The general unions are intimately involved with the Labour Party—in terms of sponsorship—and subscriptions are still relatively low. Centralized authority remained a characteristic up until the late sixties when there were considerable organizational changes in the TGWU and NUPE, for example.

Before moving on to describe the other categories of unionism that are generally put forward—industrial and occupational/white collar—it is worth noting the way in which craft unions responded to this growth in the general unions. Throughout the latter half of the nineteenth century, they continued to expand steadily and became more effective in their organization (Lovell, 1977, p. 11).

By the early part of the twentieth century, however, they realized that they needed to become less exclusive in their operation; to a large extent, this was due to changes in technology altering the nature of the craftsman's job and making it possible for firms to employ dilutees. Moreover, restrictions on apprenticeship were lifted under wartime conditions. By 1926, the engineers had 'opened their doors' to the semi-skilled and, by 1939, to women (Pelling, 1971, pp. 104 and 204). However, as Clegg suggests, 'having opened their ranks too late to prevent the development of the general unions, the craft unions did so when the result was bound to be a further complication of union structure' (1979, p. 175). We shall return to this in the next section.

The idea of industrial unions, that is, basing one union on each industry, has its roots in the syndicalist ideas of the early part of this century and was seen primarily as a step to eventual worker control of that industry. Although the original objectives behind this concept had more or less disappeared by 1920, the ideas have reappeared over the years in a variety of forms and been suggested by a wide range of opinion. In the strict sense of the word, there are no *industrial* unions in this country, although a number, such as the NUM, NUR, and ISTC all have claims to be, or have potential to become, one for their particular sector. Jackson seeks to categorize industrial unions into two types: one, the *monopoly union*, attempts to organize all workers in one industry, while the other, the *single industry union*, restricts recruitment to one industry alone (1977, p. 48). Bargaining strength of the latter type—which is mostly in evidence here—varies considerably between industries; for example, the miners and railwaymen are traditionally seen as relatively strong whereas unions in agriculture (NUAAW) or in textiles (NUTGW) have been much weaker, partly due to competition for membership in these sectors, partly due to adverse economic conditions, and in agriculture at least, due to isolation from other union members and fairly unique social conditions.

The miners are probably the best known of these groups even though the NUM is a relatively 'young' union only coming into existence in its present form in 1944 in preparation for the nationalization of the industry. Attempts had been made during the nineteenth century to achieve some kind of national integration but had met with only partial success. For example, in 1863, the National Miners Association came into being to look after the interests of Northumberland, Durham, Yorkshire, Scotland, and the Midlands. This was followed, six years later, by the Amalgamated Association of Miners, covering Lancashire, South Wales, and the West Midlands (Lovell, 1977, p. 11). Next the Miners' Federation of Great Britain was founded in 1889 and this commanded the support of most areas but for Northumberland, Durham and South Wales. There were splits in this organization over the years; for example, a 'non-political' union was formed in Nottinghamshire by George Spencer (a right-wing Labour MP). By 1927, however, this amalgamated with the Nottinghamshire Miners' Association and both then affiliated to the Federation (Pelling, 1971, p. 187). This historical description is helpful in explaining the strong area loyalties still in existence within the NUM. Furthermore, the close community links in mining serve to strengthen local organization and enable the use of sanctions against members flouting customs of the area (Cooper and Bartlett, 1976, pp. 10–11). Similarly, the attachment of miners to the industry and the specialized nature of the job (plus its hazardous conditions) make an industrial union particularly appropriate in these circumstances. The union can—and does—concentrate its resources and expertise on the industry and its related problems.

White collar workers have become increasingly unionized over the past 30 years; and now the *white collar* unions (such as ASTMS) and the white collar sections of manual unions (such as ACTSS) have achieved a voice at the TUC level. It is difficult to estimate just how many white collar workers were unionized in the past since most of the manual unions did not keep separate membership figures (Bain, 1972, p. 24). There are examples of some professionals being unionized back in the nineteenth century; for example, the teachers formed a union in 1870 and by 1888 this had not only survived but had also grown to a membership of some 14000 (Lovell, 1977, p. 15). Similarly, there is evidence of unionism in the Civil Service, banks, and local government just after the First World War (Taylor, 1980, pp. 340, 382, 420). Indeed, white collar unionism has, for a long time, been an established principle in public sector employment and over 80 per cent of the potential membership in local government is already organized. In private sector employment, there has been a considerable rise even since the late sixties; in manufacturing, for example, the density of unionization rose from 11 per cent in 1968 to 32 per cent in 1974 (Clegg, 1979, p. 181).

In many ways, white collar union growth has merely contributed further to the complex structure of unionism in this country. Some unions, such as ASTMS, have grown considerably by amalgamation; ASTMS has succeeded in attracting a number of staff associations from the insurance and banking fields and allowing them to continue with their own sections under the

ASTMS umbrella—for example, Royal Insurance and Midland Bank. The banking union (originally NUBE) has now changed its name in an effort to appeal to the insurance sector as well—it is now called the Banking Insurance and Finance Union (BIFU).

We have therefore, a situation in which unionism has grown in an *ad hoc* way to suit the circumstances of the time and there has certainly not been, even with the much later development and growth of white collar unionism, any realistic attempt at central direction. Unions have grown or shrunk in very different directions depending upon the characteristics of their memberhip, the industries in which they mainly recruit, the opportunities for amalgamation, and even the prevailing governmental attitudes of the day. The original four-fold classification of unions into craft, general, industrial, and white collar has become increasingly difficult to apply to any one union. As Hyman notes, it is 'far too simplistic to do justice to the complexity of current reality. There are no pure industrial unions . . . there are very few pure craft unions . . . and no union has aspirations as ecumenical as the notion of general unionism often implies. The picture is further complicated, moreover, by the growth of white collar unionism' (1975, pp. 38–39).

Despite a number of alternative attempts at classification,[1] however, the categorization can still be a useful one if it is seen as no more than a series of ideal types that can aid us in our understanding of the unions. It can be argued that some unions combine features of each type whereas others may correspond to an industrial union in one industry and a general in another. Moreover, the categories certainly reflect fairly accurately 'the origins and early aspirations of many unions, and may still be enshrined in their official ideologies' (Hyman, 1975, p. 38). For example, groups within the AUEW— such as toolmakers—still exhibit strong craft traditions as do members of the EETPU although both unions are more open in their recruitment strategies then they originally were. The TGWU manages to combine *general* characteristics in local government and many process industries, *industrial* characteristics in the oil industry, and it also has strong *white collar* sections in a variety of industries. Moreover, HGV drivers would probably consider themselves on a par with *craftsmen* in many industries as too would dockers. Indeed, a similar process could be undertaken for each union along the lines suggested by Clegg (1979, pp. 165–74). Such an approach must, however, recognize the dynamic nature of unionism and, just because a union fits into one or more categories at present, it is not safe to assume that it will remain there for ever.

1. Undoubtedly, the best known classification is by Turner, who distinguished between unions in terms of their openness and closedness, based largely on the degree of control that they place over entry to the union. The two ends of the continuum represent extremes and unions can be at any point along this. Moreover, a union can alter from being closed to open and vice versa. For example, it may be that an amalgamation closes up two previously open unions (see Turner, 1962 and McCarthy, 1972, pp. 89–108).

Table 2.1 The 'top twenty' unions†

1.	Transport and General Workers' Union (TGWU)	1 886 971
2.	Amalgamated Union of Engineering Workers—Engineering Section (AUEW)	1 100 000
3.	General and Municipal Workers' Union (GMWU)	915 654
4.	National and Local Government Officers' Association (NALGO)	782 343
5.	National Union of Public Employees (NUPE)	699 156
6.	Association of Scientific, Technical and Managerial Staffs (ASTMS)	491 000
7.	Union of Shop, Distributive and Allied Workers (USDAW)	450 287
8.	Electrical, Electronic, Telecommunication and Plumbing Union (EETPU)	405 000
9.	Union of Construction, Allied Trades and Technicians (UCATT)	312 000
10.	National Union of Mineworkers (NUM)	256 962
11.	National Union of Teachers (NUT)	232 397
12.	Confederation of Health Service Employees (COHSE)	216 482
13.	Civil and Public Services Association (CPSA)	216 415
14.	Union of Communication Workers (UCW)	202 293
15.	AUEW (Technical, Administrative and Supervisory Section) —(TASS)	200 954
16.	Society of Graphical and Allied Trades (SOGAT)	197 048
17.	National Union of Railwaymen (NUR)	170 000
18.	Banking, Insurance and Finance Union (BIFU)	141 042
19.	Association of Professional, Executive, Clerical and Computer Staff (APEX)	140 292
20.	Post Office Engineering Union (POEU)	130 976

† Membership figures at 31 December 1980

Multi-unionism

It is often said that questions of trade union structure—and with it multi-unionism—are central to most of the major problems of industrial relations in Britain. Back in the late sixties the Donovan Commission estimated that four out of every five trade unionists worked in some form of multi-union establishment and that one in six were in a grade of worker in which two or more unions were competing for membership (1968, p. 29). Amalgamations may have reduced this somewhat but not all mergers have led to a 'tidying up' of union structure. In certain grades, notably white collar occupations, this may have increased and Hunt has estimated that in many large engineering establishments 'at least three out of the four groups (TASS, ASTMS, ACTSS, APEX) have membership and occasionally all are represented in staff areas. Quite often the overlap between these unions is considerable and no clear demarcation pattern has emerged' (1977, p. 58).

It must be remembered, though, that multi-unionism can take a number of different forms; firstly, each main occupational group may be organized by a different union. This may present few problems to management providing that bargaining units have been clearly and adequately drawn up, and there are few grounds for inter-union disagreement. Indeed, such an arrangement may be considerably more beneficial for managers and trade unionists alike than would having one large union that runs into problems in trying to represent diverse interest groups. Secondly, a similar situation may prevail with less clearly drawn lines of demarcation as to which employee does which job—this can lead to disputes over job rights. Finally, there can be more than one union competing for the right to organize each group of employees; if manifest, this could lead to jurisdictional disputes and may need to be resolved under the TUC's Bridlington arrangements. We shall return to Bridlington later. While it is certainly true that no industry of any size is organized by just one union, we must also ask how great a problem this can be?

Problems can certainly confront management if they have to deal with a large number of unions with no well-defined spheres of influence; a greater amount of time may be spent negotiating with these unions, settlement dates may vary, and this, particularly in plants with no unified and centralized wages policy, can lead to leap-frogging claims and pressure on differentials. As was mentioned above, demarcation problems can arise as to who does what job although, as a source of overt conflict, this has been found to contribute little to the overall number of working days lost. However, to the extent that management may back away from confrontation because of fears over potential demarcation disputes, it may have a considerable effect on productivity; again, this constraint is often exaggerated.

Similarly, multi-unionism may cause problems for the unions themselves; rivalry in recruitment can lead to a waste of scarce resources and inter-union strife that could do neither the movement nor the members involved any good. Moreover, unions may 'poach' membership from others, a criticism that has often been laid at the door of ASTMS over the last 10 years or more. Finally, multi-unionism—as we shall see later—has its own solution to some degree in that shop stewards' organizations flourish and become more independent of the union hierarchy. However, this can lead to problems for the union in that it finds it hard to control local organization or for managements who seek 'outside' union assistance in their industrial relations. (See Cooper and Bartlett, 1976, pp. 22–23; and Farnham and Pimlott, 1979, pp. 104–105 for a similar list of problems.)

Despite the fact that multi-unionism is vastly overrated as a 'problem' for British industry (Clegg, 1979, p. 186), it is still *seen* by many as a problem and source of disorder. This has led to a variety of proposals for reform so as to reduce the number of unions; we can now turn to examine some of these *responses* to multi-unionism, particularly those that have sought to reduce the number of unions or to provide a more peaceful mechanism for resolving any conflict between them.

One response that has found favour from various different camps over the last 60 or 70 years has been *industrial unionism*; that is, some wholesale reconstruction of the trade union movement along a clearly defined industrial or vertical pattern. Recently, the 'success' of German industrial relations has been put forward as an adequate reason for change by a host of practitioners and laymen alike. Indeed, few ideas about trade unionism have attracted such widespread support as the notion that industrial unionism is the best trade union structure. As Clegg suggests, 'syndicalists, communists and socialists have argued for it, it has also found favour among conservatives; and captains of industry have championed it as well as shop stewards and union leaders' (1976, p. 29). Recently, there have even been suggestions for a massive public sector industrial union to cover central and local government, the NHS, and the university staff (reported in *The Guardian*, May 1980).

There have been no major resolutions at Annual TUC Conference since 1963 relating to wholesale industrial unionism; prior to that, resolutions were put forward in 1924, 1927, and 1946 (Jackson, 1977, p. 51). Each time, it has come to nought as the practical difficulties involved in such an exercise have been seen to outweigh any theoretical advantages for the union movement.

The arguments in favour of industrial unionism are, for the most part, a direct response to the problems of multi-unionism as seen by each of the parties. Namely, that it would reduce rivalry and competition between unions, that it would reduce conflict between union officials and shop stewards since all members in the industry would be organized by one union, and that there would be easier resolution of demarcation problems. Furthermore, union officials would only be required to deal with one industry and would therefore possess a more intimate knowledge about that industry. Consequently they could assist not only in making it more efficient but also serve their members better. In both the coal and steel industries, unions have put forward alternative plans for their future based on specialist knowledge, but they have also cooperated in a massive run-down in the size of their membership.

Criticisms of industrial unionism are both theoretical and practical. To define an industry would be no easy task and it may be more useful to think in terms of differing production systems; for example, does car production at Ford have more in common with assembly line work in food manufacture than it does car building at Rolls-Royce? Moreover, industrial boundaries shift and, particularly with the impact of new technology, this process may accelerate in the future. A union, such as the NUM or NUR, that ties its membership and recruitment strategy to one industry may disappear or contract with that industry. Furthermore, many companies straddle a number of industries and would, presumably, not take kindly to having to redraw their lines of demarcation accordingly. Advocates of industrial unionism also overlook the fact that some of the unions in this country nearest to the 'pure' type have been among the more militant in the past and it has certainly not removed the possibility of unofficial movements; indeed, it may increase them as members find their unions decreasingly responsive to their sectional interests. The final objection is even more practical; no big union—and especially the craft or general unions—would submit to their own dismantling in favour of unionism on industrial lines. In other words, industrial unionism, despite its superficial appeal as an orderly and 'rational' system of union structure, is very unlikely to appear in this country; unions are certainly not going to agree to a reconstruction on the basis of public opinion or pressure from non-union sources.

If wholesale reconstruction is unlikely, a much more probable development is amalgamation, in some cases of all the unions in one particular industry. At the turn of the century, there were approximately 1300 unions in this country, by 1960 this was reduced to 650, and by 1980 this had contracted further to less than 450. At the same time, of course, union membership has increased considerably, particularly among white collar workers many of whom have been keen to maintain their independence and keep separate small organizations. Most members are located in a few of the larger unions; for example, in 1977, 80 per cent of union members were in the top 26 unions. At the other end of the spectrum, less than 1 per cent of all union members were in the 263 unions with less than 1000 members (Taylor, 1980, p. 58). Mergers have tended to result in the bigger unions growing yet bigger, and there have been two big merger waves this century, one between 1917 and 1924, and the other from 1960 to 1970 (Buchanan, 1974, pp. 37–44).

There are a number of reasons why unions should choose to merge with each other. Firstly, a union faced with a decline in membership may seek another union with which to amalgamate in order to protect its membership. Added to this, there are often financial difficulties that make the process of amalgamation more attractive. Secondly, the union involved may feel that its interests are not effectively protected within the TUC while it remains as a separate but small organization. UCATT, for example, was formed from a number of unions in the building industry for this reason—as well as a number of others (England, 1979, pp. 1–18). Furthermore, by becoming *the* union for the building industry, it was to be hoped that members would have a better and more comprehensive position on any development committees or working parties examining the industry. Thirdly, Buchanan has suggested that unions may amalgamate so as to counter similar moves by employers and he cites the case of textiles where the number of unions has been considerably reduced over the years (1974, p. 39). Fourthly, unions may merge to remove competition between them for members. Interestingly enough, the law has had a sizeable effect on the rate of amalgamations as was seen for the periods after legislation on the rules for mergers in both 1917 and 1964.

At any one time, discussions are taking place between unions in the search for a more effective organization; recent talks have centred on the printing industry in which each of the five main unions has been considering plans to merge with one or more of the others. There has even been pressure from the

TUC for all five to merge together in order to combine more effectively to regulate the introduction of new technology. Indeed, the number of printing unions has been progressively reduced from eighteen to five since the mid sixties and, in many of these, the NGA—the predominately craft union—has been at the forefront. There have also been a number of unsuccessful attempts as well. Similarly, attempts to form a council of railway unions may fail because of the unwillingness of NUR delegates to give up their hopes of ever becoming an industrial union for the railways. ASLEF, on the other hand, might see the move to unification, with more clearly defined spheres of interest, as advantageous from its point of view. Not all attempts at amalgamation or federation would lead to industrial unionism of course; it is more than likely that there will be no single print union for a long time. Similarly, craft unions look for bedfellows—the case of the plumbers and electricians being an appropriate example—as do white collar unions, and here APEX is often involved in merger talks.

Nor do amalgamations remove many of the problems they were originally designed to deal with. For example, craft and non-craft divisions can still remain in unions that have merged; *inter-union* problems are merely transferred to become *intra-union* ones (Farnham and Pimlott, 1979, p. 87). Union members may still seek to preserve traditional local autonomy where this originally eixisted. Many 'rational' mergers are not undertaken due to differences in union constitution, government, or organization. Similarly, the likelihood of redundant full-time union officials may delay mergers. Indeed, overall, it can be argued that the consequence of amalgamation 'has not been a rationalization of trade union structure but increasing complexity due to the further diversification of the conglomerates' (Clegg, 1979, p. 177).

It may well be, though, that the search for structural solutions is misplaced; that, whatever the reduction in the number of unions, a more important concern is on workability of multi-unionism at establishment level. One response to multi-unionism that is local in character has been the growth and development of shop steward committees and this will be discussed in much greater detail in Chapter 5. At this point, however, we need to assess the role of the TUC in resolving inter-union disputes.

The Donovan Commission, in reviewing multi-unionism, argued that 'apart from mergers, the most practical way to reduce (it) is by agreements between unions on recruitment rights and negotiating rights' (1968, p. 812). It suggested the principle of 'one union for one grade of work within one factory' (1968, p. 184). Of course, trade unions themselves had already recognized the problem of inter-union strife and, in 1939, the Bridlington Agreement set out to minimize the likelihood of disputes between unions and particularly those resulting from union competition. The principles were geared towards unions entering into agreements with others, with whom they were in frequent contact, to establish their position over spheres of influence, recognition, transfers, and so on. They were to provide a mechanism so that new entrants would not be accepted without a full enquiry into their reasoning for and circumstances of leaving their previous union. The TUC disputes' committee is available as a buffer, in theory at least, to resolve any inter-union difficulties that could not be sorted out by the parties themselves and, each year, Congress reports on the cases that have come before it.

In reviewing the effectiveness of the committee, Kalis reports that 'a system whereby the trade union movement itself attempts to resolve disputes within its ranks is viewed as essential by many within the trade union movement. In the absence of such a system it is believed that the public image of the trade union movement could well suffer' (1978, p. 41). There are occasions, of course, when this fails as can be seen from extensive reports of the laggers dispute on the Isle of Grain where, despite a TUC ruling that jobs were to belong to the GMWU, the conflict continued since other unions felt that the 27 laggers did not have a legitimate claim to obstruct other jobs on site. There were even threats that, in the final instance, the AUEW and EETPU could be expelled from the TUC. However, the fact that 20 or 30 cases are settled by the committee each year shows that some considerable benefit does come from this body.

The structural responses to multi-unionism are, as can be seen, only partially useful in coping with inter-union issues. At best, they can lead to more effective unionization and tidier structure; at worst, however, they may do little more than confuse the structure, transfer problems so that they become internal union matters, or lead to constitutional battles between unions in the TUC. We can now move on to look at the second issue described at the beginning of the chapter; namely, the internal problems that have confronted trade unions by virtue of their development or due to amalgamations.

Internal conflict

As we saw above, different types of union developed from rather different beginnings. In the craft unions the origins were local in nature and it was only later in the nineteenth century that any attempt at national integration proved at all successful. The tradition of local (be it factory, district, area, or regional) autonomy is one that is still with us today; for example, within the AUEW, district committees still exert a powerful influence over union affairs and the national committee of 52 rank and file delegates meets annually to consider union policy. Within the NUM, strong area loyalties are very apparent and this, to a large extent, reflects the history of union development. The GMWU has strong regional traditions and so on. It is only by being aware of the historical perspective that these current-day practices can be more adequately understood.

Indeed, unions are 'distinct from most other organisations in that they explicitly incorporate a *two way system of control*. Union officials are accorded specific power of leadership and of discipline; in appropriate situations, they are legitimately entitled to exert control over the members. But at the same time they are the employees and the servants of the members, who are thus in appropriate situations entitled to exert control over *them*' (Hyman, 1975, p. 73). Local power is particularly manifest when one examines strike statistics and sees that well over 90 per cent of all disputes are unofficial in nature. In fact, as the Donovan Commission suggested, trade unions may possess too *little* rather than too *much* power, particularly in any attempts to control the membership. As we shall see in Chapter 5, the response to local power has been to devolve control within unions and accord greater institutionalized influence to workplace representatives in the way that the TGWU did under Jack Jones. Boraston *et al.* have concluded from their survey of unions that 'the extent to which the workplace organisation manages its business for itself or relies on the full-time official depends on the resources which it can deploy within the plant . . . the most general influence at work is the size of the workplace organisation' (1975, p. 178). In certain industries, local representatives are still very dependent on their full-time officials and on national agreements, footwear being a case in point (Goodman *et al.*, 1977a). In others—such as engineering—workplace organizations are considerably more autonomous and may rarely see a full-time official from one year to the next.

Amalgamations have also created intra-union problems in two different ways; firstly, when two different groups of workers have been merged into one union, different trade loyalties may still be very apparent. For example, within the TGWU, the dockers have always constituted a special group within the union and have had conflicts with other sections of the membership—say, at the time of containerization in the early seventies when they wrangled with drivers and other TGWU members. Indeed, at one stage, they even formed a breakaway union (Whitehead, 1977, p. 25). Similarly, Hemingway cites a list of some 41 postwar breakaway unions (1978, pp. 174–175), including the famous case of the Glass and General Workers' Union that was formed by Pilkington employees at St Helens dissatisfied with the GMWU (Lane and Roberts, 1971). Moreover, certain groups sit uneasily in other unions; for example, social workers became increasingly dissatisfied with NALGO during the seventies although, in many authorities, recognition facilities offer them little realistic alternative to that union. Again, the picture varies from year to year although these examples clearly demonstrate that amalgamations may merely transfer an inter-group problem to within one union.

Secondly, when a craft union has 'opened' its ranks to the lesser skilled, there is often an uneasy alliance between the two groups. Again, within a historical context, such a phenomenon can easily be appreciated. Musson describes how, in the mid-nineteenth century, 'not only was craft sectionalism extremely strong, but (also) there was an even deeper division between "artisans and others", that is, between skilled craftsmen and semi-skilled or unskilled workers or labourers. Working men . . . were keenly aware of these differences' (1972, p. 16–17). A more recent example of this occurred at British Leyland in 1977 when a breakaway body—known as the United Craft Organization—under the leadership of Roy Fraser claimed to represent 8000 toolroom workers who were demanding more adequate representation rights for skilled workers (Marchington, 1979, p. 5). This is not the first time that this has occurred within the AUEW as Hemingway documents (1979, p. 174). The problematic interface between craft and non-craft workers (and, indeed, between the crafts themselves) is likely to become even more visible with the introduction of new technology.

Responses to new technology

With the danger of becoming repetitive, new technology is nothing 'new' either. Trade unions have been responding to technological change ever since their inception and, perhaps, the major difference in the latest round of modernization is the scale and location of the changes and the speed at which they are taking place. Whitehead argues that the threat of technological change has always been present for craftsmen, that 'society will no longer have any use for their particular skill. Redundancy means more than a mere change of job. It is a blow at this status, at the basis of their self-respect' (1977, p. 20). This can lead them, according to Donovan, to 'oppose relaxations in practices which, however desirable and even essential for efficiency, may seem to constitute a threat to their whole way of life'. This is greatest, the Commission continued, in the context of technological change (1968, p. 87).

A defensive response to change has certainly been one way in which trade unions have treated new technology. Restrictive (or employment defence) practices have been employed and demarcation or other disputes have flared up. The main result can be, as we have seen in a number of cases recently in printing and television, that employers may decide to delay the introduction of change, or to withdraw new machinery on the grounds that the costs of such action, in the short-term at least, are lower than taking a series of disputes. Conversely, management may just shut down production until an agreement is reached.

However, the first policy of unions is rarely obstructive. It is more likely to be an endeavour to get control over an ordered entry of new technology. This was achieved over a two-year period at the Mirror Group of Newspapers, for example. Moreover, the TUC has produced a 10-point plan on technology agreements and has more recently been making overtures to the CBI for a joint declaration on policies, using the TUC plan as a basis for discussion (*The Times*, June 1980). Basically, the plan looks for action in *three* directions; firstly, with employers, in providing for no unilateral introduction of new technology, for information and consultation prior to change, for unions to have a say in the designing of new equipment for training, and for joint monitoring of the effects of the implementation. Secondly, on their part, there needs to be more inter-union collaboration, sharing of expertise and even 'new technology' representatives'. Thirdly, the TUC has proposed that terms and conditions should not be adversely affected in relation to pay and health and safety, that hours should be reduced, and that redundancies, if accepted, must be on favourable terms after a planned approach to redeployment (TUC, 1979). In other words, this involves accepting the inevitability of change and trying to cope with it most effectively in order to protect the membership. However, the rank and file may not see this in the same way and, once again, a historical example demonstrates the point. In the 1880s and 1890s, the same thing was happening to tailors, engineers, and boilermakers and, as Lovell reports, 'the obstinacy of the rank and file on this issue was part of a general resistance to the encroachments made by the new technology on craft status, and the discontent of the craftsmen was directed against both employers and the *national union leaderships'* (1977, p. 28). With the reality of mass unemployment, especially in certain parts of the country, it would not be unexpected to see a similar situation arising in the near future.

Conclusions

Trade unions are exceedingly complex institutions. They contain a mass of different interest groups and are influenced to a large extent by the conditions of their development. Traditions, organization, objectives, and government vary between them all and old-established classifications are becoming much more difficult to apply. There is, however, some utility in providing a simple system of ideal types in that this may help us to locate trade unions by virtue of their origins and so appreciate their development over the past 200 years. To a degree, they *are* victims of the past but, much more importantly, they have adapted in an attempt to cope with the present day. That they are not always successful in doing this is hardly surprising but the fact that, despite adverse public opinion, trade union membership has recently reached its highest ever level must be related to their giving the membership 'something of what they want'.

A number of 'problems' of trade unionism have been outlined in this chapter—in particular, multi-unionism, inter-union strife, intra-union arrangements, and reaction to technological change—in order to show their position within a historical perspective. One of the reforms advanced for reducing multi-unionism—that of a wholesale reconstruction of unions along German lines—has been dealt with in some detail if only because, despite so much evidence to the contrary, it continues to attract widespread support from a variety of quarters. Trade unionism will alter with the times and, although it may not always be in the best interests of employers or the country as a whole, *ad hoc* development would seem to offer the only realistic response at the level of structural change. More dynamic changes—through joint shop stewards committees—will be dealt with in Chapter 5.

The nature of internal conflict within unions is also complex and, in a democracy, quite understandable. The rank and file may be unwilling to support the leadership over an issue that they feel is unlikely to advance their interests or likely to damage their position. Just as the majority of union members take very little interest in their unions, preferring to leave matters in the hands of activists and/or the executive, it is true to say that, in certain workplaces, union members take action that may or may not be in line with union policy. While we can postulate that the rank and file may exert little influence over the executive, the reverse is probably just as true in a large number of unions. Democracy can be preserved through the presence of strong factions. We shall return to this subject in the latter part of Chapter 4.

Having examined the broad influences of unionism in the workplace and on employers, we can now look at the equation from the other angle and consider management approaches to industrial relations, and trade unionism in particular.

3. Management approaches to industrial relations

In the previous chapter, we confronted three basic facets of trade unionism that, to the line manager, are often difficult to appreciate. In this chapter, this approach is extended and we focus down on industrial relations at establishment level. In particular, we shall consider two alternative frames of reference, first applied to the subject by Fox (1966), that underpin a management approach to industrial relations. These two frames of reference will be contrasted by examining their response to three separate but related questions. First of all, to what extent should trade unions be recognized and accepted at the level of individual establishments? Secondly, what effect does the existence of trade unionism, as articulated on the shop floor, influence methods of decision making and especially management prerogatives? And, thirdly, what are the sources of and reactions to conflict at work? In many ways, the answers to these questions and the remainder of this chapter represent the core of the book in that we introduce ideas that will be more fully explored in later chapters.

Before commencing our discussion of these questions, however, a number of other points need to be made. Firstly, when dealing with the two frames of reference—unitary and pluralistic—there would appear to be an assumption of an underlying consistency such that one person automatically, rationally, and coherently either chooses, or unconsciously adopts, all the facets of one and rejects the other. As we shall see later in the chapter, it may be quite normal for there to be inconsistencies in any one person's approach to particular aspects of industrial relations. Secondly, despite the fact that there has been a good deal of criticism of these two frames of reference, it is suggested that the pluralistic frame of reference is the more realistic and acceptable when assessed from the perspective of the line manager in workplace relations. In the conclusion, however, we shall present some of the more prominent criticisms.

Thirdly, any discussion of management approaches to industrial relations may imply some uniformity and consistency *within* management itself, one that leads to a particular all-embracing strategy. As we indicated in Chapter 1, this is neither necessarily, nor even generally, the case. The overall objectives of the company as a whole may be translated into quite different objectives at departmental level; the conception of industrial relations held by directors will usually differ markedly from that held by foremen, for example, and we shall deal with the role of the foreman more fully in Chapter 6. Similarly, different functions within the organization may equally hold radically different ideas about industrial relations management and its place within the decision making process; again, somewhat stereotypically, the views of personnel may be at odds with those of production, as may the latter with those of finance or marketing. In this chapter, we are primarily concerned with developing an understanding of alternative line management approaches to industrial relations.

The final introductory point relates to the treatment of management approaches to the subject within the literature as a whole. On the one hand, it is often argued that there has been a neglect of the role of management in industrial relations, and this is clearly illustrated by the fact that very little space is devoted to the topic within most textbooks. Moreover, selection of suitable material for inclusion does not appear to display any coherent ordered principles. Four reasons have traditionally been advanced for this supposed 'neglect':

1. Most researchers in the subject tend to have trade union sympathies or come from union backgrounds. Consequently, their interest in unions and their ability to examine them is much greater.
2. Trade unions have generally been seen as more of a 'problem' than management and this has led to funds being directed towards researchers investigating the former. It is doubtful if this is still the case today.
3. Management has been quite happy to allow access to studies examining shop floor attitudes while refusing access to itself as a potential subject for investigation. Anthony argues that managers have been 'over-inclined to prevent access for research and too sensitive to reports which have not entirely reflected their own judgements when research has taken place'. Because of this, 'managers have done little to correct this unfortunate bias' towards union research (1977, p. 41).
4. The enormous complexity of the subject makes it difficult to generalize about management attitudes and behaviour; there may be, for example, little in common for industrial relations line management between the chemical or engineering industries, between big or small firms, or in comparisons of the private and public sectors. Case studies have been done in many industries—although there is a predominance in engineering and vehicles—but there is as yet no useful contingency model appropriate for the subject.

On the other hand, however, Wood and Thurley argue that there has not been so much a 'neglect of management but rather a lack of systematic treatment. They suggest that it is more significant to say that management *has* been treated, often in an explicit manner, largely from a particular perspective and largely on the basis of unanalysed and underresearched assumptions' (1977).

One well-known attempt at analysis has been that of Fox, and the distinction between unitary and pluralistic frames of reference. Indeed, the latter 'more sophisticated' perspective would appear to have exerted a considerable influence over managers—particularly at more senior levels and especially in the immediate post-Donovan era; this is most clearly illustrated by the associated rallying-cry of 'we are all pluralists now!' (see, for example, McCarthy and Ellis, 1973, p. 94).

Unitary and pluralistic frames of reference

In his research paper for the Royal Commission, Alan Fox outlined two contrasting frames of reference—either of which may be held by managers—and then spelt out some of the implications that would flow from this. According to Thelen and Withall (and quoted by Fox, 1966, p. 2), each person 'perceives and interprets events by means of a conceptual structure of generalisations or contexts, postulates about what is essential, assumptions as to what is valuable, attitudes about what is possible, and ideas about what will work effectively. This constitutes the frame of reference of that person'. It thus embodies 'the main selective influences at work as the perceiver supplements, omits and structures what he notices'. As we saw in Chapter 1, two people may see the same event in a totally different manner and may judge its meaning, its significance, and its outcome in contrasting ways. Its relevance to industrial relations is clear.

The unitary perspective contains the following essential ingredients; it assumes that, within the organization, there is just one source of authority and one focus of loyalty. It is seen as comprising a team with all employees (management, shop floor, office, directors) striving towards the common goal of organizational success. Each person works to the best of his ability, accepts his place in the hierarchy, and follows the appointed leader; there is no room for the development of factions either within or outside the team. For his part, the leader has to inspire the loyalty he demands (Fox, 1966, p. 3). This view was implicit in some managerial evidence submitted to the Donovan Commission. For many, however, 'this represents a vision of what industry *ought* to be like' rather than how it actually is in practice (Fox, 1966, p. 3).

The pluralist perspective, on the other hand, offers a somewhat different view of the current state of affairs. Basically, the organization is seen to contain many related but separate interests that exist in a rough equilibrium, and it is management's job to balance these competing demands on resources. Rival sources of leadership are expected and the common purpose is linked more by instrumentality and interdependence than by any moral agreement to one set of overriding aims. Rival groups cannot be unified, liquidated, or integrated totally into or out of the system (Fox, 1966, p. 4).

The two frames of reference differ in three basic respects and each of these will be considered in turn. Firstly, they see a very different role for unionism as a legitimate rival source of leadership. Secondly, management prerogatives are viewed in a very different way depending upon the frame of reference. Thirdly, reaction to conflict varies both in relation to its possible sources and in management's approach to its resolution. Since the second and third points flow very much from the former, it seems appropriate to consider the role of unions first of all.

Role of unionism

From the unitary perspective, no role is foreseen for unionism. It is seen to be encroaching upon management's territory such that unions either achieve too much for their members in that they block change and inhibit efficiency or, conversely, as being irrelevant in that management is much more able than trade unions to identify and satisfy employee needs. In addition, the paternalistic employer pays above union rates. As Fox notes, 'even managers of an otherwise high degree of sophistication can be found holding the view that, although the misdeeds and foolishness of employers in the past made unionism necessary, the growth of enlightenment means that modern workers are perfectly safe in the hands of their managers' (1966, p. 10). Some managers, however, may have no choice about accepting unions, particularly if this is 'imposed' from above by a parent company or by senior management. In cases such as this, trade unions may not be considered as legitimate by individual managers and accepted grudgingly at best.

The presence of a union is seen not only to have an effect upon efficiency or managerial prerogatives but also upon the focus of loyalty and source of authority within the enterprise. From the unitary perspective, the union represents an illegitimate intrusion into the private world of the employer and the organization. By providing an alternative source of leadership, the union *introduces* conflict into the organization and causes employees to make unrealistic demands on their employers. Again, as Fox describes, these feelings rest upon 'ideological assumptions, perhaps scarcely conscious, still less examined, that there is only one legitimate source of authority and focus of loyalty in the enterprise; that rival bids are presumptuous and lacking in decent loyalty; that men are ungrateful and therefore undeserving of consideration' (1966, p. 11).

Unionism is seen somewhat differently from a pluralist frame of reference; firstly, there is a full acceptance of its position in modern industry although, in many cases, this approval may be limited to the market relations with unions, and any incursion into the arena of management decision making thought illegitimate. That is, that unions provide a valuable service for their members through collective bargaining over wages and in representing them through grievance, disciplinary, or disputes machinery. Secondly, and linked to this, it becomes perfectly understandable to accept that employees 'owe loyalty to, and come under the authority of, leaders other than their own management' (Fox, 1966, p. 7). Because of this, the major priority is not so much how to fight off unionism as to how it can be effectively harnessed to meet the needs of the employer as well as those of its members. In other words, how to incorporate unionism into the structure of the enterprise while, at the same time, ensuring that it remains independent and legitimate in the eyes of the membership.

A strategy for management control in industrial relations in the late twentieth century could well be to 'maximise the achievement of general business objectives not through opposition to unions but by collaboration' (Purcell, 1979, p. 28). This will involve, as is done by most large corporations at the present time, an encouragement of union membership in clearly defined bargaining units, prompt recognition of unionism, and concession to the closed shop where appropriate. Moreover, the acceptance of alternative sources of loyalty is also often extended through the provision of check-off agreements for deduction of union dues at source, help with clerical matters, and facilities and training for worker representatives. Although many (though not all) personnel departments may see the efficacy of a package such as this, a large proportion of line managers may see it as little more than yet another constraint on their authority and a hindrance to their primary objectives of greater productivity.

In order to illustrate the pluralistic perspective, we shall concentrate on two particular aspects of unionism:

1. Trade union recognition.
2. The especially controversial concept of the closed shop.

The employer with a unitary frame of reference would not conceive of a role for unions and would, therefore, not plan ahead to accommodate them. Conversely, the pluralist would be mindful of their existence and would seek to establish an orderly structure that is to their own advantage and to that of the other parties. As the CIR commented, 'where membership boundaries are unclear the potential exists for inter-union jurisdictional conflicts, competitive union recruitment, and the breakdown of appropriate bargaining arrange-ments which can harm all interests. It is thus important to ensure that appropriate bargaining units are established early in the recognition process' (1973, p. 10). As we saw in the last chapter, inter-union disagreement is neither helpful for management nor for the unions themselves. Because of this, Hawkins proposes that any organization ought to have a positive policy on recognition, to come to terms with the concept of collective bargaining *before* a claim arises. He adds, that 'any management which simply responds in an *ad hoc* manner to a recognition claim, without having thought out a policy in advance, is unlikely to secure bargaining arrangements which are compatible with its own business objectives' (1979, p. 66). It needs to ensure that the policy is assessed so as to be consistent with the organization's decision making structure and needs, and be geared towards long-term effectiveness and viability (1979, p. 68).

This has been particularly apparent in recent years with management policy towards recognition of white collar unions as companies have 'encouraged' certain unions while 'discouraging' others. In the case of a union with a moderate reputation, employers hope that 'by conceding recognition *before* organisation is firmly established they can influence from the outset the nature of unionism with which they have to deal' (Hyman, 1975, p. 110).

But 'moderation' versus 'militancy' is not the only criterion on which employers may choose to recognize one particular union rather than another; in cases referred to ACAS, such as the case of W. H. Allen (1977), a number of other factors are taken into account. These would include, for example, the wishes of the workers involved in the reference, the shape of any negotiating group, the views of all parties concerned, and any existing procedures such as any industry-wide agreements to which the employer is party (Robinson, 1979, p. 30). It is assumed in general that fragmentation of unions/bargaining units is not conducive to good industrial relations. On questions of recognition, Robinson argues, we have a choice, 'Either we limit the number of unions recognised or we allow individuals to choose to be represented by any union they wish. The last option is clearly silly and unworkable. The only real issues are how much limitation there should be and by what criteria it should be determined' (1979, p. 33). Of course, this will mean some limitation of individual choice in the interests of stable industrial relations and well-defined bargaining units. Nowhere does this issue come in for more criticism than in the case of the closed shop.

Closed shops—or union membership agreements as they are legally termed—are the source of much confusion, particularly among the general public and those with no experience of them. A strict closed shop would include a clause in the terms and conditions of employment that *every* employee should be a member of a particular union. This may be *pre-entry*, in which case no one is accepted for a job unless they hold a union card, or *post-entry*, in which case the person is expected to join the specified union(s) within a certain period of time. Most of those in operation are of the latter variety (Gennard *et al.*, 1980, p. 1088). Under the Employment Act of 1980, any employee who objects on grounds of conscience or other deeply-held personal conviction to being a member of any trade union whatsoever or of a particular trade union will effectively be exempt from membership. This extended the previous 'escape' clause that was related to religious beliefs alone, and that had to conflict not just with a particular union but with the concept of trade unionism as a whole.

The major objection put forward against the closed shop is that it is fundamentally at odds with the concepts of liberty and freedom and inconsistent with the idea of trade unions being seen as voluntary bodies. As we have seen above, in the case of recognition, orderly industrial relations may often conflict with individual aspirations; the essentially pragmatic manager may prefer to accept the closed shop, even if it does appear distasteful from his personal political standpoint because of its implied restriction on personal freedom (Purcell, 1979, pp. 29–30).

However, adherents of the closed shop would argue that one of *their* primary reasons for wanting to extend membership to everybody is to prevent the existence of the 'free-rider' who gets all the benefits from the union without paying the subscriptions. From a *collectivist* standpoint, this is just as distasteful as is the restriction of personal freedom from an *individual* perspective. Furthermore, Taylor notes that most employers have little time for free-riders either, seeing them as nothing more than a potential nuisance (1980, pp. 46–47). Moreover, very few union membership agreements provide for 100 per cent unionization; in the post-entry cases, while all new employees would be obliged to join the union, there are usually loopholes for existing employees. This essentially pragmatic approach has much in its favour as it does at least safeguard the position of the existing employee who is a non-unionist and may provide an acceptable compromise between the two extreme views of 'the freedom of choice' supporters on the one hand and the 'trade union solidarity' enthusiasts on the other. Similarly, 100 per cent union membership exists in many factories without the need for a formal agreement. Only in rare cases, such as the well-advertised activities of SLADE in the late seventies, will unions push their position on UMAs too far.

A second major objection to the closed shop relates to the way in which it may serve to increase trade union bargaining power due to their greater ability to control and, if necessary, discipline their members. Trade union solidarity can be increased and there will be restrictions on management's freedom to manage, especially in its recruitment of the 'best man for the job' (Hawkins, 1979, p. 79). Some would say, however, that the closed shop merely acknowledges formally a power position that already exists.

Furthermore, one would expect the pluralist to assess whether a UMA is necessarily in his worst interests just because it may benefit a union concerned and its membership. Taking recognition policy to its extreme, a closed shop further reduces the potential for inter-union competition and this avoids a number of industrial relations problems. It can also help to stabilize industrial relations even more with negotiations being conducted centrally through one body and being channelled through one source of representation. It may encourage the growth of plant-level shop stewards committees that work together, and with management, in a more effective way. And, finally, UMAs may help management by increasing union control over the membership so that they ensure that terms and conditions are observed by all (Hart, 1979, p. 353).

According to Hawkins, the balance of opinion in industry would appear to have swung in favour of the closed shop (1979, p. 80). The IPM, while asserting that the aim of their paper had not been 'to come down in favour or against the principle of the closed shop' were encouraging managements to plan ahead, to consider the options, and certainly not dismiss the closed shop as a possible development with favourable consequences for companies (1976, p. 12). Indeed, fairly strong arguments were put forward to counter objections to UMAs. Hart concludes her analysis by noting that many employers have conceded closed shops in the interests of compromise and enforceability. Moreover, 'the practice should be seen increasingly as a source of order and discipline in industrial relations—goals which many of its most vehement critics espouse and which explain why employers have learned to love the closed shop' (1979, p. 354). By conceding or even encouraging a closed shop, management will be more able to ensure good relations with the unions involved.

With regard to recognition in general, it has been argued that a principle of 'cumulation' takes place in which 'early experiences in developing industrial relations in a company influences subsequent behaviour. Where a long and bitter recognition battle took place or where initially management was strongly anti-union, industrial relations are liable to remain tense and unstable' (Purcell, 1979, p. 31). Conversely, a policy of encouragement may help to create an 'initial fund of goodwill (that) will help both sides to overcome the problems of adjusting to the new relationship' (Hawkins, 1979, p. 67). Interestingly enough, this had led some writers to argue that those who should be most worried about management policy on recognition and the closed shop should be trade unionists themselves, and this is something to which we return in a later section (Hart, 1979, p. 354; Nichols and Beynon, 1977, p. 114).

Governmental attempts to amend closed shop legislation, through the 1980 Employment Act, would appear to have had relatively little effect on industry. If management has become used to working in a closed shop situation, and has found it to its benefit, it is unlikely to want or use any available legal machinery. Despite pressure from certain quarters to emasculate the closed shop even further, the government may be more usefully advised to leave the current situation as it is. Indeed, opinion during 1981 would seem to have focused upon the level of compensation for unfair dismissals and with ballots rather than with outlawing the closed shop altogether.

The acceptance of unionism, and the attempt to incorporate it into the current structure of the organization, is thus central to pluralism. Managements utilizing this frame of reference are keen to find ways of achieving this partnership, accepting alternative sources of loyalty, and encouraging membership. The presence of a union, however, also has some effect upon managerial prerogatives, especially in the workplace as articulated by shop stewards. We can now move on to examine this factor from both perspectives (unitary and pluralistic).

Management prerogatives

In simple terms, the difference between the two frames of reference lies in its willingness to accept a curbing of management prerogatives in the face of workplace representation. On the one hand, the manager with the unitary perspective would expect the shop floor to trust him to make the correct decision on 'impartial' and 'objective' grounds. Since all employees contribute to their *own* particular jobs to the best of their ability, the manager will obviously do the same in his job. Of course, on occasion, he may ask for assistance but the decision as to whether to do so or not rests upon his shoulders alone and cannot be catered for through any sophisticated and regular consultative machinery. He 'knows', it would be argued, when to consult and when not to.

On the other hand, the pluralist—accepting the role of an alternative body in the workplace—believes in a policy of working *with* the unions to achieve the best possible solution to a particular problem. To be sure, he does not consult on all issues but believes that it is only fair and correct that, especially on major aspects of change, he should have to justify his actions to shop stewards or other union representatives. Similarly, accepting the role of jointly agreed procedures, he would be unwilling to chance losing the trust of the stewards by, for example, failing to observe a status quo agreement or taking unilateral action before testing opinion and listening to alternative viewpoints. On many occasions, the *substantive* outcome of joint decision making may be little different from that which would have been achieved by direct management action; the *procedural* element is, however, considerably different and seen as vitally important. The trade union—or its representatives—comes to be seen as a body that 'participates with management in a process of joint decision-making on issues of day-to-day management. It is the *method* that is valued here, not necessarily the *results*' (Fox, 1966, p. 7).

Many would argue that this adherence to joint decision making is no more than a realistic assessment of the current state of affairs and, as should have become apparent already in this chapter, 'the pluralistic frame of reference, which openly concedes the severe limitations on management power, constitutes thereby a source of potential strength rather than weakness'. Fox continues that 'any notion that this full acceptance of the representational rights of organised work groups is necessarily conducive to a permissive stance on mangement's part would therefore by fallacious' (1966, p. 14). Indeed, the opposite is usually the case; shared decision making (in whatever form) involves managers in considerably more work than the alternative approach, primarily due to the need to ensure employee commitment.

Managers clearly vary in their willingness to accept a curbing of managerial right, both between individuals and with the subject matter under consideration. In a previous study by the author, managers were most willing to negotiate (with the proviso of an eventual management decision) on issues relating to methods of payment, methods of working and job design, design and operation of disciplinary procedures, and the numbers to be made redundant should the situation arise (1980, p. 103). Similar types of issue were outlined in a sample of managers studied by Storey; namely, job content, overtime allocation, manning, and shifts were all felt to be most open to negotiation. Many others were also negotiated but there remained several aspects of the business on which management wished to retain its prerogative. These, as might be expected, related to aspects such as investment and pricing policies, promotions, and product development (1980, p. 134). Therefore, the manager with the pluralistic frame of reference feels that certain issues are not up for negotiation at the present time nor should they be in the foreseeable future.

Three areas in which pluralism has had more than a limited effect will be mentioned below. Firstly, the role of the foreman has undergone a massive transformation from its position before the growth and development of strong shop floor unionism. Now, the foreman is increasingly urged to work *with* the shop stewards rather than compete against them for the leadership of the workgroup. This implies that 'at shop floor level, where the corporation needs the compliance of the trade unions, it is quite prepared to share control with the union in order to maintain control' (Purcell, 1979, p. 41). The way in which 'shared control' is seen and responded to by the foremen will be dealt with in Chapter 6.

Secondly, this also implies a new role for stewards; one in which they are encouraged to sit on a variety of joint bodies with management and they are given facilities for undertaking their duties and time off for training courses. Moreover, in some companies at least, they are encouraged—by being given time for joint shop steward meetings—to form their own inter-union committees to negotiate with management. This, it is argued, helps joint union–management meetings to concentrate on the more important topics since the minor irritants or irrelevancies have already been filtered out at pre-meetings. Furthermore, a more consistent and well-conceived union policy is expected to emerge. This we deal with in Chapter 5.

Finally, we have the development of diverse forms of employee participation. These, from the more formal consultative committees to the less formal working parties on topics such as job evaluation or working methods, and so on, will be analysed in Chapter 10. Management by agreement, according to McCarthy and Ellis, implies that '*all* proposals for change ought to be viewed as opportunities for improving and extending techniques of joint control' (1973, pp. 99–100).

With the emphasis on joint control, these authors go on to reassure managers that this 'is not a system of workers control. These proposals are not intended to challenge management's ultimate responsibility for running the enterprise. As in all forms of collective bargaining this remains intact' (1973, pp. 106–107). Because of this, we would not always expect a peaceful resolution of all issues, and this leads us on to the final strand in the pluralist perspective—the inevitability or acknowledgement of conflict.

The acknowledgement of conflict

From the unitary perspective, given the doctrine of common purpose or basic harmony, conflict is unlikely to emerge. If it does, however, it must be caused by one of a number of factors; there may be incompatible personalities on the management and union negotiating teams, or individual stewards and line managers may not get on with each other; faulty communications may cause rumour and produce conflict; employees may be stupid and not grasp the essentials of a message that management is trying to get across; or conflict may be the work of troublemakers, agitators, or wreckers inciting moderates on the shop floor and leading them into industrial action that is imposed on them against their will (Fox, 1966, p. 12).

The implication of an analysis such as this is simple; either managers must improve their communications and become better at 'educating their employees or the 'agitators' have to be rooted out. From the former point of view, and given that from the unitary perspective, 'the really fundamental interests are shared by management and managed alike, then management may have to be cruel to be kind by overriding what it asserts to be "irrational" beliefs, purely short-term preoccupations, and limited perspectives produced by ignorance' (Fox, 1973, pp. 197–198). Fox continues by suggesting an analogy between the treatment of employees by a unitary employer and that of children by a father, in that the latter may try to impose his interests on the former, regarding himself as trustee of their 'true' interests (1973, p. 188). This line of reasoning has also been heard on a number of occasions by the author.

Conversely, in the case of troublemakers, the suggested unitarist solution would be to weed out the individual in order to stop the 'root' of the conflict. Perhaps, if there is an individual asserting his will on a reluctant membership, such a policy may prove effective—in the short term at least. Moreover, employees may become unsure about action for fear of similar retribution. However, such a policy can only be of limited success in quelling the conflict. More likely, if the steward is merely responding to or articulating shop floor demands, others will come to the fore, and the resulting action may be considerably more explosive than it was previously.

The pluralist, on the other hand, rather than attributing unrest to an individual or to ignorance, will recognize that a certain degree of conflict is inevitable in any organization trying to balance competing demands for scarce resources. Trade unions do not 'introduce conflict into the industrial scene. They simply provide a highly organised continuous form of expression for sectional interests which would exist anyway' (Fox 1966, p. 8). A certain level of conflict—whether expressed through strike action or grievances passing through procedure—may be perfectly normal and it can be argued that 'overt and palpable expressions of conflict are no more a reliable indicator of low morale than their absence is of a clean bill of health' (1966, p. 9). Low productivity, for example, may be just as likely in companies that experience no strike action as it is in those that do. Conflict may also lead to change that is beneficial for the organization as a whole.

However, this is not to assume that conflict is, conversely, always good for an organization. What the pluralist frame of reference should do, according to Fox, is to 'convince us of the need for close, painstaking inquiry into specific situations rather than for blanket solutions derived from false identifications of industrial health and ill-health' (1966, p. 9). The willingness to try to appreciate conflict from the other side and to see why and how it arose may be a necessary 'precondition of success in modifying behaviour' (1966, p. 10).

Much of the pluralist approach to conflict will be examined in considerably greater detail in Chapter 7 when we look at the nature of power and conflict resolution, and in Chapter 8, when we examine the role of procedures in containing and channelling conflict through jointly agreed institutions. Certainly, a major advantage of the pluralistic frame of reference is that, within it, there is an acknowledgement of the possibility of conflict. Since this is acknowledged, it then follows that managements ought to be willing to seek to discover mechanisms either for reducing this or for channelling it through agreed procedures. In other words, management policy is 'to create a set of institutions and procedures through which conflict can be expressed and resolved at least on a temporary basis without recourse to overt industrial action' (Purcell, 1979, p. 39). If management can also persuade union leaders to follow these procedures as a matter of course, their objectives are furthered even more. And if union leaders have been involved in drawing up these procedures, they can be more appropriately seen as a mechanism 'for dealing with these differences rather than a formula for apparently dissolving them' (McCarthy and Ellis, 1973, p. 108).

In addition, conflict would not be seen as destroying a relationship; rather, industrial action—if taken—is seen as purely temporary and the parties expect their relationship to continue in the future. For example, Anthony quotes the convention in coal mining that safety work will continue during disputes. Similarly, he cites other incidents in which where 'there was evidence of management going beyond what was absolutely necessary for it to do in order to give strikers pay-in-hand, tax rebates and other payments' (1977, pp. 153–154). This, for him, represents 'our realisation that the employment relationship is a continuing one and that co-operation is necessary to it, despite temporary interruptions caused by a dispute' (1977, p. 154).

But, to acknowledge that conflict may exist is not an excuse for sitting back and waiting for it. On the contrary, such a perspective may lead management to develop more appropriate contingency plans in the event of action, and to try to predict which groups are most strategically placed for action and the likelihood of their taking it. Also it may lead to improved working conditions and so remove 'irritants' from the work situation. These again will be discussed in Chapter 7.

Criticism of pluralism

Having outlined the two frames of reference and spent some time developing the pluralist perspective, it might be helpful to reiterate the primary assumption underlying this approach. Pluralism, with its emphasis on joint arrangements, offers a much more realistic perspective than does its unitary counterpart. The overall implication is one of forward planning and a commitment to developing joint procedures where possible in the expectation that this may lead to more orderly and, hopefully for the manager, more predictable industrial relations. But, there are limitations to this approach, and pluralism has certainly attracted its share of criticism; in order to conclude the chapter, we shall make some reference to these.

Firstly, the pluralist standpoint has been attacked by those holding a unitary perspective. In the main, the assault has been from those with little knowledge of unions or large-scale industrial relations; for example, small business owners who possess both an ideological and a protectionist dislike of unions. Despite the fact that such a perspective might appear increasingly attractive as unemployment increases (and consequently union power decreases), it would appear to have little, if any, role to play in fostering good long-term industrial relations. On pragmatic grounds, unitarism cannot be viewed as a coherent strategy for the future in the majority of establishments. Indeed, Fox is particularly condemnatory of arguments by its proponents, accusing them of a lack of coherence and tendency to practise 'double-speak' (1973, p. 205).

Secondly, pluralism has been criticized from a more radical perspective and, in his later works, Fox himself takes the lead in this. Hyman, for one, issues the challenge that 'originally radical in orientation, pluralist ideas have increasingly tended to serve as a conservative legitimation of established institutions and ultimately as a cloak for essentially repressive programmes' (1978, p. 35). Other critics do not go quite as far but argue that pluralism rests on a number of basic assumptions and leads to a number of implications that are questionable to say the least.

First of all, pluralism rests on the expectation that there is a rough balance of power between the competing interest groups; critics argue that this is patently untrue, and the owners and controllers of resources (that is, employers) exert control in a variety of ways and 'rarely need to exert publicly and visibly in open conflict more than a small part of the power that lies at their disposal' (Fox, 1973, p. 208). By control of most of the dominant institutions of society, they are able not only to influence employees directly at work but also through the underlying ideological perspectives that permeate the media and society at large. Trade unions do not restore the balance but merely mitigate the imbalance. However, 'a great imbalance remains, symptomised by the fact that there are many other types of management decisions which employees might aspire to influence were they conscious of having the power to do so, but from which they are presently completely excluded' (Fox, 1974, pp. 15–16). While they may fight to preserve autonomy at work, they do not attack the principle of hierarchy in the organization; and while they may fight for better health and safety at work, they do not, in general, fight for the principle of 'socially useful products' In other words, while there may *appear* to be a rough balance of power in issues fought out at the workplace and in what is visible, the overall power imbalance remains relatively unaltered. However, the point remains that a pluralistic perspective offers a more realistic assessment of present-day industrial relations, and one with which many line managers would be able to identify as a way forward in achieving greater cooperation at work. That is, one that may enable both employers and employees to satisfy at least some of their basic objectives in relation to work.

A further implication of the pluralist frame of reference is that collective bargaining or joint regulation actually enhances rather than reduces management power. Management is seen to have a more 'human' face and, because of this, likely to achieve consent for, and legitimation of, its policies. Again, Fox notices that 'greater effectiveness . . . is achieved, first by frank and open recognition of divergent group interests and values, and secondly, by a patient and honest working-through of these differences towards a compromise or synthesis which is freely accepted by all parties as being fair' (1973, p. 215). If pluralism is more likely to achieve efficiency than either unitarism or a more radical perspective, it will gain adherents not just in management circles but also among many trade unionists who do not wish to fight for more radical or revolutionary change. As we have seen, a pluralist approach certainly alters the style of management to one of operating by greater consent and, by recognizing and institutionalizing alternative interest groups, it may also serve to increase management control. It may also, however, increase union control through more well-defined bargaining units, higher levels of membership, and the concession of the closed shop. To assume that what is good for one side is *automatically* bad for the other would be a fundamental misinterpretation of industrial relations.

There is, however, some danger that procedural principles may be elevated above substantive outcomes in the bargaining process (Hyman, 1978, pp. 32–35). That is, that 'reformed' industrial relations is primarily tied to engineering more appropriate structures for joint regulation—procedures, job evaluation, joint consultation, and facilities for representation—to the neglect of what these are likely to achieve for the stewards who become party to them; to take a 'Hawthorne' type view that to participate is what really matters and ownership of decisions—which may not be very different from those made unilaterally—is all important. No doubt, as we shall see later, there is some truth in this. Recently, however, there have been warnings that this strategy of enhancing the procedural status of trade unionism is not necessarily capable of improving industrial relations. Batstone, for example, has suggested that 'while personnel managers may have suceeded in formalising and centralising industrial relations procedures and decision-making, they have done little about the *content* of those procedures and decisions. As a consequence, they may have exacerbated labour conflict' (1980, p. 37). He goes on to note that there is a possibility that higher levels of conflict may have been caused because stewards have become 'frustrated both by centralisation within management and by the failure of management to take (sufficient) account of personnel and industrial relations considerations' (1980, p. 39). Similarly, Turner *et al.* noted a correlation between the degree of formalization and strike levels (1977, p. 72).

Perhaps, the major advantage for the manager adopting a generally pluralistic frame of reference (rather than any other) is that it causes him to plan ahead, to be more aware of other parties to industrial relations, and to find ways of working with them rather than against or in ignorance of them. Adoption of a pluralistic approach may certainly increase management control in one sense by helping to make industrial relations more predictable. In another sense, however, by forcing management to reconsider previously held ideas on prerogatives and modify its approach to joint regulation, it may be seen to increase union or employee control. To some, this may be seen as little more than sophisticated managerialism; to others, it may offer the only realistic approach for reform in workplace industrial relations.

Consistency and frames of reference

Before moving on to look at the way in which employees feel about their employers, their unions and possible conflicts between the two, something must be said about the consistency of these alternative perspectives; that is, is one person always a unitarist or a pluralist or is there likely to be variation between the two depending upon the situation? The two frames of reference are in reality two ideal types; in practice, as Clegg notes, 'neither is commonly found in its pure form' (1979, p. 163). Not only must we expect managers at different levels to display different tendencies—that is, that managers or foremen at 'the sharp end' would be more aggressive towards unions since they face the day-to-day manifestations of their power—but also that individuals will shift according to the issue before them. Winkler describes the existence of contradictory stereotypes that the directors in his sample were liable to articulate; 'in the course of a single conversation, one man would advance contradictory interpretations of workers' behaviour or agree with opposed theories advanced by colleagues' (1974, p. 207). Two of these are interesting for our discussion; in talking about strikes, opinion would veer from the assertion that 'it's all a few agitators' to a more philosophical concern that 'there's a deep malaise in British industry'. Similarly, in discussing motivation, there would be variation between a statement such as 'the old loyalties are dead; they don't give a damn about the company' to one of 'they'll pitch in if you let them know what the score is'. He concludes by suggesting that 'the implication for industrial relations is that we must expect instrumental inconsistency in attitudes to be the normal state of affairs . . . men adopt the attitude that best achieves their goals' (1974, p. 208).

We can also note some inconsistencies in relation to the subject matter of three sections we have dealt with in this chapter. For example, unionism— while acceptable to the pluralist—must also be seen to be 'responsible'. The role of unions is to be limited, the argument goes, to making a valuable practical contribution to economic progress and to be limited by public opinion and the law (Fox, 1974, pp. 253–254). Within the sophisticated modern pattern of management, the role of the union is defined as acceptable provided it lies between certain upper and lower limits of militancy and limited aspirations towards encroachment on management prerogatives (Fox, 1974, p. 303). Nichols and Beynon note that, for the foremen at ChemCo, it is clear that for them 'trade unionism (on the shop floor) has an important role to play in the future of ChemCo . . . they are also clear that it must be a particular type of trade unionism. "Real", "responsible" trade unionism' (1977, p. 116). In other words, a pluralist acceptance of unionism is required, with a unitarist definition of its role as assisting managerial goals that may be at the expense of the membership.

Similarly, in relation to management prerogatives, it is often felt that 'participation should not "upset" current systems of decision-making and company objectives but should be integrated into the framework so as to provide more opportunity for employee opinions to be taken into account' (Marchington, 1980, p. 101). On the one hand, participation in management decisions is recognized as a legitimate social function while, on the other, it is considered unnecessary because management already possesses sufficient information and skills to make decisions in the best interests of the company as a whole, employees included. Since management represents 'common interests and aspirations . . . given its technical competence there (is) no reason for workers or other groups to question its right to authority' (Child, 1969, p. 223). That is, participation is quite justified from a representational angle but totally unnecessary from an efficiency angle since decisions are best made by 'impartial' managers. Indeed, this is clearly an important issue in Great Britain where line managers often come from a technical background or from the shop floor, and are less likely to possess technical qualifications or degrees than their counterparts from abroad. However, management authority is regularly legitimized by reference to technical expertise, and this is regularly questioned by the shop floor. Consequently, there is a danger that managers, unable to draw upon a broader scientific or technical background, may be especially sensitive to criticism on the grounds of technical expertise. The implication of this is that they will be unwilling to 'open-up' decision making for fear that it shows up any inadequacies on their part.

Finally, we might expect to see the greatest confusion between the two frames of reference in the event of industrial action. Although, as pluralists, the likelihood of conflict may be accepted, the search for solutions and for its causes may easily rest upon unitarist assumptions about troublemakers and the like. From previous research by the author, otherwise pluralist managers would fall back upon unitarist ideology at times of dispute. They would argue that the stewards had manipulated the shop floor, and support for their assertion came from 'trusted' employees who were quite categorical—when asked by the manager—that they themselves had not wanted to go on strike. Because of this, the search for solutions was misdirected and generally irrelevant. It even led some to articulate their fears about employee *loyalty* in the event of union membership and *commitment*. We shall now look at this in Chapter 4.

4. Motivation, loyalty and commitment

As we saw in the last chapter, it has been difficult for some managements to adapt themsleves to the extension of trade unionism since they fear that the latter merely represents an intrusion into what, they feel, should be a private relationship between employer and employee. Because of this, the union involvement of an employee may be taken as a sign of disloyalty, and loyalty is a concept that often emerges during discussions with mangers about industrial relations.

With this in mind, we can assess the manager–employee relationship by dealing with a number of key issues; how can the manager motivate people at work? Can he manage without loyalty or commitment? Can he count on these or do they have to be earned? To what extent does unionism represent disloyalty, if at all? To answer these kinds of question, we need to appreciate management approaches to motivation, the concept of loyalty, and employee commitment to unionism. In the rest of the chapter, we shall examine each of these in turn.

Before commencing our discussion of motivation, however, one further point needs to be made about loyalty. It may be common for the manager to question the loyalty of the people who work for him and to wonder why it is in his eyes, that they lack loyalty to his and the organization's primary goals. On the shop floor, this query can be posed the other way round; that is, do managers have any loyalty and commitment to us as employees, or are we merely seen as a cost to be treated in much the same way as machinery. If the latter, is it then realistic for the company (and its managers) to expect loyalty and cooperation from the shop floor without demonstrating its own commitment first? We shall return to these issues later in the chapter.

Motivation
It is clear from a historical perspective, that certain universal visions of 'the worker' have led to the subsequent development of strategies aimed at

Table 4.1. Theories of man and management strategies

Theory of man	Primary exponent(s)	Management strategy
Rational-economic man	Taylor, Gilbreth	Scientific management of work
Social man	Mayo	Human relations and participative supervision
Self-actualizing man	Maslow, Herzberg, McGregor	Job enrichment and enlargement
Complex man	Schein	Contingency approaches

ensuring effective levels of work from such a person. Over the course of the last century, the vision has been amended on a number of occasions; basically, we can identify four dominant themes that have predominated among management theorists, and four distinct strategies which have emanated from them (see Table 4.1).

The picture of employees as being *rational and economic* in their approach to work was tied to the development of scientific management and, particularly, to the work of Taylor and Gilbreth. The former, in his role as consultant to the Bethlehem Steel Company, held a firm conviction that it is possible to give the workman what he most wants—high wages—and the employer what he wants—a low labour cost—for his manufactures. The implication for management is this; namely, that 'the principal object of management should be to secure the maximum prosperity for the employer (profits, long-term success), coupled with the maximum prosperity of each employee (higher wages, efficient performance in the highest grade of work for which his natural abilities fit him)' (Pugh *et al.*, 1971, p. 97). The assumptions underlying this picture of rational-economic man are therefore as follows:

1. People are motivated by economic incentives.
2. There is one particular job at which each person will excel.
3. People (on the shop floor) are basically lazy and have to be motivated by management.
4. People are incapable of self-discipline and control.
5. Jobs have to broken down into their smallest constituent parts.

If people are motivated primarily by money, Taylor felt it essential to ensure that the jobs they were doing were capable of providing them with the opportunity to maximize their earnings. For this reason, jobs needed to be scientifically examined, broken down into their constituent parts, and then put back together in the most efficient manner. He would devise the 'best' method by observing the 'best' workman on each particular task. Once he had achieved the best method, this could then be taught to other workmen who, if necessary, were to be retrained until they were proficient at the job. It may be that some people would never become proficient at a particular job, so they were moved until they achieved a satisfactory level on another job. Much of his early work was based upon the handling of pig-iron and from this came his famous phrase 'that the science of handling pig-iron is so great that the man who is fit to handle pig-iron as his daily work cannot possibly understand that science; the man who is physically able to handle pig-iron and is sufficiently phlegmatic and stupid to choose this for his occupation is rarely able to comprehend the science of handling pig-iron' (Pugh *et al.*, 1971, p. 130). He then turned to shovelling—which is 'a great science compared with pig-iron handling' (1971, p. 131)—and, with Gilbreth, to bricklaying. In each, the basic idea was to devise a method that was universally correct and then train people in this way. Since he felt it was management's duty to provide an environment in which it was possible for workers to earn as much as they could, he developed the principles of method study and work measurement.

Taylor has, of course, been roundly condemned over the years. As Schein notes, his managerial conception of rational–economic man led to a self-fulfilling prophecy that 'if employees are expected to be indifferent, hostile, and only motivated by economic incentives, the managerial strategies used to deal with them are very likely to train them to behave in precisely this fashion' (1965, p. 49). Rose also points to Taylor's tendency to equate men with machines, assuming that there is one universal best method and that the *individual* incentive to earn more money is the primary, if not the sole, motivating factor at work (1978, p. 62).

It was against a backcloth such as this that the picture of *social* man emerged. This developed out of a piece of research designed to test the effects of fatigue at work on productivity. Elton Mayo is generally assumed to have been the leader in this research although, according to Rose, he never conducted the Hawthorne studies and never led the diffuse human-relations movement (1978, p. 113).

The groups under investigation (at the Hawthorne works) were studied over a number of periods and the changes that were introduced related to alterations in rest periods, refreshments, starting and finishing times, payment systems, and—probably best known of all—lighting levels. Much to the researchers' surprise, variation in these 'objective' conditions of work did not appear to correlate with productivity. Even at the end of the experiment, when conditions were back at their original state, production was over 30 per cent higher than at the beginning of the studies. The researchers concluded that there was nothing else but increased satisfaction—through being given special attention, working in a close tightly-knit group, and being involved in decision making by their supervisors—that could account for the higher productivity. Accordingly, the 'initiative for work shifts from management to the worker. The manager, instead of being the creator of work, the motivator and the controller, becomes the facilitator and sympathetic supporter (Schein, 1965, p. 51).

As with Taylor, there is a substantial body of criticism surrounding this approach to motivation; it is unlikely that every employee wants to be part of a closely-knit group or to engage in joint decision making with management. The human relations approach did not incorporate any treatment of trade unionism within its model. Furthermore, the research methods have been strongly queried; in particular the choice of group members appears to have been biased towards those who were the more cooperative; autocratic supervisors appeared to get just as high a production as did their more 'democratic' colleagues; and the economic position of the thirties enhanced cooperation through fear (see Rose, 1978, pp. 125–142).

In the forties, Maslow postulated his 'hierarchy of needs' approach to motivation. To some extent, it incorporated the previous two 'theories' of motivation—economic and social—before moving on to identify higher-level needs relating to *self-actualization*. Basically, the theory goes, people are satisfied by a number of factors at work. However, they need to satisfy one particular need before moving on to attempt to satisfy the next in the hierarchy; for example, basic security needs, such as food, job, and house, have to be satisfied before someone begins to consider their social and affiliative needs. Once they feel secure and part of a group, they can then turn to satisfy their personal needs for ego satisfaction and self-actualization (Pugh, 1971, pp. 27–41).

Much of this approach is observable in Herzberg's two-factor theory of motivation that had such a big influence over many large companies in the sixties; for example, it can be observed in ICI's consideration of the move to the Weekly Staff Agreement (WSA) in the late sixties and early seventies. Since most people are probably aware of Herzberg's work, we shall merely recapitulate the central argument and the research approach, among other things, Herzberg asked two questions; firstly, 'when was the last time you felt exceptionally or pretty *good* about your job? Describe the situation, telling me what happened and how long the feeling lasted for?' Secondly, a similar question was posed with 'bad' substituted for 'good' (Pugh, 1971, pp. 324–344). Respondents were asked to ensure that certain criteria were observed; that is, that the feelings related to the 'job' and not factors external to the work situation; that they must be centred around an event or a series of events; that they must be bounded by a time factor; and that they must have taken place while the respondent was doing his present job or one broadly comparable with it.

His major finding was that satisfiers and dissatisfiers were not necessarily related and that, just because a person did not feel satisfied about a particular aspect of his work, it did not mean that he was automatically dissatisfied. Conversely, if he did not feel dissatisfied about his work, it did not mean that he was automatically satisfied. The *motivators* that tended to be identified with the 'good' feelings were aspects such as achievement, responsibility, recognition, advancement, and the work itself. The *hygiene* factors—which tended to be identified with the 'bad' feelings—were factors such as company policy, working conditions, supervision, and pay. In other words, if a respondent talked about his feeling good, it was generally related to having achieved something, being recognized as a good worker, and so on. Conversely, if he talked about his feeling bad, this usually referred to bad supervision, insufficient pay, or poor working conditions. However, unless the hygiene factors were satisfied, no amount of motivators would be of any use; Herzberg argued that many jobs did not even satisfy hygiene factors let alone motivators. Therefore, pay or conditions needed to be above a certain 'acceptable' minimum before the motivators could take effect.

As with the other approaches, Herzberg too has attracted his share of criticism; again, the assumed universalism of his theory failed to allow for people who did not want to be motivated at work, or to be involved in management decision making. Herzberg assumed work to be of central life interest and, consequently, neglected external factors and their effect on performance at work. Closer examination of his findings does not suggest such a clear-cut distinction between motivators and hygiene factors—particularly with regard to pay—as he maintains. Indeed, it has also been suggested that the phraseology of his questions left respondents with little alternative to answering in the way that they did (Schein, 1965, pp. 56–60). Moreover, the ideas have been applied to a much wider range of employees than was originally covered by the research; for example, his research was conducted on professional people (accountants and engineers) whereas many of his findings have been applied to manual workers. Similarly, his work was undertaken for the most part in the USA where there are probably different cultural meanings to work.

Our fourth and final group of theories can be referred to as those positing the existence of *complex* man. This does not lead us to any automatically universalistic picture of the employee but one in which he 'has many motives which are arranged in some sort of hierarchy of importance to him, but this hierarchy is subject to change from time to time and situation to situation' (Schein, 1965, p. 60). Similarly, in the UK, the universalism of other theories has been increasingly questioned, particularly by those utilizing an action frame of reference such as Goldthorpe and his colleagues. The *Affluent Worker* study (Goldthorpe et al., 1968) was originally designed to test the embourgeoisement theory that manual workers would become progressively more middle-class as they earned more money and gathered more material possessions. Despite finding little evidence to support this thesis, they did discover a group of workers who wanted little else from work other than enough money to enable them to enjoy life to the full outside the workplace. Few of the respondents were particularly satisfied with their work but neither were they dissatisfied; as a priority in their lives, work was not important.

They came to work for purely instrumental reasons and their attachment to workmates, company, and union was of a similar order.

Clearly, this has important implications for theories of motivation. Rather than assuming one universalistic approach to employee relations, managements need to assess what the subjective priorities of their employees actually are. Schein argues that the manager will need to be flexible and prepared to accept 'a variety of interpersonal relationships, patterns of authority and psychological contracts' (1965, p. 61). Although the *Affluent Worker* study is a major milestone in our attempts to understand employee motivation (and industrial sociology) this too has attracted criticism. It has been argued that the researchers over-emphasized the factors *external* to work to the neglect of those operating within the factory.

Furthermore, as we saw above, attitudes and priorities can and do vary considerably over time and it is insufficient to treat attitudes to work on entry to an organization as being maintained after entry. Nevertheless, at least this is a much more realistic approach to work attitudes than those of its predecessors and, along with certain aspects of the Herzbergian model, offers a better prospect to enhance our understanding of motivation. As Schein comments 'every manager makes assumptions about people. Whether he is aware of these assumptions or not, they operate as a theory in terms of which he decides how to deal with his superiors, peers and subordinates' (1965, p. 47). In view of the large number of attitude surveys that has been undertaken recently, we can move on to examine employees' attitudes to work, to supervision, and to the organization for which they work.

Attitudes, loyalty and teamwork

In view of the argument advanced towards the end of the previous section—that is, that in order to understand employee attitudes to work, one needs to assess their *priorities* and place these within a suitable context—it would be misguided to set out to demonstrate some universal employee attitude that is fixed in nature and consistent over time. Similarly, responses to survey questions may vary depending upon the research methods used. Nevertheless, it is useful to report the results from a number of studies in order to illustrate employee priorities in a variety of situations.

The 'affluent workers' in the Goldthorpe *et al.* Luton study did not report any great degree of satisfaction with the jobs that they were performing; in fact the general impression was that for most of them work was 'regarded as an expenditure of effort made with the aim of extrinsic rather than intrinsic returns; in other words, the *meaning* which was given to work was essentially that of *labour*' (1968, p. 25). When asked what it was that kept them at their current work (in view of their low attachment), by far the most important reasons offered were those relating to pay and security of employment (approximately 55 per cent of all reasons) (1968, p. 29).

Security was also seen as a vital factor in research undertaken at about the same time on employees working at a large chemical complex in the north east of England. It was situated in an area in which fears of unemployment remained alive after its consequences in the thirties. For the general workers, the company was seen in a predominantly favourable light because of its international reputation and its policy of avoiding redundancy whenever possible '. . . there was undoubtedly still a fund of goodwill towards the company because it had succeeded (in the inter-war years) in maintaining its employment level when other industries in the area were not' (Wedderburn and Crompton, 1972, p. 35). Also high on their list were good working conditions and fringe benefits; pay came much lower down the list. Nevertheless, in both these surveys, the attachment of the employee to the company was largely of an instrumental nature and there appears to be little, if any, desire for more intrinsically rewarding employment.

A similar finding emerged in a more recent piece of work undertaken by the author on employees of a kitchen furniture manufacturer situated in an urban environment in the West Midlands; the area has a long tradition of factory employment. Respondents were asked to indicate the extent to which their present jobs offered them a certain number of rewards and opportunities; a supplementary question then asked how much they felt that jobs *ought* to offer these factors. For most of the 'basics' of the job, the sample were fairly satisfied; for example, they already felt that their pay and hours of work were as much as they felt they 'ought' to have. A series of other factors—such as working conditions—were also fairly well satisfied by their current jobs. Because of the insecurity surrounding the kitchen market, however, they felt somewhat uneasy about their current degree of job security and felt that this ought to be much higher. When we turn to examine their current and desired level of intrinsic rewards, we find them wanting considerably more opportunity to learn new things in the trade, chances for advancement, and recognition of qualifications to name a few. At present, they felt these were sadly lacking in their jobs. However, despite the wish for a much greater amount of intrinsic rewards in their jobs, this was not the priority for their employment; interestingly enough, it was the extrinsic factors that remained as the priorities and top of the list came the feeling of working for a good employer. Security of employment was also a priority (1980, pp. 44–47).

These results have been given not to show any universal response to work but merely to demonstrate the type of things that appear to have been priorities for particular groups of employees in different parts of the country and under very different economic circumstances. Nevertheless, despite this, we can observe a fairly calculative attachment to work displayed by all these groups of employees, one that could well increase with high levels of unemployment when security becomes of paramount importance.

Indeed, it is hardly surprising to find that the major attachment to an organization, which maintains one's presence by payment, would be of a calculative manner. That is, what companies get 'in the way of involvement is in line with what they give in the way of rewards and the kind of authority they use . . . (if) a manufacturing concern expects its employees to like their work, and be morally involved, it may be expecting workers to give more than it gives them' (Schein, 1965, pp. 45–46).

This is not to say that business organizations do not—or should not—try to develop a higher level of employee identification with the company; this often emerges under the umbrella of *loyalty* and we can see numerous examples of this in industry as a whole. Fox, for example, examines a number of strategies that managements have used in order to secure some degree of compliance and, if possible, moral involvement, identification with, and commitment to the goals of the organization (1974, p. 3). In more recent surveys, authors have noted the objective of senior management in two large companies (ICI and BP) to gain the *loyalties* of its employees and so ensure identification with the aims of the company rather than with the wider trade union movement (Gill *et al.*, 1978, p. 150 and Gallie, 1978, p. 183). In these cases, it did not imply that these companies were seeking to undermine the union in the workplace but rather, by different means, to integrate the union representatives into current structures of decision making operating within the organization. Similar exhortations have been made at both British Leyland and Chrysler in attempts to secure not only the *compliance* of the workforce but also to stimulate *cooperation* through a difficult business cycle.

In these cases, management—even though it may have gained a high level of cooperation over a considerable period of time—is trying to overcome any opposition to its policies. On occasions such as this, managements come close to equating opposition with disloyalty; this has been observed by the author on more than one occasion when observing joint consultative meetings (1980, pp. 158–159).

Managements have demanded complete loyalty and, when total loyalty is not forthcoming, assume absolute *disloyalty* and opposition. This equation of opposition with disloyalty is even more apparent when the ranks of management, themselves, start to join trade unions; however, this does not appear to have caused any great problems for public sector managers.

It would seem that loyalty and cooperation are an even more crucial consideration with increased competition and greater job complexity. Indeed, Fox has even suggested that 'changing circumstances may call for more than passive uninvolvement even among those performing the most humble jobs. Quickening foreign competition and accelerating technical change may require a ready and cooperative acceptance by the rank and file of adaptation and flexibility' (1974, p. 43). But, if management requires a more loyal and committed workforce, it too will need to change its approach in relation to its subordinates; that is, that trust and security of employment may become even more paramount considerations for employees. However, it is during times of economic recession that managements are probably least able to give such assurances. For Fox, there is no doubt that this is where they have demonstrably failed (1974, p. 25).

Recent work undertaken by the author has revealed, particularly on Merseyside, that manual workers have questioned not so much their own loyalty but, rather, that of their management. In some cases, the former may have remained with the company through a series of takeovers and variety of managements. They certainly appeared to resent the management team, drafted in to 'sort out' the company, which had little commitment to their future or to that of the area. Management decisions were interpreted within this framework (of loyalty and commitment) rather than on technical or financial criteria. In a very different area (the south coast), White reported very similar feelings, and argued that it is useless for managers to ask for moral cooperation or commitment from the workforce when it is regularly reconfirmed that 'the firm has little moral commitment to them' (1981, p. 71). Clearly, the concept of loyalty works both ways.

On this theme, one question has been asked in a number of surveys in an attempt to discover employee perceptions of the company for which they work. Although varying slightly in its wording, it basically asks employees to say whether their firm is more like a football side (because teamwork means success and is to everyone's advantage) or whether teamwork is impossible (because people are really on opposite sides). The responses to this question have been remarkably similar in most cases as we can see in Table 4.2.

Apart from the study by Willener, which was undertaken in France, the results show a fairly high proportion of employees endorsing the conception of a firm being like a football team. The French result is interesting in that

Table 4.2   Firms and football terms (%).†

Researcher	Site	Team	Opposite sides	Don't know
Willener	France— steel and iron	28	69	3
Goldthorpe *et al.*	Luton— affluent workers	67	28	6
Wedderburn and Crompton	North east— chemicals			
	(Tradesmen)	71	22	6
	(General)	69	23	8
Brown and Cousins	North east— shipbuilding	79	17	4

† Some of the percentages in the table do not add up to 100, presumably because the researchers have either rounded up or rounded down the scores in the appropriate columns.

more recent work by Gallie has demonstrated similar differences between employees' conceptions of the firm in the UK and France, with French workers appearing much more oppositional in their stance towards their employer than are their British colleagues (1978, pp. 113–115 for one example of this).

Goldthorpe *et al.*, in noting the generally 'harmonistic' view of the Luton workers, suggest that they have 'a conception of the enterprise in which the recognition of the interdependence of management and labour is generally more powerful than awareness of conflicts between them . . . in the eyes of the majority; a co-operative attitude towards management was important to the effective operation of the plant and would also, in most cases, or "in the long run", turn out to be in their own best interests' (1968, p. 74). They felt that the 'affluent' workers did not show any moral commitment to their organization but, recognizing the need to work together in order to achieve *their own ends*, were quite willing to go along with the 'teamwork' view. Indeed, they continue, 'notwithstanding the prevalent "teamwork" image of the enterprise, they recognise that their relationship to their firm may well, on certain issues, become one of opposition and contention' (pp. 84–85). That Vauxhall workers went on strike not long after the report was published—no likely connection between the two— shows the frailty of the link between a teamwork view and industrial peace.

Other commentators have argued that, in answering the 'teamwork' question, respondents are not really identifying what actually is best but rather what it *ought* to be like. When the shipbuilders in the Brown and Cousins' survey were asked the same question but with the qualification 'is this how it works at Swan-Hunter', the percentage supporting the teamwork view fell to just over 50 per cent (Ramsay, 1975, p. 397). Moreover, Gallie notes that the major criticisms by the BP workers he interviewed related to 'technical matters' or 'the efficiency with which management carried out its duties'. He continued by noting that 'these criticisms were not accompanied by a demand for greater control by the workforce . . . (they) appeared to reveal a high level of identification with the underlying objectives of management—a commitment to increased rationalisation and efficiency' (1978, p. 298).

In order to test out the possibility of a purely calculative attachment to the company, Ramsay added a third alternative to the football team question and also amended the 'agree' response. He found, in fact, that very few manual workers (just 8 per cent) agreed with the statement that 'a firm is like a football team because managers and men have the same interest in everything that matters', whereas 46 per cent agreed with the amended version of 'agree *but only* because people have to work together to get things done'. Nearly half, 41 per cent disagreed with the football team analogy (1975, pp. 398–399). While accepting that the original question was probably biased in favour of a harmonistic reply, this one would appear to be unduly biased against it and towards a calculative response.

Nevertheless, his eventual conclusion seems about right when he argues that 'the view of the employment relationship is thus not one of normative integration of the employee but rather a chiefly pragmatic acceptance by employees who accept that one way or another the current relation has to be lived with' (1975, p. 339). It is wrong to equate consensus with loyalty, and cooperation may be offered on a negotiated basis. By asking questions at a certain level of generality, respondents are more likely to answer in a strictly consensual way. On the other hand, reactions and replies will be very different to more concrete questions, ones directly applicable to their own situation.[1] If results from the general level questions were used as a basis for management, there could, in Ramsay's words, be a rude disruption.

In other words, it would seem that there is not outright opposition to managerial objectives in most cases; conversely, however, cooperation has to be won and employers have to illustrate their technical competence and their willingness to manage by consent. For many employees, attachment to work could be said to be highly calculative at one level and highly indifferent at another; how about their commitment to their trade unions?

Union commitment

Judging from the results of any opinion poll, or hearing discussions about trade unions through the media, one could easily gain the impression that the majority of union members are unwillingly forced into membership and often manipulated by political extremists. Indeed, in August 1980, *The Sunday Times* reported on the results of a poll showing that a clear majority of union members felt that trade unions had got too much power (58 per cent), that they were controlled by extremists (55 per cent), and that the closed shop was a threat to individual liberty (59 per cent). Moreover, only just over half the union members questioned were satisfied with their own leaders. If this were the case, it could be argued, why do people remain in trade unions if they perform such an unsatisfactory service? Below, we shall examine this question from a somewhat more balanced viewpoint than that presented in this and other opinion polls where dubious use of statistics (and research methodology) enables headlines of sensational proportions.

Most people join trade unions for primarily instrumental reasons; as one would expect, given their low-key attachment to their employer, the 'affluent workers' joined their unions for the benefit of insurance against either accidents or protection against arbitrary decisions (Goldthorpe *et al.*, 1968, p. 97). A similar picture emerges from studies of union commitment undertaken by the author in which, across a number of sites, protection against

1. See Parkin (1972) for a discussion of the variety of value systems that can be adopted by people and the way in which they choose between them depending upon the situation.

victimization and accidents was the crucial reason for joining. In some cases, and again particularly that of Goldthorpe *et al.*, membership was not a matter of choice and quite a number of members felt they had been compelled to join in order to get the job. In others (by the author) there was a surprisingly high proportion of union members who felt it was morally right to be in a union; indeed, in the survey at the kitchen furniture manufacturer, in which a post-entry union membership agreement was operated, almost one-third of the sample reckoned that this was *their* most important reason for joining (40 per cent felt that some more instrumental reason was the most important). And this is not just confined to manual workers. However, the insurance function is probably the one that comes to mind most readily. That is, one in which they have the backing of the union in the event of injury, discipline, dismissal, or dispute.

Because of this, participation in union affairs is generally of a fairly low order. The average branch attendance has been estimated at a little under 10 per cent of the total membership on a regular basis. This varies, of course, between workplaces, occupations, and unions; skilled workers are more likely to attend as are those whose institutional and community arrangements make participation an easier or more normative affair. For example, of the Luton workers, only 7 per cent attended branch meetings regularly while 60 per cent claimed that the never went at all (Goldthorpe *et al.*, 1968, pp. 98–99). Other studies of union commitment show similar results across a number of industries; for engineering workers, only 14 per cent said they attended regularly, for furniture workers it was 6 per cent, while for a sample of metal workers it was 13 per cent (see Marchington, 1979, p. 136). Taylor's results also support this level of attendance, although unions such as NALGO, NUT and NUM traditionally *report* higher levels (1980, pp. 176–179).

As we shall see below, participation in union affairs rises considerably when a concrete problem confronts the membership. One has to take into account an individual's reason for joining and remaining in the union; as Child *et al.* argue, 'viewed in this perspective a low level of membership participation may imply an adequate degree of democratic involvement for members who regard their union almost exclusively in an instrumental light' (1973, pp. 74–75).

Despite their criticisms, it is interesting to note the response that the unionists sampled in *The Sunday Times* (August 1980) survey gave to a more concrete question relating to union membership. In fact, 90 per cent of them felt that trade unions were *essential* to protect their interests; just 6 per cent of them disagreed. From our own surveys, the union was seen as a very important element in their working lives, not only at their present place of work (where, on average, just 11 per cent of all the samples felt it to be unimportant) but also should they go elsewhere for work. Quite a large number regarded the presence of a union in their next place of work as a primary factor that would influence their choice of accepting employment. Moreover, when asked whether they would be willing to pay higher subscriptions, if the union were about to collapse for lack of funds, approximately 60 per cent of the furniture and metal workers said that they would and, in about one-third of these cases, it would be twice as much again. Continuation of union membership is seen very much as the norm.

Unions are seen very much in *local* and *economic* terms since this is where the union performs its service and is most visible, particularly through its lay representatives, to the ordinary member. This localized conception of union membership—and, with it, the development of what has been termed a factory consciousness—is also apparent when we assess the degree to which union members care about which person is elected to a number of offices in the union (see Table 4.3).

Clearly, we can see that the office of steward is considered as the most important position for the rank and file member; there is considerably less interest in the election of more senior full-time officials, particularly at national level. This relative lack of caring related to feelings of remoteness from the official channels of the union. Goldthorpe *et al.* report a similar situation with their Luton workers who, they argue, 'fail to identify at all closely with their unions above the level of the workplace, and in effect see little connection between the unionism which they themselves practise and the national organisations to which they formally belong' (1968, p. 133). Nichols and Armstrong continue in the same vein when they report that their ChemCo sample 'only have a hazy impression of what they (national negotiators) do, or even of who they are . . . quite simply, the officials are not part of the workers' world' (1976, pp. 30–31).

This localized conception of unionism is further supported by attitudes

Table 4.3   **Degree of caring about election to offices in union.**

| | Caring score† | | | |
Office	Engineering	Furniture	Metal	All
Shop steward	4.61	4.30	4.37	4.38
Convenor/chairman	4.09	3.83	4.08	3.95
Local full-time official	3.31	3.40	3.66	3.45
General secretary/president	3.27	3.29	3.54	3.35
N	88	231	116	435

† Respondents were asked to indicate how much they cared about election to a number of offices on a scale from 'not care in the least' to 'care very much'. For the former we assigned a score of 1, for the latter one of 5; in between, 'not sure' was scored as 2, 'care a little' was scored as 3, 'care somewhat' was scored as 4. Although the scores in themselves mean little, the comparison between different samples scored on the same basis is perfectly acceptable. These results are based on surveys carried out between 1974 and 1977.

towards strike action. From our own studies, the vast majority of union members felt that, in the abstract, strikes should not be called until procedure had been exhausted although nearly 90 per cent of our engineering sample had taken part in one strike or more during the course of their working lives. In other words, there is a realization—when concretely experienced—that workers may (and do) need to go on strike on occasions in order to put pressure on management, so as to press home an advantage or react against some form of supervisory treatment. On the other hand, other people's strikes seem to be for petty reasons, precisely because so little is known about the underlying reasons for the action. It is hardly surprising, therefore, that a seeming contradiction should exist between negative attitudes towards unofficial action in general and its high level over the past 20 years (relative to official action). Results from opinion polls can create the misguided impression, and lead to the incorrect assumption, that most strikes are for stupid reasons or are the work of agitators.

Moreover, attitudes in times of industrial peace or calm are also likely to be considerably different from those observed during crisis; as Kellner (in *The Sunday Times*, August 1980, article) suggests, it may be 'that many union members are intrinsically neither radical nor right-wing, but simply defensive-conservative in the way they want the world ordered but militant when their own direct interests are threatened'. The 'affluent workers', instrumental though they were, were not unwilling to take strike action should the need arise; similarly, participation in union affairs and attendance at branch meetings have also been found to rise dramatically in crisis situations.

As Beynon notes, in his study of Ford car workers, attendance at the branch jumped from an average of 80 members (out of a membership of 5000) to several hundred if there was anything important to discuss. For example, he reports that 'the branch meeting that made the final decision on the 1967 wages structure was attended by 400 members' (1973, p. 203). Similar 'explosions' were noted by Lane and Roberts during the lead up to and during the course of the strike at Pilkingtons (1971, pp. 235–240).

For the most part, then, union members are perfectly willing to allow their leaders (at whatever level) to run the union in accordance with predetermined policy; there is certainly a danger in exaggerating the differences between member and organizational interests, and too much reliance on the concept of a passive and moderate rank and file could lead to a severe shock for management and union leaders alike. Above, we have seen occasions when management has been surprised; events during 1979 and 1980 also demonstrated that union leaders cannot take membership support for granted either in calling an official strike or, conversely, refusing to make a local skirmish official. What is apparent, however, is the nature of union members' commitment to local matters, whether these be at departmental or factory level, and the different meaning that unionism can have for the rank and file. The ordinary membership relies to a very large extent on the shop floor leadership of the steward movement, whether this be in relation to local management or to the union outside of the workplace. Indeed, as Clegg suggests, in relation to voting at branch meetings, this may 'be represented as to some extent a form of indirect election in which trade union members rely on their representatives to make a choice among candidates for elective posts within the union' (1979, p. 222). We can now turn to an examination of this and other aspects of the stewards' role.

Conclusions

Clearly, the commitment of most people either to their work or to their unions is predominantly calculative in nature. As we have seen above, in relation to union involvement, interest can wax and wane, and is very much tied to the significance of the particular issue at hand. Similarly, employee loyalty to an organization is very much dependent upon the approach of management to employee relations. It would appear unrealistic for managers to expect loyalty from their employees when they, themselves, appear to show little interest in the people who work for them. As with many other aspects of industrial relations, it is up to management to take the initiative in the anticipation that employees will respond to this. As we shall see below, in relation to steward organizations, positive management action has exerted a considerable degree of influence over the development of steward bodies.

5. Working with the shop steward

Who needs the shop steward? There seems to be no question in industrial relations that elicits a negative response as easily as this one! Further probing reveals that the superficial reply glosses over a wealth of reasons why the steward is seen as a valued member of workplace relations whether it be from the standpoint of the individual members, the full-time official or the member of management who has to deal with him. Unfortunately, the 'Fred Kite' image still takes a long time to die and the manager coming into industry for the first time should be 'forgiven for approaching his first shop steward with some trepidation. The new manager may well expect to meet a monster-like figure representing the archetypal shop steward and it may surprise him to find that the average shop steward is in reality a very ordinary person' (Hunt, 1977, p. 18).

Since the time of the Donovan Commission, a mass of evidence has been produced that shows the steward in a somewhat more favourable light. For example, stewards are now more conventionally seen as reasonable and moderating influences, as lubricants of the industrial relations system rather than as irritants to it. Managements have increasingly not only accepted stewards in the workplace but also *sponsored* their development and organization in some cases. In other words, managements have found that the principle of working *with* the shop steward is a considerably more appropriate response to their existence than is continually working against them and viewing them as a potential enemy.

As with other chapters, it will be useful to organize the argument around a number of simple questions. What has led to the emergence of the steward as a key figure in workplace industrial relations? To what degree does the steward attempt to lead his constituents, or does he merely respond to membership demands? How do steward organizations operate? And, finally, in what ways can managers effectively learn to work with shop stewards, bearing in mind the role that the steward occupies?

Reasons for steward emergence

Although it is since 1945 that there has been a real growth in the number of shop stewards, there are reports of workplace spokesmen as far back as the seventeenth century. In printing, for example, there is mention of their presence in 1682. The term 'shop steward' was actually used nearly 200 years later by the Amalgamated Society of Engineers; it was the duty of such a person to check that all fellow employees were in the union, to ensure that craft rules were observed, and to report infringements to the district committee (Clegg, 1979, p. 20). Their role expanded later in the century to include some workplace negotiations and, by 1918, the Whitley Committee of Inquiry saw fit to try and integrate them into a three-tier system of joint regulation within each industry.

There have been several estimates of the number of shop stewards in British Industry since 1945, and recent evidence suggests that there are now in excess of 300 000 shop stewards. Added to this can be safety representatives, people who are union nominees on pension committees, consultative committees, and suchlike, and the number of workplace representatives will total over half a million. Since estimates for 1960 would suggest about 100 000, and those for 1970 around about 200 000, we can see how there has been a mushrooming in their numbers over the past 20 years. Quite a proportion of these representatives will be responsible for members who are new to trade unionism, particularly among white collar workers and, especially in the public sector, relatively senior levels of management. Much of this is a response to specific managerial or governmental initiatives. At least five reasons have been put forward to explain this growth in numbers:

1. Decentralization of collective bargaining to establishment level.
2. Reluctance/lack of resources to appoint more full-time officials.
3. Development of company procedure agreements.
4. Increase in labour law.
5. Increased acceptance of stewards by management on an informal basis.

The duties undertaken by stewards have also undergone something of a shift during the seventies due to the formalization of the role and to the massive increase in legal intervention in the employment field. Stewards may now have much less to do with negotiating payments and considerably more to do with workplace rights in relation to such issues as dismissal, health and safety, maternity, and redundancy. Moreover, there has been a development in steward hierarchies over a much broader range of industry; now, we can estimate that, in manufacturing, three quarters of all establishments with 50 or more employees have stewards for manual workers and a third have them for non-manual employees. In all but the smallest workplaces, a senior steward will be recognized. In addition, Brown estimates that there are between four and five thousand full-time stewards in manufacturing, with possibly an equal number in the public sector (1980, p. 20). While it is estimated that, on average, 12 per cent of manufacturing establishments had a full-time steward present, this does vary between industries; for vehicles, it is 30 per cent and mechanical engineering 20 per cent. On the other hand, in paper, printing, and publishing, it is just 4 per cent (Brown, 1981, p. 64).

Turning to the micro-level, it is interesting to see why it is that people take on the often time-consuming job of a shop steward. It is clear that a large number take on the job without being particularly keen on the prospect or committed to the broader principles of unionism. For example Chinoy, back in the fifties, identified three different ways in which people came to occupy the role of office-holder—by *accident*, because they were *ambitious*, or because they were *ideologically* committed to it (1965, pp. 162–167). This categorization has been amplified and extended by Nicholson; he outlines seven reasons for taking office that basically fall into two distinct categories—those of external and internal direction (1976, pp. 15–26). The former occurs when the person is either pressurized from elsewhere to stand for office or simply falls into the job by virtue of undertaking some or all of the duties in the absence of a regular steward. For example, after the previous steward resigned, a number of people come to take on the job merely because no one else is willing to do it—in a sense, the 'new' steward is the one who is the last person to step back! As Nicholson notes 'in such cases, the slightest sign of interest above a lowest common denominator is sufficient to catapult an individual into a job' (1976, p. 18). In a similar vein, though slightly less negative in orientation, is the case of the individual who is either the popular choice of the section for whatever reason or is nominated either by the previous steward, the convenor, and even, more indirectly, a member of management. Support for this concept of external direction comes from several pieces of research as the following quotes demonstrate:[1]

The girls voted me on, so I had to stand.

The job just kind of fell on me. I felt we needed stronger representation on the section so, when I was approached, I took it on. I didn't go out of my way to become steward.

The branch chairman persuaded me to stand. I knew no one else would put in for it . . . . I had to do it. Someone had to do it.

When the previous steward left the company he recommended me to take over from him. I wasn't too keen as I'd had experience of the job before.

Not all the reasons were so negative or externally-directed as the preceeding comments; the stewards who, following Nicholson's categorization, stood for office for 'internally-directed' reasons are perhaps characteristic of about half the number of people who take up the position. For example, there are cases of people feeling that they are better at some aspect or other than the rest of their

1. These quotes are taken from research both by the author (Marchington, 1980, p. 69) and by Beynon from his work at Ford (1973, pp. 189–196). The 'internally-directed' reasons are also from these sources.

constituents and this motivates them to stand for office. Similarly, and in line with Chinoy's ideas, other potential stewards were either motivated by some careerist ambition or some ideological belief. The latter need not be associated with the issue of 'political' motivation; recent evidence would seem to indicate that the 'politically motivated' steward only succeeds at remaining in office for as long as he remains in touch with the membership. Once he tries to manipulate his constituents towards the achievement of broader long-term aims that they do not share, he is soon pulled back into line or ejected from office (Hunt, 1977, p. 21). A shop steward will be tolerated—and as we shall see in the next section, be allowed to hold quite different views—by the membership only so far as he is successful in defending or improving their position. Quotes to illustrate the 'internally-directed' reasons are shown below:

> I like finding out whats going on . . . . I wanted to get involved.
>
> I felt that I could do a better job than the rest of the lads.
>
> I could see the injustices being done every day so I thought I'd have a go.
>
> I wanted to do it to look after the interests of my fellow workmen.

Although we can get some idea of steward behaviour from looking at their reasons for wishing to be elected in the first place, the situation can be far from static. Those pushed into occupation may later become highly motivated to remain in office, feeling that it provides an extra satisfaction that is not present in their 'normal' job or that they become quite successful at it. Similarly, a large minority of foremen have been promoted from the shop floor after having been seen in action by management. Conversely, the enthusiastic and positive steward may become disillusioned either with his section or with management; the role may not develop as he had previously imagined. However, as Nicholson comments' 'once in the job, the reluctant steward sometimes found it hard to shake off' (1976, p. 19). Managers clearly need to be aware of the stewards own motivation and expectations if they are going to work with him in an effective way. But, as we have mentioned before, the steward is also very dependent upon the people he represents; it is now time to explore this relationship in a little more detail.

Membership attitudes and steward behaviour

Since the steward 'emerges', so to speak, from the shop floor, there is a good case for arguing that he would hold fairly similar attitudes to the people he represents. To some extent, this idea of the democratic, populist, and responsive steward gained a considerable degree of currency in the early seventies as observers sought to destroy the previously held myth—prior to Donovan—of the agitator or troublemaker aspect of the steward's role. That is, that stewards, since they are the people who articulate grievances to management, must therefore be the *source* of any discontent on the shop floor.

As we saw in Chapter 3, such a view is a key point in a unitary management ideology. The 'responsiveness' stance goes to the other extreme and pictures the steward as completely dependent upon his constituents, adopting the role of spokesman or mouthpiece, and never attempting to redefine or reorientate issues before presenting them to management. For example, Whitehead expresses the view that 'it remains axiomatic to nearly every shop steward that he or she should intuitively react to a given situation in the way that his or her members expect' (1977, p. 106).

As we shall see later, the steward does have certain sanctions at his disposal by virtue of his position; moreover, he may receive support from other stewards—particularly through bodies such as a JSSC—in order to help him 'control' the membership. As Terry suggests, the idea of stewards *merely* responding to membership wishes is almost as misguided as was the 'agitator' thesis (1978, p. 2).

Even if stewards in general did possess similar attitudes to the membership at the time of election, it is unlikely that they will continue to do so once elected. For a start, they become exposed to different pressures and are in receipt of different information from their constituents; this may either emanate from other stewards, the outside union, or from management. Moreover, in taking up issues, they begin to realize which of the membership is 'trying it on'. One of the most common problems expressed by stewards soon after they are first elected to office is one of establishing the seriousness of a member's grievance; in assessing whether the grievance is real or genuine, or whether it is merely a passing whim. Stewards are 'tested-out' by the membership and many feel they have graduated into the role once they can establish some independence from the membership and not automatically be 'conned' into taking up every issue.

Surveys have shown that steward and member attitudes can vary quite considerably without this posing any threat to the relationship. To a degree, stewards are *expected* to be more union-conscious than their constituents yet also to take a responsible attitude towards management. Similarly, they are also expected to lead on issues yet also to be responsive to membership pressures should the situation arise. In other words, the steward-member relationship is considerably more complex than either the democracy or agitator theses would have us believe.

Recent research by Nicholson *et al.*, on a group of NALGO stewards, illustrates the way in which stewards and members' attitudes may be at variance. They conclude that 'attitudinally' the white collar stewards are more similar to blue collar stewards than they are to their own members' (1980, p. 238). In a survey by the author, in relation to the demand for employee participation, the stewards wanted considerably more influence over management decision making than did their members. However, the membership was keen on its steward, rather than itself, having more influence over decisions taken at departmental level and above. That is, that the steward is given the freedom to act on his own initiative above a certain level, and over issues on which the membership feels he has access to more information and is in a better position to make a realistic judgement of the appropriate line to be taken (1980, pp. 71–78). What the membership appears to demand from its stewards is an adequate degree of consultation prior to decision making if the issue is one that interests the shop floor. Conversely, it also appears to expect its steward to ensure that its point of view is made known to management.

There is a danger, however, in trying to establish a *dominant* style or pattern to steward–member relations. Even if it could be argued that one pattern appears more regularly than another, or that members prefer—on average—that their steward responds to their wishes, this still means that other patterns appear from time to time or that the style of the stewards varies with his experience or the issues at stake. For this reason, the recent research of Batstone and his colleagues is particularly helpful in that their analysis of shop steward activity provides a number of rich insights into the complexities of shop floor life. While a detailed discussion of the conceptual framework is beyond the scope of this book, suffice it to say that a number of criticisms—primarily of a methodological nature—have been made of their model of steward activity.[2]

They conducted an in-depth study of two 'domestic (local shop steward) organizations'—one on the shop floor and one in the offices of the same company—in order to examine the way in which these two bodies operated in practice. They made a distinction between stewards on the basis of two dimensions—the steward's commitment to union principles and the extent to which the steward leads or merely transmits member opinion. They then concentrated on exploring the attitudes and activities of two very different types of steward; firstly, those who were high on union principles and took the initiative *vis-à-vis* their members—known as *leaders*—and, secondly, those who were low on union principles and expected to be mandated by their members and merely carry out their wishes whatever these might be—known as *populists* (1977, pp. 23–53 in particular).

Therefore, by moving discussion away from the concept of the average or typical shop steward, it became possible to examine *differences* between

2. Their model is described in *Shop Stewards in Action* (1977). Probably, the major criticism relates to their treatment of leadership as a generalized property of certain individuals rather than varying on an issue-specific basis. Similarly, there is doubt over the adequacy of their two dimensions—leadership and pursuit of union principles—due to problems of overlap and the non-ambiguous nature of the definition of union principles (see, for example, Willman, 1980, pp. 39–40). Their treatment of 'power' has also caused some concern. Added to this we could argue that their categorization reflects a predominantly shop floor image of union principles, that stewards' activity may change over time and in relation to the type of mangement with whom they are dealing as well as an issue-specific basis. Finally, it could be argued that other dimensions are more important than the two that they outline. See also Pedler (1973, pp. 43–60) for a further discussion on stewards and leadership.

stewards and to see the way in which these two types of steward interacted
with the other parties in the workplace. It is useful for this analysis in that we
can concentrate on the variety of networks stewards utilize at work and, of
crucial importance, what implications this may have for the management of
industrial relations. We shall concentrate our discussion on stewards who
adopt a leadership role in relations to their constituents since this is the more
complex of the two; to quote from Batstone *et al*. again:

> The very idea of steward leadership involves an ability both to undertake certain
> courses of action without direct resort to the membership and to *influence member
> attitudes*. But steward independence is necessarily limited . . . shop steward organi-
> sation . . . cannot continue without the backing of those who elect the stewards and
> from whom their basic power derives. (1977, p. 99—my emphasis)

In the remainder of this section we shall look at some of the ways in which
stewards influence their constituents; firstly, the steward—rather than
progressing every issue that his members bring to him—can 'squash' these at
source. As we noted above, the ability to decide which issues to progress and
which to squash is one that confronts every steward at some time during his
period of office—usually, fairly early on. Hunt, for example, states the point
quite simply when he notes that 'the experienced shop steward who knows his
job will be loath to take on issues which he knows he cannot win and he will tell
the member involved that the issue is not worth pursuing' (1977, p. 29). By
definition, if the issue goes no further than the steward, this is an aspect of the
steward's job about which management may never be aware; in this sense, the
steward acts as an informal first stage in the grievance process. He may act not
only to squash claims that he knows he cannot win but also those that he feels
may damage *unity* in the section or the factory even if he knows that he *can* win
them. Also, the steward can, at times, act as the person who 'disciplines'
individual employees for regularly coming in late, being absent, skiving, or
anything that can reduce the steward's ability to push other issues that may be
of greater importance. In other words, the steward's power over his
constituents may be an important source of his ability to exert power for them
(Hyman, 1975, p. 65). Paradoxically, this may not always be to the
disadvantage of management in that leader stewards may 'control' membership militancy.

Of course, not all issues are squashed by the steward; many of them will be
taken on board and progressed through the appropriate procedure. Once
again, the steward who adopts a leadership style will work out whether to let
the issue go forward as it stands or whether to redefine it in some way. He will
need to explore the facts behind the case, know the people involved, and
anticipate likely reactions from other constituents, the stewards committee,
the union, and management. Only when this has been undertaken can the
steward then decide how the issue should be defined and what is the most
appropriate channel through which to pursue it. If the steward does not need
the support of the membership, via the threat of collective sanctions, the

individual member(s) may know little of the case until it is resolved. If support is needed, however, the steward has to ensure that he legitimizes the grievance such that he gets the appropriate backing. In other words, in this type of case, 'the steward cannot define the issue in any way he likes—he has to present the issue in a manner which is congruent with the minimal frame of reference held in common by his members' (Partridge, 1978, p. 193). However, the steward is in a position to mould issues and consequently influence the eventual course of action.

The two ways we have just described in which leader stewards influence member opinion—that of *squashing* and *redefining*—both relate to issues that are initiated in the workplace by the members themselves. Stewards can also initiate action themselves or mobilize opinion in support of JSSC resolutions and recommendations. For example, stewards may try to persuade the membership to follow their proposed course of action by outlining a plan for which they would like a mandate from their constituents. In order to do this, stewards in a section may plan *before* a shop meeting what course of action they would like to follow; this could then be put to the shop floor for a vote and, if successful, presented as the 'view of the section' to management. In doing so, however, the steward has to be careful not to isolate himself from the membership or conclude by bowing to membership opinion that he feels is not in the best interests of the workforce as a whole. (For examples of this, see Batstone *et al.*, 1977 pp. 92–98; Marchington, 1980, p. 89.)

In other words, it may be too simple to talk of a single style that stewards adopt in relation to their members; as Pedler argues, the style of the representative varies with the issue at hand: 'on some issues where the representative has access to the necessary information, a "leader" role tends to be adopted. On other issues, where the matter in question is central to the norms of the group, a vote is taken and the representative is simply a "mouthpiece"' (1973, p. 56). It may well be that the 'leader' steward has a greater repertoire of skills that he can adopt depending upon the issue, whereas the 'populist' does not; if this is the case, training needs to be directed towards this end. Equally, it should not be overlooked that underlying much of the discussion on stewards is an assumption that they *know* and *logically choose* the best course of action; this is dubious to say the least and is just as absurd as perfection in any other job. At the end of the day, though, the steward is judged by his 'success rather than in terms of procedural nicety. That is, the steward maintains the support of his members because he is successful in substantive terms—rather than because he always refers issues back to them' (Batstone *et al.*, 1977, p. 52). One essential ingredient in this 'success' is the effectiveness of the steward network and the support this gives to the individual steward.

The steward network
One major development during the seventies has been that of joint shop

steward committees and steward hierarchies across large sections of British industry, particularly in workplaces over the 500-employee size. For example, on the manual side, 90 per cent of establishments of 500 or over have recognized senior stewards and over 70 per cent have regular steward meetings, although this is slightly lower (about 60 per cent) in multi-union workplaces. For establishments over 1000 in size, nearly 70 per cent had a full-time steward present for manual workers and over 60 per cent reported their involvement in multi-establishment combine committees. For non-manual workers, the percentages were a little lower, particularly those relating to the presence of full-time stewards; for combines, interestingly enough, the proportion of non-manual establishments attending such a meeting was slightly *higher* than for the manual (Brown, 1980). And this development is not just confined to the engineering industry; across manufacturing as a whole, once establishment size has been taken into account, it is the *similarity* of steward organizations that is particularly noteworthy. There is less complexity of development in public services, however (Brown *et al.*, 1978, pp. 139–159). Interestingly enough, there is a divergence between the estimates made by management and steward respondents as to the presence of full-time stewards or the likelihood of regular meetings, particularly for smaller manufacturing establishments (Brown, 1981, p. 66).

Two different influences can be seen to have had an effect on this growth and development of steward organization; firstly, the building of JSSCs represents a response to the problems created by multi-unionism in the workplace. Stewards from different unions saw the need to establish links and, as such, this illustrates the way in which trade unionism adapts to the pressures that confront its historical organization. Since wholesale reconstruction is most unlikely, it is the stewards who 'mend fences and prevent conflict between unions wrecking the harmony of the workplace' (Taylor, 1979, p. 207). Shop steward committees then begin to establish their own organization, resources, and ideology at establishment level; this has important consequences for union organization in general, and this localized commitment to unionism has been termed 'factory consciousness'. Indeed, as Brown *et al.* suggest, 'multi-unionism stimulates the development of steward organisations, and steward organisations, as they develop, become more able (and probably find greater necessity) to cope with multi-unionism' (1978, p. 151). The second influence—that of management organization and attitudes—is one we shall return to in the next section.

It is quite usual for convenors or senior stewards in large plants to operate very independently of the unions to which they belong; due to insufficient union resources and a lack of full-time officials, the latter are often happy to let the 'experienced' stewards in well organized plants operate very much on their own since this allows the officials to concentrate their efforts on those workplaces where unionism is weaker or less stable.

Despite the relative lack of contact with larger plants, however, there are ways in which the union movement can rely on these stewards to follow traditional principles. Firstly, it is more likely that these senior stewards will espouse union principles as a matter of course. Secondly, there is often considerable informal contact between full-time officials and experienced stewards; this may take the form of officials supporting JSSC principles where these ensure unity among the membership or by implying that a JSSC should use its discretion on whether or not to recommend action in support of national policy; the full-time official may imply that stewards should not follow policy without explicitly advising them to do so (Batstone *et al.*, 1977, p. 209). Thirdly, stewards may actually seek the assistance of an official—say, by going through procedure—on an issue that they feel unable to handle themselves. In other words, the likelihood of breakaway unions at factory or establishment level is much reduced because of the way in which experienced senior stewards and officials utilize a similar frame of reference, even though formal contact may be minimal and stewards do not express much desire to increase that contact.

Within the establishment, JSSCs act as both a means of *support* for, and as a potential instrument of *sanction* against, individual stewards. In terms of support, the committees can provide individual stewards with valuable information that they may find hard to get elsewhere, and that would enable them to get a more coherent picture of management and union policy. They provide a source of advice on how to act on specific issues and guidelines on future strategy; this is particularly important for the new steward who is experiencing problems coming to terms with his new role. This 'educational' function goes deeper as well in that new stewards become aware not only of how to handle strategy but also how to cope with their own members. Both Beynon and Batstone *et al.* cite examples of stewards learning to 'lead'—and not just respond to all membership pressure—through the help and assistance of more senior stewards. The JSSC can, therefore, prove an invaluable source of support in attempts to maintain unity.

It can also utilize sanctions to pull 'deviant' stewards back into line; this can either be direct or indirect. Batstone *et al.* report that 'the possible reaction of JSSC was an important check on the behaviour of many stewards. . . . In the main, for example, JSSC policies are followed on the shop floor. . . . Certainly, strong sanctions are imposed upon those who are found to be acting contrary to these resolutions. Stewards have occasionally been banned from the JSSC' (1977, pp. 78–79). In a similar vein, Hyman reports of senior stewards gaining support from management in controlling 'unruly sections and stewards' (1975, p. 168).

In order to adopt such a role, however, there needs to be a considerable degree of stability within the steward organization; the issue of high shop steward turnover or unstable organization is a problem not only for the stewards (and the membership) but also for management in its attempt to forge strong bargaining relationships with experienced and respected leaders of shop floor opinion. Such channels can be an effective way of assessing shop floor opinion and getting feedback on possible reactions; turnover and instability can, consequently, reduce the probability of this being achieved (Winch, 1980, pp. 52–53).

The maintenance of unity within steward organizations is hardest for inter-establishment committees, usually known as combines. Potentially, combines possess similar advantages for stewards as do JSSCs only to a much greater degree; that is, they are a valuable source of information about management policy, they can ensure greater consistency and cohesiveness in approaching company initiatives, and they could, if taken to their extreme, provide an appropriate focus for sanctions against management and against recalcitrant or unruly establishments that are threatening to endanger unity and solidarity. Despite interest in them, however, very few have succeeded in achieving an effective level of organization once the crisis that gave rise to their birth has either passed or faded away. The problems posed by distance, differing products, and occasionally different interests have restricted their activities. Beynon and Wainwright, in describing the Vickers' combine, report that 'interference' by the combine in plant affairs is a delicate one and this had led the combine to accept that it 'cannot *instruct* the workers or the shop stewards of any plant to follow a particular line of action. It can offer information, support and, on specific policy issues, recommendations . . .' (1979, p. 152). Consequently, and particularly in times of economic depression, their ability to achieve unity and solidarity is somewhat limited. Unless, that is, they are officially recognized by management; there can only be a key role for steward committees if they have someone with whom to negotiate, and it is important to assess the influence that management can exert on stewards' behaviour.

Management organization and steward activity

As we saw in Chapter 3, managers holding a pluralistic frame of reference are likely to accept the role that the steward plays in workplace industrial relations, and to do all that they can to improve their bargaining relationships with individual stewards. Even prior to Donovan, a survey of senior managers revealed that not only did the vast majority find the steward fairly or very reasonable to deal with but also there was a marked preference for dealing with him rather than the full-time official. Since then, managers have probably become even more used to working with the steward—particularly in well-organized workplaces—and much can be learned by examining some of the approaches of what might be referred to as the 'more enlightened' manager. We can analyse this perspective by examining the manager–steward relationship at two different levels; firstly, the *informal* face-to-face relations that develop, mostly at departmental level, between individuals; and secondly, the more *formalized* influence management has had on the development of steward committees.

On the informal side, much of the discussion hinges around the concept of a 'strong bargaining relationship'. According to Batstone *et al.* this occurs when both parties are 'concerned with protecting the relationship and the other party. The basic opposition of interests which exists within negotiation is therefore mediated by personal relationships which facilitate the constructive resolution of problems' (1977, p. 169). They continue by arguing that this 'means that both stewards and managers are "on the same wavelength". Bargaining occurs on the basis of shared understandings and definitions. At the extreme, many arguments are known to each party before the other states them' (1977, pp. 174–175). This rests to a large degree on the level of trust between two parties since, particularly with the informal 'chat', it depends on a dropping of caution because information private to one's own side can be imparted. Both leader, stewards, and managers feel that this rests upon an acceptance of 'the facts of life' and the continuance of bargaining with the other party who, it is felt, has sufficient power to deliver the goods if necessary (1977, p. 172).

This has a number of implications for both managers and stewards. The informal chat, for example, is a valuable mechanism for sounding out opinion, for checking upon the efficiency of a projected proposal, or for softening the blow of a future announcement. The manager or steward may want to make it clear to the other side so that he can avoid any problems that may arise or prepare the ground for dealing with the issue. For example, in a recent interview with the author, an individual talked of his first few days on the shop floor as a newly promoted manager. He explained how he wanted to alter some of the practices and went ahead as logically as he could to consult opinion on a proposed change. The stewards stood by and watched him do this. After a few days, one of them came into his office and explained to him quietly that, with his proposals, things would go wrong and he ought to reconsider his approach. He ended the conversation by 'advising' the manager to have a 'chat' with him prior to taking or initiating action in future. He did so and found that things were implemented much more smoothly. This same manager then went on to explain how, several years later, he had been on the point of disciplining an employee for perpetual lateness; he explained this to the steward and, between them, they worked out a joint proposal. Firstly, the manager talked of harsh action such as suspension; then, the steward pleaded for a reprieve. When this was successful, the steward asked for a few minutes with the man on his own; the manager agreed and, on returning to the office, found the employee ready to accept a warning instead of suspension. Indeed, the steward was even more annoyed with this man than was the manager since, he felt, incidents such as lateness reduced his bargaining power with more senior management. Undoubtedly, there are similar instances of such close bargaining relationships in other factories.

The principle is the same, however, in that the manager and the steward had seen greater value in working together towards the joint resolution of problems than in trying to argue against each other, thus being at perpetual loggerheads. On the shop floor, managers are concerned with 'maintaining good relations with those stewards who are able to control their members and hence reduce some aspects of management uncertainty . . . those stewards who lead their members tend to have strong bargaining relationships with managers' (Batstone *et al.*, 1977, p. 155).

This can work the other way as well, of course, in that managers only 'reward' those stewards who they feel are 'cooperative' and use sanctions against those they feel are not. As Beynon was told by a Ford senior executive, 'while a quiet, more reasonable bloke may be less dramatic, he'll probably get more for his members because if he's in any trouble we'll help him out. We make concessions to him that we wouldn't make to the other bloke' (1973, p. 158). This has implications for his relations with the membership; when stewards are 'cooperative' or 'reasonable'—and this is not necessarily linked with being weak—management will endeavour to see that they are successful and that the members are aware of this. The more uncooperative steward will be met by the full force of management, either directly or through a body such as the JSSC. What this means for management, in its relations with stewards, is that its environment becomes more *predictable*; however, if action is taken by the membership, it is likely to be more centralized and more united.

While the majority of the concessions by management in an informal context tend to be of a *de facto* nature, there is also an important role for more constitutional methods of sharing control—by, for example, at shop floor level, allowing joint control over issues such as overtime allocation, manning levels, and line speeds. In many cases, these aspects are now almost totally handled by the stewards (Beynon, 1973, pp. 139–147). At establishment level, stewards and managers may both sit in equal numbers on job evaluation committees; even if there has been little in the way of *substantive* change in terms of job grading, at least the shop floor sees that its representatives had been allowed access to, and have a good deal of control over, decision making in such bodies. And, at even higher levels, recent decisions by a number of companies to 'open-up' their books would seem to have increased the likelihood of acceptance of, or at least acquiescence with, the level of pay that has been offered.

Indeed, by the increasing centralization of bargaining and related matters, and the consequent development of a committee structured on a hierarchical basis, management has come to influence the form of shop steward organization in both a direct and an indirect way. Since shop steward organization tends to mirror that of management, the centralization of authority on the management side will lead stewards to do the same thing. Purcell suggests that 'shop stewards will quickly recognise that power resides among senior management and will feel the need to develop appropriate central control in their own organisation . . . in short they will develop an integrated shop stewards committee' (1979, p. 36). Moreover, this is particularly advantageous for management in that it becomes easier to reach agreement with a single body rather than a multiplicity of separate union bodies.

Management organization can lead therefore in some indirect way to the sponsorship of steward organizations; but, management needs to be aware of the fact that this body will not *always* operate to its advantage. If it does, and is seen to do so by the shop floor or other sections, action is likely to explode, trust can be lost for good, and the stewards replaced by individuals who are unlikely to enter into any informal bargains with management. Furthermore, as we mentioned above, if authority is vested in a single committee at establishment level, management may merely experience conflict being expressed in a different *form* than it has previously. Again, any attempt to discredit respected stewards is bound to destroy existing relationships. In other words, working *with* the steward is a strategy that must not be mis-read as a technique for manipulation; if it is, the stewards may return the compliment and use it to manipulate management as quickly and effectively as they can.

Conclusions

One conclusion that emerges from this and other discussions of the role of the steward, and particularly the development of steward organizations, is the importance of management attitudes and organization in this process. This has led Brown to suggest that 'in the long run, management itself is the most important influence in shaping the behaviour of its shop stewards' (1973, p. 157). Certainly, there are a host of examples that illustrate the way in which management organization of bargaining has led to the development of parallel steward bodies; there is little point in stewards being effectively organized if they are only allowed access to totally non-influential levels of management. Furthermore, managements have also found it advantageous to support the activities of centralized steward bodies since these may act as a potential source of control over membership.

Management has been helped in this process by the fact that several of the traditional trade union goals have now become convergent with those of management, as epitomized by the interest of the personnel function in 'ensuring the consistency and reliability of the "equitable" rules it administers, and an interest in observing at least the letter of regulatory labour legislation . . . in these changed circumstances, one can plausibly expect a certain amount of collusion in such areas' (Willman, 1980, p. 48). Certainly, in an organization with well-developed procedures or with a proactive stance on industrial relations, it may be easier for the line manager to work with the shop steward.

There are dangers of course with the increased formalization of the steward's role; by providing training, for example, there is the possibility that a gulf may open between stewards and their members as the former adopt a more professional approach (Pedler, 1974, p. 57). Moreover, the steward may begin to sit on so many committees that his constituents never see him, that he becomes divorced from them and their point of view, and that rival leaders begin to emerge in the workplace. The steward has to be allowed, and encouraged to use, mechanisms for remaining responsive to membership opinion. Similarly, as we mentioned above, the steward also has to remain, and be seen to remain, independent of management.

Our discussion in terms of leader and populist stewards can also be extended. The leader probably offers the potential for greater predictability in workplace relations; however, he is equally likely to ensure unity *against* management proposals as he is to *favour* them. The populist, on the other hand, offers less certainty but might have a 'quieter' section most of the time; when conflict does explode, though, it might be unexpected and not conform to 'the rules of the game'. Although leader stewards may constrain managers, they may also enable them to manage with greater certainty (Goodman and Whittingham, 1973, p. 209).

While this more formalized relationship may be appealing to managers and stewards, it may not look so rosy when seen from the position of the foreman. For him, such developments may seem to reflect nothing more than pandering to the shop floor, and lead to a further reduction in his status and authority. We shall now move on to look at modern industrial relations from his perspective.

6. Problems for the foreman

A common fear regularly expressed by foremen is that they are 'losing control'; losing control of their function as shop floor managers not only to specialist departments—such as personnel—who increasingly are felt to take away their individual discretion and replace it with laid down procedures, but also to shop stewards as we illustrated in the previous chapter. For many, their own perceived loss of control is directly correlated with the steward's seeming increase in control.

Many managements are very aware of these fears and, on visits to companies, it is quite usual for senior managers to discuss their 'supervisory problem', their attempts to 'win back' the foreman, and their concern about a lack of adequate personnel to fill this crucial role. In a similar vein, the literature uses phrases such as 'the forgotten man of industry', 'the marginal man', or 'the lost manager' to describe the current-day position of the foreman. How has this state of affairs come about? What are the kinds of problems that foremen, themselves, feel affect them at work, and what have they done to try and alleviate these? Finally, what has management done, and what can it do, in order to cope with its 'supervisory problem'? The remainder of the chapter is organized around these questions.

Historical developments

Prior to the First World War, the foreman was quite clearly the *man-in-charge* in his relations with the shop floor and in organizing the workflow and related production requirements. To a large extent, he had sole control over the people who worked with him; for example, he had the power to hire and fire without reference to higher authority, the ability to influence the size of the employee's pay packet by the way in which he allocated work, and the power to impose sanctions that, in most cases, would not be challenged by the shop floor. Moreover, due to smaller company size, he had relatively easy access to the boss and, consequently, could be closely involved in departmental matters.

For a number of reasons, the position changed considerably between the wars. Foremen were increasingly expected to manage by consent, rather than coercion. Companies began to develop specialized departments that took over many of the duties originally undertaken by foremen. Growth in trade unionism on the shop floor reduced the unilateral powers of the foremen, particularly where union organization was strong. Overall, these changes—both from above and below—reduced his discretion and led to the description of the foreman as the '*man-in-the-middle*' (Child, 1975).

These trends, along with others, have continued to impinge upon the role of the foreman; union membership has increased to well over 50 per cent of the labour force; management by consent has become even more acknowledged as a fundamental aspect of securing good industrial relations; specialization in both the technological sphere and in that of aspects of personnel policy—such as legislation, procedures, job evaluation—has continued to reduce his 'expert' role for the groups he supervises; this, too, has resulted in a lessening of opportunities for promotion. From an industrial relations angle, most important of all has been the post-Donovan formalization that has taken place in much of manufacturing industry at least, and has led to a reduction in the discretionary elements of shop floor management. In a sense, his position has become increasingly untenable; as Clegg states, 'he remains responsible for the section's performance but without the freedom he once enjoyed to choose his workers to suit himself, to organise their work as he sees fit, and to offer them incentives and rewards' (1979, p. 157). The foreman's position in the management system 'appears to have become increasingly *marginal* and even *redundant*' (Child *et al.*, 1980, p. 364—my emphasis).

What kind of people enter into supervision then? There have been a number of categorizations put forward.[1] Rather than deal with all of these, we shall concentrate on just one, by Nichols and Beynon, in which foremen were divided into two groups—the *traditionals* and the *management men* (1977, pp. 44–67).

The traditionals tend to be the older foremen who have worked their way up from the shop floor (often after a long time there), have very little in the way of education after 14 (apart from an apprenticeship in some cases), spent a long time with the company, and were generally promoted on the basis of superior skills or being noticed for achievements in the job of shop steward. Usually, they will share a common bond or culture with the men they supervise rather than with the managers. The management men, on the other hand, tend to think and *act* like managers, they have outside contact with them and they 'have a style, an ideological stance and a technical ability which marks them off from the rest (of the foremen)' (1977, p. 48). In the company studied by

1. See for example, Fletcher (1969), Child (1975), Dunkerley (1975), and Nichols and Beynon (1977) for a list of categorizations. Some of these leave a lot to be desired in my view and the search for ideal types has tended to obscure some of the realities in the situation.

Nichols and Beynon, these men were in a minority (just six out of the forty foremen) and they were generally earmarked for promotion. In fact, two of them were promoted during the course of the study.

These descriptions, and the distribution between the two different types, would seem to be a fairly accurate representation of much of British industry. To some extent, the problems we shall outline below are more likely to affect the traditionals than they are the management men; the latter are more likely to be involved in decision making and to get any promotions that come about. The former are unlikely to go much further. In addition, they may have been foremen a number of years ago under very different conditions, and the reality of their current role neither conforms with their expectations nor as they remember it from the past.

Problems for the foreman

From several studies of the foreman's role, it is possible to draw together a number of common worries expressed by the foremen either in interview or during observation of them at work. Basically, they illustrate a mismatch between expectations and reality, and most are indicative of the insecurity currently experienced by foremen. For ease of analysis, we can break these down into six areas and deal with each in turn. They are as follows:

1. Lack of *involvement* in management decision making.
2. Being *by-passed* by stewards going direct to management.
3. Not receiving *communications* from management before the shop floor do.
4. Fears of not being *backed-up* by management.
5. Lack of opportunities for *promotion*, and fears about *job security*.
6. Lack of *identification* with management.

These are not meant to be in any order of priority, nor is it claimed that this list is necessarily exhaustive. Furthermore, not *all* of these problems are likely to be present in *all* workplaces at any one time; it would be unusual, though, to find none of them present. Bearing this in mind, we can turn our attention back to the perceived problem areas.

Firstly, a common complaint is that foremen feel excluded from decision making bodies to the extent that they have problems understanding or identifying with the decision or in ensuring that it is upheld on the shop floor. This lack of 'involvement' issue can be seen under three different headings; firstly, supervisors are resentful of the fact they do not get asked for their opinion nor involved in making decisions even on matters that they feel are directly applicable to their own section or department. Alternatively, particularly when a company moves its young managers around the group, foremen feel that their involvement merely serves to advance another person's position within management. Generally, though, the foremen has now become a 'recipient, not a contributor, to union–management relations' (Dunkerley, 1975, p. 64). That this can have disturbing implications is reported by Weir and Mills from their case study of organizational change at shop floor level. They note that supervisors were given little or no chance to influence the objectives or the plans for the change to the new system, nor were they given much information about it. Consequently, they found themselves in the position of having to implement a change about which they had more doubts than confidence (1975, p. 64). Secondly, since decisions tend to be made without their involvement, this has served to constrain them more tightly in their relations with the shop floor. For example, they no longer possess—as we saw above—the formal authority to dispense rewards and punishments to the people who work for them. This, it has been argued, leads them to question what techniques they have available to motivate the shop floor or to sanction them should the need arise. The foremen observed by Terry were almost unanimous in regarding rewards as the only effective practical tool to improve shop floor behaviour, and disciplinary powers were often applied loosely within the framework of a pattern of indulgency (1977, p. 86). Finally, the foreman is likely to resent being obliged to consult with his subordinates if he is not effectively (or at least *perceives* that he is not) consulted by his superiors—a feeling that any increase in shop floor involvement with senior management is likely to reduce their already limited control.

The second major 'problem' area is *by-passing* by stewards. Theoretically, procedure agreements would generally make provision for a steward to approach his foreman in the first instance and, should he fail to get the issue resolved at this level, to then move the matter up the chain to management level. Of course, this does not always happen in practice, and the Workplace Industrial Relations survey of 1974 reported that 72 per cent of managers felt there were ways for the steward to avoid the first stage in procedure (WIR, 1974, p. 45). Similar views are expressed by the foremen themselves although they attribute much of the blame for this state of affairs to management for allowing the steward easy access without first ensuring that they have gone through procedure. In Bowey's study of supervisory status, about one-half of all the supervisory grumbles related to this (1973, p. 398). Some of the foremen who were interviewed at Kitchenco (by the author in a previous study) describe this problem quite eloquently:

> The shop steward goes above my head . . . sees managers at departmental level before he's even spoken to me. Management should not allow this to happen . . . they shouldn't listen to their moans and groans, procedure should *always* be enforced.

> Communications are not what they should be . . . stewards are always popping in to see the personnel manager—don't even bother asking me any more.

> We do get forgotten . . . managers come down and sort things out without even telling us what's happened. Gets me needled, this.

As we saw in the last chapter, the use of the 'informal chat' can often be a key characteristic of good bargaining relationships between managers and stewards; because of this, the manager has to judge whether this is more important to him than supervisory resentment. He does, however, need to be aware of foremen's reaction to this activity and take appropriate steps to allow for this. Indeed, it is ironic that the TGWU shop stewards' handbook now gives specific advice to stewards *not* to jump over their foremen or boast about victories to them since this may only lead to further trouble.

The third complaint relates to being missed out in the flow of *communications* from management to the shop floor. The 1974 WIR survey reported that five out of six managers felt that they *always* kept their juniors informed; the foremen, conversely, were not so sure. About half said that management usually told them of new developments whereas a further quarter reported that the information usually came from the shop floor. The remainder got information from both sources (p. 32). Bowey also observed the regular practice of senior managers discussing and sorting out grievances with stewards before they become a major source of trouble. Since, she continued, 'there were no ancillary mechanisms for keeping other members of the organisation informed of and involved in these communications and decisions . . . as a result, many managers and supervisors felt by-passed and thought their authority was being undermined' (1973, p. 397). As companies get larger of course, this problem is likely to increase although supervisors may demand or be granted their own representative who can tap information from senior management at the same time or before shop floor representatives. Overall, foremen appear to be relatively satisfied with the amount and the timing of information from management and it is only on occasion that they learn things from the shop floor. White, in a book that he recommends as appropriate for NEBSS students, tries to reassure supervisors when he suggests that managers need to give the shop steward *recognition* and *information* in order to do his job correctly. Because of this, he tells the student that 'you can play your part in seeing that he receives both, and can appreciate why management sometimes unintentionally makes the mistake of giving more of these two commodities to him than to you' (1975, p. 137).

This leads us on to probably the most crucial of the foreman's worries; this is that he will not be *backed-up* by management when he does make a decision or implements some instruction. Again, the 1974 WIR survey can give us some information on this; of the foremen they questionned, 42 per cent said that they could always rely on management backing, while another 36 per cent felt that they usually could. However, approximately one in six felt that this only happened 'sometimes' (p. 22). Similarly, Bowey found that the fear of not being backed up was a major concern of the foremen (1973, p. 398) and this may only need to happen once to undermine a supervisor's confidence and affect his future ability.

A sample of quotes from our research interviews also illustrates this particular point:

> We're scared to make decisions now in case it goes against management policy . . . on discipline, for example, it is impossible to do anything because management won't back us up any more.

> Generally, we are backed-up . . . occasionally we're not though and then you're made to look very silly.

> Yes, you can feel that you've been *dropped* in it sometimes . . . remember, if the men are 'gunning' for a foreman, they'll find some way to get him.

It is probably fair to say nowadays, for the 'traditionals' at least, the job of foreman represents the highest rung that they will reach on the managerial ladder. For this reason, blockage of *promotion* is also seen as a potential problem in their jobs. With the growth in specialization, especially in high-technology industries such as chemicals, there is a need for more highly qualified people in the management team. Foremen are known to feel resentful of young graduates coming into industry in a superior position to themselves; this is made even more problematic when the foremen feel they have to 'teach' the new entrant all about the job (Bowey, 1973, pp. 399–400). Similarly, Child *et al.* found that only a small minority of foremen, at the two factories they observed, had actually been promoted over the last decade or so; in one works, for example, only two foremen had been made up to managers during the course of the last 15 years—and the average number of foremen employed over that period had been of the order of 60 (1980, pp. 370–371). Some of the foremen became resigned to this state of affairs whereas others became increasingly resentful; either way, they may become a potential source of problem for management.

While fears about promotion blockages may be common in some factories, in others attention may be more exclusively focused on job security; in particular, when a company has introduced autonomous working groups, those that work without any supervision but elect leaders from within their membership, these fears are bound to be enhanced. Reports on companies moving to this kind of system suggest at least two different types of response. On the one hand, management feels it *ought* to delegate some of its responsibilities to the supervisor, who can then become a facilitator or a technical expert; in practice, foremen often act as little more than quality controllers or providers of work (Mansfield, 1980, pp. 11–15). In other cases, where the job has been eliminated altogether—as at Christie-Tyler—some of the foremen have gone back to their original trade and formed their own cell (autonomous workgroup) within the factory (Maude, 1977, pp. 16–18). Of course, this may be neither desirable nor appropriate in many companies.

One final problem area concerns the degree of *identification* that supervisors have with the management; this is where much of the uncertainty and ambiguity is most apparent. They are repeatedly told by their superiors that they are 'a part of management and a line manager in every respect', and that they are more closely identified with management than with the shop floor. In

Child *et al.*'s study, supervisors generally 'gave strong approval to statements representing them as part of the line management and enjoying promotion opportunities. Portrayal of the supervisor as a breed on his own, not enjoying acceptance into management also generally met with disapproval' (1980, p. 388). In other words, they *want* to be part of mangement in many ways, feeling that they have, to quote one of the foremen interviewed by the author, 'lifted themselves out of the mire and don't want to be considered as part of the mass again'. Perhaps this is an extreme statement of the position, but the general feeling of lack of status is there; sometimes they feel they are treated as part of management, sometimes not. After noting what supervisors felt would be desirable, Child and his colleagues then went on to report that, in reality, the supervisors felt that 'their position was less managerial than it should be, and also that they had a closer identity of economic interests with workers than was desirable' (1980, p. 388). The marginality of the role is consequently all too apparent to them. Since the foreman is usually promoted from the shop floor, he still identifies with many of the people in that position. However, to them, he begins to represent the management view and consequently is felt to be losing touch with them. From the other angle, although management 'claims' him as a team member, he is often accused of displaying shop floor tendencies that render this identification with the management team as dubious. Using an army analogy, Fores, Sorge, and Lawrence suggest that 'he is in the position of the corporal who reports to senior NCO's, but still "messes with the men"' (1978, p. 87).

Overall, therefore, the foreman occupies an increasingly ambiguous and uncertain position within industry; many companies and senior managers have become all too aware of this over the last few years but the problems still remain. By identifying these problems, it is possible to analyse the nature of the issues at stake and, consequently, examine some of the managerial efforts to alleviate the strain on the foreman. But foremen too have responded to increasing formalization, uncertainty, and ambiguity in at least two different ways; one of these is unionization and we shall look at this in the next section. The other is by failing to enforce a strict application of the rules and, by managing with a degree of indulgence, both allowing and promoting custom and practice on the shop floor.

Response through custom and practice
Up until recently, it would have seemed unusual to discuss custom and practice (C + P) in a chapter on the role of the foreman. C + P was assumed to be a device operated and applied by workers *alone* in an attempt to mitigate the worst effects of managerial pressure, and one that management could do little to prevent. Recent research investigations have, however, illustrated quite graphically the manner in which supervisors and line managers not only allow C + P to flourish but also help to create it by their own interpretation of company rules. Indeed, as we saw in Chapter 1, even the most structured and

detailed of rules and procedures are not always strictly enforced on the shop floor; this has led Terry to argue that, to a certain extent, informality is inevitable.[2]

This can operate in a number of ways; firstly, even if rules are prescribed in a fairly clear and unambiguous way, the foreman still has some discretion whether to apply that rule or not in the same way that a policeman 'decides whether to ignore, warn or report the speeding motorist' (Purcell, 1979, p. 1040). Secondly, the supervisor may use the rules and apply them liberally in return for worker cooperation on other matters; in a sense, operating as a form of *trade-off* to ensure production. This kind of usage has been well documented by Terry and he gives one example relating to a three-minute factory rule concerning lateness. In this,

> a man was allowed to be three minutes late, but any further lateness had to be reported to the foreman, who had the authority to accept or reject any excuses given. If an excuse was accepted, the man concerned would not lose any pay, if it was rejected he would. . . . In practice the situation was very different. It was accepted, by the workforce and the foremen, that a man could be up to ten minutes late before he even needed to start thinking about an excuse. For lateness in excess of that 'limit', there was a well-established and growing list of excuses which had been accepted once and had passed in to the list of 'accepted excuses' (1977, p. 80).

It may seem strange why such a situation should develop particularly when foremen were sticklers for punctuality themselves. But, as Terry goes on to suggest, it 'seemed to be the case that these concessions of lateness were made by the foremen to try to get cooperation from the workforce over certain aspects of job mobility and flexibility—issues that were unpopular with the shop floor' (1977, p. 80). Senior management was aware of these 'concessions' and put the blame firmly on the foremen for their lack of competence. However, such a reaction misses the point—and presumably the advantage to the company—of these developments. Foremen were reacting against a tight agreement and also building discretion into their own jobs—a response that is quite understandable bearing in mind the worries we have discussed above. Goodman *et al.* note similar 'understandings' that foremen negotiated informally in order to assist them in their objective of 'getting the work out' (1977a, p. 172).

Arising out of this point is a third point; that foremen do not accept a management rule as either sensible or legitimate and so apply that rule 'without enthusiasm'. Fourthly, C + P can be created not just by acts of

2. See Chapter 1, pp. 13–14. Also see, Terry (1977). The pioneering work on C + P from a position of 'worker strength' was undertaken by Brown (1973) and can also be seen in other products of the Warwick school in examining the engineering industry, for example, Batstone *et al.* (1977). A study of the footwear industry has more recently examined C + P creation in a position of 'management strength' and shown the way in which rules may also be interpreted more strictly by foremen and junior managers (Armstrong and Goodman (1979)). Of course, we should not forget the contribution of Gouldner to the discussion of an 'indulgency pattern' by managers and supervisors.

commission but also by error or by overlooking practices that develop on the shop floor. In other words, the foreman may turn a 'blind eye' to events that take place as do many senior managers if they think it is neither worth the time nor the potential disruption to eradicate that custom. Moreover, senior managers may unwittingly accept new C + P during a factory walkabout or at times when the ability to resist shop floor pressure is low. Finally, and from the other angle, we can see the way in which foremen may apply rules more strictly than is laid down in procedure. Particularly if they are in a position of comparative strength *vis-à-vis* the shop floor, supervisors may 'try it on' and push through an issue and interpret a rule from above so as to squash worker demands or to discipline a particular subordinate.

Whatever the outcome of this C + P creation, management needs to be aware of *why* it arises and the fact that it is, to a large extent, a response to its more formalized, centralized, and bureaucratized approach to industrial relations. In this sense, it is wide of the mark to speak of 'incompetent' foremen because of a failure to apply rules in the prescribed manner. Since foremen are seriously affected by formalization, it may be unrealistic to expect them to accept a lessening of their discretion over their subordinates without them developing C + P in the manner we have described above.

Responses through unionization

A second, and not unconnected, response to the increasing uncertainty in their position has been for foremen to join unions although it is difficult to determine how many have actually taken this step. Some, for example, will have retained membership of the manual union to which they previously belonged merely transferring their membership to the white collar section (e.g., MATSA in the GMWU; ACTSS in the TGWU). In other cases, such as TASS, the link with the manual union (AUEW) is less direct. In yet others, there is no link with a particular union and supervisors form one part among many different groups covered by such a union; ASTMS is a good example of this. In 1964, Bain estimated that just under 9 per cent of all supervisors belonged to a trade union, compared with an average of 12 per cent for *all* white collar workers and considerably higher percentage for occupations such as draughtsmen (nearly 50 per cent) (1972, p. 35). At that time, foremen in textiles were the most highly unionized of any industry (28 per cent). Since that time, however, white collar unionization has increased considerably and it is safe to suggest that supervisory unionization has at least kept pace with, if not exceeded, this. In large companies in particular, it would be unusual to find many cases of non-unionized foremen and many of them have gone so far as to make union membership a condition of employment.

As one would expect, given their possible identification with management, foremen have sometimes been unsure about joining a union, particularly if they have never held membership before. In interviews conducted by the author, this feeling has been repeatedly emphasized although, now they are members, they appear to accept and even defend their need for collective organization. It is possible to discern at least four different strands of reasoning as to why they joined the union in the first place. Firstly, there was the desire for protection—in its broadest sense—and for monetary benefits; that is, for the union to provide some kind of a back-up job as an insurance function and to provide, as one respondent put it, 'an annual dividend in the form of a pay increase'. Secondly, foremen are concerned about what they see as the growing power of shop floor unions and the effect that this may have upon their position; they feel the need for some kind of security and protection from the shop floor should they become involved in disciplinary matters. In other words, they search for backing from the strength of an outside collectivity rather than their more traditional source of support, the company. This leads on to the third set of reasons, which are the depersonalization of management, rationalizations, redundancies, and basically, being treated as a number by some kind of 'faceless bureaucrat'. Their own words probably describe this best:

> When the new managing director came along, the first thing he said to us was 'if you don't want to work with me, you might as well get out now.' I joined the union the next day.

> One guy was made a scapegoat by the last boss . . . we resented this power but we couldn't do anything about it. We've all joined the union now.

> I joined because of fears when we were taken over by (the parent company) . . . didn't join for a few months. Had loyalties to the directors, but I also have loyalties to myself . . . needed protection. I would never have joined if it had still been (the subsidiary).

All of these foremen joined a union in response to what they saw as an increasing distance between themselves and senior management, or the key decision makers. As can be seen, one was unsure about where his loyalties lay whereas the other two joined in direct response to a managerial act or attitude. Unionization—despite the unsureness—often takes place fairly quickly and, nowadays, senior management may actually promote the process as we saw in Chapter 3. The final reason for joining unions relates to the need for some kind of representative influence in company decision making; and a union was seen as *the* way to achieve this (Bowey, 1973, p. 405; Nichols and Beynon, 1977, p. 64).

Supervisory unionization has now become an established aspect of British industrial relations. Following Donovan, the Commission on Industrial Relations reported in 1969 that there was no evidence that unionization would adversely affect relations between foreman and management. In addition, many supervisors adopt an instrumental rather than a moral or political orientation towards their union, with the majority favouring a union with management rather than shop floor associations. However, it may still be hard for some managements to accept the mere fact of unionization for a group that they have usually identified as the first line of management; that the two can coexist is, to some, inconceivable.

Management activity

We can conclude this chapter by considering the steps that management has taken, or may be in the process of taking, in order to reassess, reevaluate, and possibly redefine the role of the foreman and to help him come to terms with an increasingly marginal position. Dunkerley, for one, is in no doubt that this is the responsibility of management and that supervisory effectiveness is affected by the way in which management defines the job, allots functions to it, and allows responsibility and authority to rest at this level (1975, p. 3). What action can senior management take then?

First of all, it needs to appreciate the kinds of fears that are articulated by foremen. Of the six categories of 'problem areas' outlined above, management can do much to overcome supervisory unsureness as to where it now stands. For example, involvement and communication can be more effectively catered for by the provision of places for supervisory representatives on joint consultative or other similar committees. In one plant we are currently investigating, in the chemicals industry, management has made allowance for two representatives to sit on the works committee and then have an opportunity of reporting back to the rest of the foremen early the next day. Others have organized briefing sessions the same day or the day after the works meeting when foremen can have a chance to hear senior management plans first-hand and put forward their own viewpoints.

Similarly, line and personnel management can try to ensure that procedure is followed by the stewards and can make a point of referring issues back for resolution whenever appropriate. It is widely believed (by foremen) that steward access to management is too easy and is even promoted by individual managers; as we saw in the last chapter, this may be true and may help in the industrial relations management of a company. If this is the case, however, foremen also need to be made aware of the advantages that such a strategy may have for management in sorting out *potential* issues before they explode. Tied in with this, of course, is the requirement for managers to clearly and positively back up their foremen (and be *seen* to be doing so) in their dealings with the shop floor. Lack of confidence and uncertainty about direction have caused foremen many a problem in the past. Recent events in the car industry would appear to indicate that foremen are being involved in the development of more positive management plans in relation to discipline and are being backed up in their enforcement of them. The foremen feel greater 'ownership' of these proposals and are, consequently, willing to observe them more closely; in other words, they are seen as *legitimate* by supervisory staff.[3]

But just how much support can management give to foremen, and how

3. This point was made recently to the author by a senior ASTMS representative in one of the car company's plants in the UK.

much discretion can it formally allow them in the workplace? It makes little sense to devolve decision making to shop floor level without taking into account not only the changes in procedures and employment law since the foreman used to occupy a central role in industrial relations, but also the relative increase in shop steward strength since that time. Stewards nowadays are much more likely than foremen to have been trained in negotiating skills or have greater knowledge of procedures and legal enactments. Foremen need to undergo basic training as well in order that they can manage with greater confidence and act positively on the basis of better information. If they receive this, foremen may be in a better position to resolve problems before they escalate rather than merely passing issues straight through to departmental or personnel management.

Of course, this assumes that the role of the foremen will continue to exist, even if in a somewhat modified form. As we noted above, autonomous group working and movements to new technology are likely to reduce the significance or necessity of a supervisory role still further; in some cases, it may even disappear. Managements clearly need to confront this question and ask whether or not there should be a role for the foreman. If there is to be one, they then need to resolve exactly what the foreman should be doing and what knowledge is required in order to do the job. And, in so doing, managements need to come to terms with the fact that power on the shop floor has moved away from the foreman, and therefore plan accordingly with this in mind (Jenkins, 1979, p. 144). It seems an appropriate point, therefore, at which to turn to an analysis of power in workplace industrial relations.

7. Power in workplace industrial relations

Power permeates all aspects of organizational life; in one way, it can be seen in the day-to-day power (usually called authority) that a manager has over his subordinates in relation to their contracts of employment or, conversely, in action by employees—usually through their unions—against managerial decisions. This latter form of power is often considered illegitimate by much of the general public and by managers as well (see Chapter 3). Indeed, the terms used to label this type of action—disruption, holding the country to ransom, destruction—reflect this perspective.

The manager, however, needs to go somewhat deeper into the subject in order to appreciate both the sources and nature of union power. In this chapter, we shall concentrate on what has been called 'negative' power rather than on 'positive' power; that is, on action taken against management in order to persuade it to change previously made decisions, and a strike would be a clear example of this. On the other hand, 'positive' power refers to action before decision taking in which employees try to influence the final outcome, say through schemes of employee involvement, and this will be analysed in Chapter 10 (Hebden and Shaw, 1977, p. 204; Marchington, 1979, pp. 3–7). More particularly, we shall focus down on a number of questions; what is meant by the concept of power? What are the sources of workgroup (or union) power and why are certain groups more willing or able to use their power than others? And, finally, what have managements done in order to counteract or contain workgroup power? It is important to begin our discussion with a broader analysis of power so that the rest of the chapter may be seen in its true perspective; that is, that despite an increase in shop floor power over the last decade or more, management still possesses significantly more power and has greater resources at its disposal.

The concept of power
The concept of power has always attracted a considerable degree of interest

from academics and practitioners alike. It now has such general usage that its exact meaning is somewhat hard to determine; for example, are power, influence, authority control, and domination merely synonyms for one another, or do they really describe different concepts. From the mass of literature on the subject (see Lukes, 1974; Clegg, 1975; Martin, 1977, to name but a few), we can identify a number of important characteristics of power:

1. Power is concerned with both the *capacity* of someone or thing to affect others and also with its *exercise.*
2. Power is a *property of a relationship* and not, despite general usage in this way, a general capacity held by an individual irrespective of situation.
3. It is important to focus on the *subject/object* that is influenced as well as the *wielder* of power.
4. It is crucial to consider power that *prevents* conflict from becoming manifest in addition to actual observable exercises of power.

Probably the most concise and comprehensible of the recent attempts to analyse power has been that of Lukes and we shall consider his distinction between three different dimensions of power. Firstly, there is the *one-dimensional view* as characterized by the work of political scientists, such as Dahl (1957), on voting patterns of United States' senators. In this work, the researchers observed the way in which 'important' issues were decided in relation to legislation over foreign policy and on tax and fiscal policy. Certain senators were found to initiate more alternatives that were successful or vetoed alternatives initiated by others that, due to their intervention, were turned down. Such a senator was then ranked as powerful if he had more successes—that is, prevailed in decision making or got his own way—than the others. Certain senators were found to be predominantly successful whereas others were found to be generally unsuccessful in these situations. From this, Dahl concluded that 'A has power over B to the extent that he can get B to do something that B would not otherwise do' (pp. 202–203). Applying this to industrial relations would require us to examine a range of 'decision situations' that could be described as important within joint union–management committees and then seeing who 'won' on the majority of them. From this, following the one-dimensional view, we could then see whether particular stewards or managers were more powerful than their colleagues or their counterparts. For example, we could assess which party most adequately satisfied their demand/offer in the event of a pay claim, and which side most usually won in a shop floor negotiation over manning or in joint union–management committees examining issues such as job evaluation or disciplinary hearings. Clearly, such an approach is absurd for a variety of reasons; first of all, an initial offer or demand may not be a realistic figure on which to base the intentions of the two parties—this could be improved by assessing their realistic expectations or their initial 'sticking point'. However, there are more problems than this; both sides may 'win' on the issue, managing to gain things other than pay that enter into the negotiating arena during the course of discussions—for example, fringe benefits, new pay structures, new technology agreements, and so on. Most important of all, the one-dimensional view only allows for observation when both parties sit down together in some committee; it may well be that all the *really* important decisions influencing the enterprise, and consequently its employees, are taken at meetings where there is only a senior mangement presence. That is, that joint decision making is confined to relatively safe and non-controversial issues.

This led to the development of what Lukes has called the *two-dimensional view* of power as articulated by Bachrach and Baratz (1962, 1963). As they, themselves, argue 'power is also exercised when A devotes his energies to creating or reinforcing political values and institutional practices that limit the scope of the political process to public consideration of only those issues which are comparatively innocuous to A' (1962, p. 948). In other words, a satisfactory analysis of power must incorporate both decison making and *non-decision making*, to examine which issues are *excluded* from union–management discussions and to assess their effect upon employees. It is often argued that participation or consultation is confined to relatively safe issues; in relation to the BSC experiment, Brannen *et al.* report that the worker directors felt they were not originally sitting on the committees at which 'key' decisions were taken and so, consequently, did little more than to rubber stamp issues that had been decided elsewhere (1976, p. 236). However, once someone finds out that they have been excluded from decision making, their response is likely to be one of anger, mistrust, and frustration. Participation schemes without clearly defined objectives might therefore fall into disrepute.

For Lukes, although this view of power goes some way towards an effective model, it does not go far enough and he therefore proposes his own *three-demensional view*. The two-dimensional view is insufficient, he argues, because it is wrong to assume that power and conflict are necessarily related; the likelihood of conflict is apparent under the two-dimensional view when the subject of the power imbalance comes to realize that he is being excluded from crucial decisions that he thinks he should be helping to take. If A can get B to not even *desire* any involvement on an issue, surely this is an even more effective use of power. As Lukes suggests, 'A may exercise power over B by getting him to do what he does not want to do, but he also exercises power over him by influencing, shaping or determining his very wants . . . the most effective and insidious use of power is to prevent such conflict from arising in the first place' (1974, p. 23). It is wrong, therefore, to assume that the absence of grievances equals genuine consensus. During the latter part of the seventies and early eighties, we have seen—in a number of companies—employees being exhorted by their senior management to moderate wage claims or accept redundancies in order to streamline the company and ensure its survival. That these 'pleas' are realistic is not necessarily in doubt. What does demonstrate the three-dimensional aspect of managerial power is the fact that these should be so readily accepted. In other words, it is possible to assess consensual employee values by effectively structuring expectations. Furthermore, it could be argued that many of the dominant values in society socialize us into acceptance of traditional roles and values that we may unquestioningly accept as the automatic 'natural order' rather than the product of social institutions—for example, consensus politics, rigid sex-stereotyping, and harsh attitudes towards minority ethnic groups.

This more theoretical treatment of power has been important for two reasons; firstly, it illustrates the way in which power can be used to *support* the traditional prerogatives of management in industry and to show that the agents of capital have more resources at their disposal than do the agents of labour. Secondly, since the remainder of the chapter is going to focus on the role of union or workgroup power, it is important to place power in perspective and not to imply that our concentration on union power is meant to indicate the supremacy of the latter. For the average line manager (or foreman even more so), the overall balance of power, however, may seem somewhat distant when he is confronted with action or potential action in the workplace. Indeed, power does not *necessarily* have to be used in order to be effective; it could be argued that power is at its greatest when an individual's or group's reputation or threat of sanctions is sufficient to enable it to have its demands met by the other side.

A model of union power

Very little work has been done in order to tighten up the concept of workgroup power or to provide a satisfactory analytical treatment of it. While, at a macro-level, we can suggest that the miners are a powerful group, from what basis do they derive this power? Is it purely because of their centrality to the continued functioning of British industry, or is it also important to take into consideration their solidarity, their willingness to take action, the ability of their leaders to organize a successful strike, their reputation, or what? Similarly, it is pertinent to ask whether other groups may be more strategically placed than the miners, for example, but unwilling to use or unaware of their potential muscle. For example, where would nurses or solicitors or computer staff stand in this analysis?

For this reason, it is important to try and identify the different stages that a group—and this is loosely defined from a small number of people up to a whole union—may go through in the process of putting its power potential or capacity into action. Below, we shall deal with a sequence of four stages in this *power generation* process and each will be considered in turn. These are:

1. Power capacity.
2. Power realization.
3. Power testing.
4. Power outcomes.

Clearly, the process may break down at any of the stages; also, there is an important role to be played by feeding back information that may then increase the likelihood of a successful progression through this sequence. First of all, though, we shall look at *power capacity* or the potential for action. There are four elements to this, and their identification owes much to the work of Hickson *et al.* (1971) and Hinings *et al.* (1974). We shall summarize each of these elements in tabular form later in the chapter.

Firstly, a group's *pervasiveness* has been defined as the 'degree to which the workflow of a sub-unit connects with the workflow of other sub-units. It describes the extent of task interactions between sub-units, and for all sub-units in an organisation, it would be operationalised as the flow chart of a complete systems analysis' (1971, p. 221). Therefore, the higher the pervasiveness of a work group, and the more central it is to workflow, the greater its power capacity within the organization.

This point has been noted by a number of students of industrial relations. Most notably, Sayles has stated that 'the way jobs are distributed and flow into one another . . . moulds the types of work groups that evolve within the plant' (1958, p. 4). Kuhn emphasizes that a number of product lines reduce the power of units as the rest of the work can always flow on (1961, p. 156). It may well be that groups in technically strategic positions receive more favourable treatment from management in order to prevent them from taking action. In other cases, treatment may not be forthcoming and small groups of employees— say, internal truck drivers—are able to close down a whole factory. Indeed, in certain instances, management may actually unwittingly create a greater dependence upon key groups of people in order that it satisfies other technical and economic criteria of efficiency. A good case in point here would be the increasing reliance upon computers and consequently the people who work with them, something that did not go un-noticed by the Civil Service unions in drawing up their plans for selective action against the government. Computer staff are now in a very strategic position to disrupt workflow (Purcell *et al.*, 1978).

However, higher pervasiveness is only technologically determined up to a point. Action may be spread so that a whole department or plant is disrupted in order to press home a sectional claim. In order to do this, though, strike leaders have got to ensure sufficient solidarity, unity of purpose, and identification with the original group in dispute for it to be effective. As a strike is escalated, it becomes more difficult to ensure cohesiveness; we shall return to this later.

Secondly, a group may possess the ability to close a plant down quickly and this we refer to as *immediacy*. It differs from pervasiveness in that it relates to the *speed* with which the rest of the organization may be affected through disruption by one particular group. For a mass production system, this factor is especially important; since work flows quickly from one operation to the next, there are short cycle times, and a lack of storage space between operations. The *exact* position within the production flow of a highly interdependent system may not necessarily be important since groups at the beginning of the operation can clearly stop the supply of work to other operations but, equally, groups at the end can prevent work earlier on the line due to lack of storage space. Indeed, most groups within a plant possess some immediacy since they have the ability to close down a factory or department.

Beynon has described how stoppages of work in the paint shop at Halewood soon stop production elsewhere so causing other workers to be laid off within a few hours. When there are high schedules during periods of market boom, the workers were willing to press home their advantage (1973, p. 131). We have seen, over the last few years, the efforts by the miners to move their settlement date back to November when the effect of a stoppage would have much more *immediate* effect due to the greater demand for coal over the winter months. Similarly, the success of a seaman's strike partially depends upon the speed with which the residue of food or other imported goods already in the country is used up. It also depends, of course, on their pervasiveness as both an importing and exporting channel. The influence of technology, or position in the workflow, is therefore quite marked.

The other two sources of power relate less to the ability of a group to disrupt production on a short-term basis and more on their long-term ability to maintain control over their work, usually by preventing other people from being able to do it. Whereas the first two sources are related to the position in production flow (in its broadest sense), these two relate to the labour market. Firstly, there is the fact that there may be a lack of appropriate *substitutes* available to undertake the work of a group of people, on an individual or a departmental basis. Other factors remaining constant, 'a person difficult to replace will have greater power than a person easily replaceable' (Mechanic, 1962, p. 358). This form of power is less obvious than the short-term disruptive capacity since it is less overt; it may well be that management automatically gives in to key personnel without even attempting to combat this power.

This is especially marked for apprenticeships, through which there is often trade union control over the supply and training of future tradesmen. By controlling entry into the occupation, a craft union can limit the possibility of substitutes and so enhance bargaining power. Management, for its part, may be forced to accept this process in order to ensure a continued supply of labour to the organization. In the case of craftsmen, trade union control is simplified by the way in which adherence to the norms of the occupation is upheld by socialization during apprenticeships.

Moreover, a 'strong' trade union may have negotiated formal undertakings from management that work cannot be contracted out in the event of an industrial dispute. The union may have links with workmen in other local and competing firms so as to prevent contracting out. In fact, for most organizations, this facet of substitutability is well controlled by the workforce, but not always; two examples in which management stepped in to complete work during a strike are the hospital dispute of 1973 and the 1975 stoppage by some British Airways clerks. Similarly, the employer may borrow money in order to keep operations going as the government did during the Civil Service dispute of 1981.

Control through lack of substitutes is also apparent through restrictive practices, notably demarcation and battles over routinization of work (de-skilling). Craft unions have generally been most unwilling to allow routinization of their members' work since this would remove their major power capacity. In shipbuilding this can be observed in the delicate preservation of individual job skills even though the jobs themselves may now be relatively simple. In most factories, there is a clear demarcation between the jobs of maintenance fitters and electricians.

The final source of power capacity is *control over uncertainty*. Units do not necessarily aim to remove uncertainty but merely to cope with it, and this is where the power capacity is generated. Hickson *et al.* note that 'coping by a sub-unit reduces the impact of uncertainty on other activities in the organisation, a shock absorber function' (1971, pp. 219–20). Thus a group that copes with uncertainties possesses considerable power over the groups to which it passes work since it routinizes their activities. It holds the threat that it can transmit the uncertainty to an area that has become conditioned to accepting certainty.

The major research in this area was by Crozier in his study of maintenance personnel in the French tobacco industry. Since machine breakdowns are unpredictable—more so in the absence of planned maintenance—the groups who repair machinery are likely to be powerful since continued operation of the factory depends upon their work. Moreover, not many people can understand what mechanics are doing or how long it should take them to complete a job (1964, p. 109). Therefore, the need to prevent the introduction of planned maintenance was of vital importance for shop floor control.

As with technology, groups on the shop floor that are in a strategically powerful position within the labour market possess a considerable power capacity by virtue of their low irreplaceability. Management may acknowledge this strength and so treat such groups with greater respect, thus limiting the possibility of industrial action. Nevertheless, the privileges often accorded to these groups, in terms of higher wages, better facilities, and greater job security, demonstrate their high-power capacity and potential control.

This leads us to the second stage of the process; that is, the degree to which a group *realizes its power capacity*. It is clearly important to consider why individuals or groups with high power capacity fail to take advantage of this—indeed, it may well be that the groups neither realize their power nor desire increased control. This stage can also be broken down into four parts.

Firstly, we have to look at the issue of *group cohesiveness* and individual attitudes to work and to their workmates, factors that are brought most sharply into focus when preparing to challenge management. In a recent book by Friedman and Meredeen, which assesses the dynamics of a strike from the standpoint of two of the principal protagonists, this concept of cohesion and its linkage with power capacity was introduced on a number of occasions. For example, the ex-personnel specialist (Meredeen) wondered why the union had not escalated the strike so as to incorporate key workers. The ex-convenor (Friedman) replied that, while this was considered, it was rejected since 'by introducing supporters without an immediate interest in the outcome, you risk diluting the strength and cohesiveness of the strikers' (1980, p. 198). In other words, there has to be at least some minimal shared understanding of issues in order for a group to be cohesive.

Clearly, this can vary by virtue of the type of work done, opportunity for interaction and sociability, and work expectations. The research on the 'affluent workers' in Luton demonstrated a very low attachment to work and a lack of contact with workmates. The calculative or instrumental attitudes of these workers meant a lack of cohesiveness although, on occasion, they did take action against management. Similarly, other groups—and perhaps most notably those in rural or agricultural areas—may indicate high levels of sociability and group cohesion alongside a willingness to defer to management decisions. Other groups may be more collectively based and challenge management. We shall return to the relationship between group cohesiveness and willingness to oppose management in just a moment.

The second part of this *group realization* process is one in which the group may possess a significant power capacity but *not be aware* of this. Purcell and his colleagues asked their computer respondents if they were unaware of their considerable power capacity and, perhaps not surprisingly, they dismissed this as a reason for their inactivity; they did, however, concede that they may be inept in the *use* of their power (1978, p. 35). A group of internal truck drivers interviewed by the author some years ago certainly appeared unaware of its disruptive potential. Moreover, one could argue that many sections of public service workers were not fully aware of their power capacity until after the dustmen's strike in the late sixties.

Thirdly, if a group is sufficiently cohesive and is aware of its power capacity, it may still not think that it is legitimate to take action in order to press home its advantage; in other words, it may not be *willing to use its power*. In the computer case mentioned above, it was felt that the group did not choose to take advantage of its power capacity. Its values and beliefs were such that it was reluctant to challenge management's decisions, and its professionalism inhibited it from using the power it had. However, 'if the values which appear to have restrained the use of power by (these) staff were to change, then the power of computer technology in industrial relations might suddenly be unleashed'. Indeed, during the research, these people were joining unions and beginning to question their old loyalties (Purcell, 1978, pp. 35–38). There are other indications, too, of a greater willingness to challenge management and to become involved in action against it. Perhaps, other groups have gained from their opposition to management and this stimulates another group to test out its ability to influence management on a particular issue (Brown, 1973, p. 144). Events during the late seventies and early eighties have shown that professional workers such as teachers, airline pilots, and even civil servants have been prepared to take industrial action. Similarly, continual argument takes place among the nursing unions and their members about the legitimacy of industrial action; feelings such as these were relatively unknown up until a few years ago.

But, despite this growing mood of militancy, the prevailing one still tends to be that of moderation, particularly in sectors where either human life or professional values might be at stake. Nurses, for example, will generally be most unwilling to take action that seriously endangers their patients. Teachers may be too concerned about their pupils to prevent them taking full-scale action. Similarly, many office workers or managers will be unsure about the potential damage they may do to the company. Indeed, it could be argued that those groups with the greatest power capacity are, due to a mixture of personal feelings and the pressure of public opinion, *unwilling* to use this in order to satisfy their demands.

Conversely, other groups may be less hesitant about taking action. For example, the craft ethic fosters a similarity of interests and a rejection of dependence upon management (Batstone *et al.*, 1977, pp. 142–143). Similarly, in printing, stereotypes of conflict appeared to be 'essential in order to maintain the internal solidarity of the group' (Hill, 1974, p. 221). This certainly involves some re-interpretation of past events in order to 'demonstrate "bad faith" on the part of management . . . things which at the time were considered merely coincidental now become defined as a part of a larger strategy on the part of management' (Batstone *et al.*, 1978, p. 51).

Often, the shop steward plays a key role in articulating this discontent and this takes us on to consider the final stage in the realization process, someone with the *ability* to lead employees should they decide to engage in industrial action. It should be remembered, as we saw in Chapter 5, that stewards also exert their influence over the membership by *restraining* them from taking action and the role of translating power into action is not the only one that the steward plays. Partridge, in suggesting a process of leadership on the shop floor, sees the steward doing four things in defining and articulating a grievance; first of all, the issue has to be defined in such a way as to mobilize the appropriate values among his constituents and to help mould group identity. Having done this, he then has to choose the most appropriate network through which to progress the issue and, in so doing, minimize opposition and maximize cooperation from other groups and, if possible, management. Finally, and particularly if the outcome leads to a reaffirmation of the group's power, he will use some form of feedback in order to maintain group identity, to get them to identify with previous experiences as a commonly felt 'good' or 'bad' time (1978, pp. 193–196). The role of the steward, however, important as it is, is often over-emphasized in the event of industrial action and, as we shall see later, leads to superficial and possibly ill-conceived managerial responses—such as dismissal of a so-called trouble-maker.

We can now see the second stage in power generation; that in which the group realizes its potential power, organizes itself in opposition to manage-ment, and articulates its discontent through the steward. Having got this far and perhaps threatened action, the group may now move onto the third stage in the process if it has failed to resolve, to its own satisfaction, the issue at hand. This we call the *power testing* stage. There are two crucial elements to this; firstly, the group has to attempt to choose the 'right' moment at which to press home its claim. Obviously, it has greater chances of success if management is unable or unwilling to resist due to pressure for production, the need to satisfy an important order, or even, perhaps, the need to maintain a good company image. Secondly, the 'right' method must be chosen in order to win the claim. Again, the method may vary from time to time and it may well be that 'cut-price' industrial action—such as working-to-rule, overtime bans, going slow, or working without cooperation—may be more harmful to the company than an all-out strike. Recently, for example, NALGO members have taken action by refusing to process rate demands so starving the authority of in-coming cash. In a similar vein, Post Office Telecommunica-tions workers held up the dispatch of phone bills, although, in this case, the GPO borrowed money to help them through the action. In other words, a strike *may* not *always* be the most cost-effective form of action for union members to take.

Finally, if action is taken, the group needs to ensure that it leads to a strengthening or reaffirmation of the group's power; that is, that the *outcome* needs to be favourable in order to provide a basis for the future and maybe even prevent the *need* for action the next time an issue arises. In other words, to build up the solidarity of the membership to the extent that management is willing to comply by virtue of its reputation. As we mentioned above, a union's negotiating strength 'may derive ultimately from the threat of a strike, but such a threat need not be put into practice. Indeed, the most powerful unions may rarely resort to strike action, since a threat to do so modifies the employer's attitude' (Armstrong *et al.*, 1977, p. 94). There have been occasions in which strategic and quite militantly active groups have become much quieter and less likely to resort to industrial action. It may well be that these groups have been 'cushioned' by management and their reactions anticipated so as to minimize the likelihood of their needing to take action (Sayles, 1958, p. 109). However, if their expectations do not continue to be satisfied, they may resort to their previous activity. Conversely, they may 'forget' how to act as a unit. The role of feedback—to both members *and* management—is a crucial factor in preserving one's power and in trying to ensure that the need to take industrial action is rarely required.

Hopefully, it is now apparent why this model of power generation involves a number of stages; it is insufficient to focus upon the technological and labour market sources of power capacity alone, important though these are. Similarly, consideration of a group's willingness to take action will only paint a partial picture. It is the interaction of the two—the largely structurally influenced facets of power capacity and the largely behavioural or attitudinal aspects of group solidarity and willingness to act through power realization—that a group is able to test its potential for influence over management and hopefully (for it) reaffirm or strengthen its perception of its relative power. Clearly, there are other interactions between the stages; for example, the technological arrangements in an organization provide certain conditions that facilitate or impede group cohesiveness. Similarly, the leader or experienced steward may be able to mobilize support for action from other sections of the membership in order to enhance power capacity. It is useful to consider these factors separately, however, so as to distinguish between them from a conceptual standpoint. It also helps us to organize our examination of *management responses* within the same relatively simple framework.

Management responses to union power
From a variety of examples, it is clear that management has not been slow in devising strategies to combat the exercise of union power. It has sought to find ways in which to reduce the power capacity of strategic groups or prevent the likelihood of power being used to the detriment of the company. Activities can be aimed at seeking:

1. To reduce the dependency on a particular group.
2. To inhibit the development of solidarity and beliefs in the legitimacy of industrial action.
3. To ensure that, if power is tested, the outcome is to weaken rather than affirm the group's perception of its power (Purcell, 1979, pp. 49–53).

Firstly, in trying to reduce a group's *power capacity*, management has taken action in response to each of the four characteristics of this stage in the power generation process. In the pursuit of economies of scale, mangement may decide to centralize aspects of its business; in particular, if it becomes dependent upon one site or part of the organization, it increases this unit's *pervasiveness*. Purcell describes a major toy manufacturer making a decision such as this only to be confronted by annual stoppages at peak distribution time that effectively disrupted its business. Being successful one year led the drivers to re-test their power the next. Eventually, management reverted to the old system (of four depots) having realized that it had failed to take sufficient notice of the potential industrial relations implications of the original move (1979, p. 51). Similar effects were seen through strikes in NHS laundries, those with several alternative plants servicing different parts of the hospital being able to keep going more easily than those with a central laundry operation.

Companies can also insulate themselves against power through *immediacy*. By building up or allowing for stock banks between operations, sectional disruption—even by a strategically placed group—may be minimized and work restored to normal before there is any effect on the supply of completed goods. Batstone *et al.* report that, from their research, management may 'purposely build up stocks when it expects a strike . . . (in one instance) for several months it expanded production beyond immediate requirements and stockpiled completed vehicles at various locations outside the plant so that, if the strike were to occur, it would still be possible to meet orders' (1978, p. 31). Of course, this is dependent upon a number of factors; that union members are prepared—if they are aware of management strategy—to work overtime if this is required; that the company has enough money to stockpile; that it has sufficient physical resources to store excess work; and that it feels it is more appropriate to do this rather then resolve the issue.

Management can also attempt to ensure that the work of the group can be *substituted* by other people or indeed goods. For example, in hospital disputes back in the early seventies, management turned to the use of disposable sheets rather than be dependent upon laundry facilities. Similarly, one company investigated by Purcell *et al.*, realizing the importance of a computer to its continued operations, replaced its sophisticated system with a slightly less efficient, but more easily substitutable, one that could be used in the event of an emergency (1978, p. 34). Moreover, new technology may reduce dependence upon certain highly skilled jobs while, at the same time, transfering power capacity to groups or even individuals who may be even more willing to exploit their pervasiveness.

Finally, there may be attempts to routinize jobs that possess a high power capacity by virtue of their ability to *cope with uncertainty*. For example, Crozier's maintenance men were against any company move towards planned maintenance since this would make them less indispensable (1964, p. 165). There are, therefore, quite a number of ways in which management has been able to reduce its dependence on key groups of employees. However, it may not always be possible to do this—obviously, a group with a high power capacity may be able to resist the introduction of changes designed to weaken its position—and consequently management has also attempted to influence the *power realization* aspect of the process.

Again, in relation to computer staff, Purcell has noted the increasing popularity of separating these departments, often on green field sites away from the main centre of the organization, so as to prevent them becoming *aware* of their potential power. It then becomes possible to pay special attention to such staff and helps to create, if possible, a professional ethic that is more likely to work in favour of the company rather than the union. In addition, by reducing contact with other workers, it may then be possible to inhibit the development of solidarity with them (1979, pp. 51–52).

There have also been attempts to reduce the *willingness* of groups to use their power; this can take quite a number of forms. For example, a common policy during the seventies has been the use of the lay-off of other groups in a factory if there has been a sectional dispute. That is, rather than attempting to soldier on until work for other groups has dried up, to lay off most other sections—and particularly large production or assembly shops—soon after the dispute has started. By doing this, other groups learn of their *vulnerability* to action elsewhere in the company and, it is hoped by management, they will put pressure on the group that has taken the action to return to work. Moreover, since many agreements (in the car industry for one) do not make allowance for lay-off pay in the event of an *internal* dispute, this then tends to thrust the problem onto the union instead.

Management has also used more direct methods, aimed especially at individuals, to hinder the development of solidarity. Personal letters have been so commonplace at companies such as BL that they even become the butt of cartoonists. Warnings about the dire consequences of continued action and the use of ballots over the top of the union's head have certainly caused employees to acquiesce with management proposals for fear of more dramatic action. During final negotiations in the Water Industry in 1981, one or two comments from the employers referred to the water workers having 'a lot to fear from the public' in the event of their taking all-out action. Perhaps most apparent of the attempts to reduce *willingness to act* have been the threats to all strikers that they will be dismissed should they fail to return to work on a certain date; to an extent, this may be used more as a bargaining tactic.

Finally, management can attempt to influence power realization by taking action against the leaders of shop floor groups. Again, at BL, the dismissal of the then senior steward, Derek Robinson, in 1979 can be seen in this particular light. Management may be willing to risk the likelihood of action or a visit to an industrial tribunal in order to get rid of someone whom it considers to be a troublemaker. Moreover, management may hope to 'teach' other employees on the basis of this approach. Although such a policy may achieve short-term success in stabilizing industrial relations, it is altogether more dubious whether its long-term effect will be beneficial to a company (Sayles, 1958, p. 167). It may well be that when the opportunity presents itself to the shop floor to fight back against management, its reaction will be even more determined and possibly less ordered. In line with Chapter 5, it is suggested that a far better policy is to work with stewards and involve them in more centralized company bargaining provided there are appropriate mechanisms for effective shop floor involvement. Hunt, for example, describes the way in which he was able—as an industrial relations manager—to get the agreement of the stewards to ensure that sectional action must first be ratified by a JSSC. While this did not rule out industrial action altogether, it did make it far less likely to occur (1977, pp. 132–134).

Much of the previous argument assumes that management is trying to *avoid* strike action; this may not be the case, of course, particularly if it seems important to bring out an issue that has been bubbling under the surface for months. In that case, management may actually *promote* strike action. Similarly, if management feels that a stoppage is likely sometime in the near future, it makes more sense to have the strike when it is *least* likely to affect it; that is, if there is to be action, management wants to choose the best *time* for it to occur so as to minimize the costs on it, and also to try and influence the *method* by which the conflict will become overt; for example, by 'converting' conflict from 'cut-price' action into a strike. Timing is influenced by many of the factors we have discussed—for example, when finished goods levels are high, when the market is slack, when it is likely that employees want to maximize earnings, or at times when willingness to act may be lower than usual—but the primary objective is to ensure that, if action is taken, it serves to *weaken* rather than strengthen the group's perception of its power.

Whereas many of the responses made by management are primarily oppositional in character, a number of them—particularly under the umbrella of 'power realization'—are intended to incorporate shop floor employees and stewards more effectively into line with company policy. This strategy of incorporation reflects a long-term approach to industrial relations; conversely, certain facets of the oppositional response reveal a short-term objective to 'win' the issue at stake. Yet again, some of the aspects covered under power capacity illustrate a longer-term strategy with regard to technology and labour market conditions. Perhaps we can most adequately sum up this process of power generation with the aid of a diagram (see Table 7.1).

Conclusions

In this chapter, we have attempted to focus on the importance of analysis in industrial relations; to see the way in which power can be assessed in such a way as to increase the predictability of likely action and so direct the line manager to adopt a longer-term contingency approach as a response to workgroup power. It is certainly true to say—as we can see from a number of examples described above—that managements have not always thought through the industrial relations implications of technical or organizational change. That these also need to be taken into consideration—not just coped with in a fire-fighting way—should also now be clear.

Both parties will (or should) use their analysis of conflict as part of a learning process; on the part of the stewards, the emphasis will be upon feedback to members and management, and on the form of action most suited to particular circumstances. On the part of management, feedback is also important, but so too is the need to restructure industrial relations to ensure that conflict is usually channelled through jointly agreed mechanisms (procedures) for its resolution. If industrial action is taken, management needs to be aware of how to contain this and ensure that power perceptions are weakened. But, in line with the rest of the book, we shall now move on to

Table 7.1. **The process of power generation, management response, and philosophy**

Stage	Aspect	Management response	Management philosophy
Power capacity	Pervasiveness	Dual sourcing, not centralizing	
	Immediacy	Stock banks, store finished goods, borrow money to help increase resistance	Long-term strategic opposition
	Substitutability	Other materials, simple machines, management do the work	
	Coping with uncertainty	Routinization of work	
Power realization	Group cohesiveness	May be to management's advantage	Opposition and incorporation
	Awareness of power capacity	Reduce contact, green field sites	Long-term opposition
	Willingness to take action	Lay off other workers, letters, threats of dismissal, public opinion	Short-term opposition
		Action to increase company loyalty open-the-books'	Long-term incorporation
	Steward ability to lead	Sack 'troublemakers',	Short-term opposition
		Work *with* steward committees	Long-term incorporation
Power testing	Choice of 'right' timing and 'right' method for union	Choice of 'right' timing and 'right' method for management	Short-term opposition
Power outcomes	Strengthening or affirmation of power perception	Weakening of power perception	Short-term opposition

concentrate on the mechanisms available to management in order to institutionalize conflict and promote cooperation. The next three chapters deal, therefore, with strikes and procedures, legal controls, and employee involvement. First, we shall deal with the extent of strikes and other industrial action in Britain today.

8. Industrial action and the role of procedures

In Chapter 7, we examined both the nature and sources of workgroup power in industrial relations; in this chapter we concentrate on industrial action—both strikes and action short of stoppage—as a manifestation of this power, and on mechanisms that have been used in order to contain and channel this discontent through agreed procedures. In other words, to assess the extent of industrial action, particularly strikes, in this country and to see the way in which procedures may help to contain the consequences of disputes. Again, we shall pose three questions to introduce the rest of the subject matter. How extensive is industrial action in this country? What value can procedures hold for the line manager in order to institutionalize conflict at work? What are the fundamental facets of procedural design?

The extent of industrial action

Despite the fact that strikes are the most visible manifestation of conflict at work, they are by no means the only form of action that can be taken by employees. For example, it may be more appropriate to take action short of a strike such as a work-to-rule, an overtime ban, a go-slow, or a work-in, instead. Brown and his colleagues asked the sample of senior managers in their survey of 970 manufacturing establishments, which, if any, form of action had been taken by employees at their establishment over the previous two years. For manual workers, 46 per cent reported some form of action whereas, for non-manual, it was a little less than 10 per cent. For both groups, however, strikes were less popular than other forms of action combined; approximately 40 per cent of all incidents were strikes (1981, p. 81). Whether employees choose to strike or take cut price action depends upon the situation at hand. In general, the ratio of strikes to other industrial action is fairly similar across the manufacturing industry although it is interesting to note a likely preference for strikes in textiles and clothing and a greater likelihood of other forms of action in printing, paper, and publishing (p. 84).

In order to get some idea of the extent of strike action, we can turn to the published statistics collected by the Department of Employment (DE). Before analysing these a number of reservations need to be made about their accuracy. First of all, the definition of a strike used by the Department involves a cut-off point that excludes very small stoppages; that is, those stoppages that involve less than 10 workers or last less than one day, unless the aggregate number of working days lost exceeds 100. Consequently, we can expect some degree of under-reporting because of this; however, the same criteria have been applied since 1893, which at least allows for comparability over time. Secondly, companies are under no obligation to report a stoppage of work to the Department, so we can expect under-reporting here also; representatives of the DE, however, do defend this on the grounds that they 'find out' through a variety of channels about most stoppages that would come within their definition (Smith *et al.*, 1978, p. 156). This has been queried recently by Kelly and Nicholson based on work in South Yorkshire in which they found that, while most plants accurately reported strikes to the DE, there was evidence of under-reporting in the most strike-prone establishments (1980, p. 29). This leads us onto the third reservation; namely that reporting accuracy may vary not only between plants, but also between the private and the public sectors, and also over time.

The Brown survey of manufacturing establishments estimated, however, that the official figures are very accurate when it comes to accounting for 'number of days lost'—94 per cent are captured so to speak. For 'number of strikes', the official figures may under-report by a factor of up to four times, due mainly to stoppages lasting less than one day that would not be covered by the Department's definition anyway (1981, pp. 98–101). Since the definition and the method of collection are consistent, we can at least compare strikes between companies or industries and over time.

Certainly, the nature of strikes has varied over the course of the last century; the number of working days lost was much higher than nowadays for the period between 1893 and 1926—for example, approximately 150 million days were lost over a three-year period following the end of the First World War. Between 1933 and 1967, the yearly average only exceeded four million working days on three occasions. Since then, the number of working days lost has averaged over 10 million but has varied enormously.

The number of stoppages has increased regularly since 1893 and, as can be seen from the Table 8.1, this was recorded as 2598 for the seventies, a figure two to three times higher than the period prior to the Second World War.

A number of points need to be made about these figures in order to clarify the position regarding the nature of our strike 'problem' today. First of all, the upward trend in the number of stoppages through the sixties and seventies has not been that steep; in fact, from 1978 onwards, we have seen a reduction to a postwar low in 1980. Secondly the vast majority (usually in excess of 95 per cent) are unofficial and of very short duration; this is even more apparent if we

Table 8.1   Strike statistics 1960–1980†

Year	No. of stoppages beginning in year	% known to be official	Working days lost in all stoppages (millions)	% known to be official
1960	2832	2.4	3.02	16.4
1961	2686	2.2	3.05	28.3
1962	2449	3.2	5.80	70.9
1963	2068	2.4	1.76	30.0
1964	2524	2.8	2.28	30.3
1965	2354	4.1	2.93	20.8
1966	1937	3.1	2.40	48.9
1967	2116	5.1	2.79	14.1
1968	2378	3.8	4.70	46.9
1969	3116	3.1	6.80	23.6
1970	3906	4.1	10.98	30.2
1971	2223	7.2	13.56	74.2
1972	2497	6.4	23.82	76.2
1973	2873	4.6	7.19	27.9
1974	2922	4.3	14.75	47.7
1975	2282	6.1	6.01	19.1
1976	2016	3.4	3.28	14.4
1977	2703	2.9	10.14	24.8
1978	2471	3.6	9.41	43.1
1979	2080	3.9	29.47	79.8
1980	1262	7.3	11.91	85.7
Average 1960–1979	2522		8.20	
Average 1960–1969	2446		3.55	
Average 1970–1979	2598		12.85	

† Most of the detailed information on stoppages is taken from C. Smith *et al.*, *Strikes in Britain*, HMSO (1978), which provides comprehensive information on the statistics.
Source: various

take into account stoppages of less than one day. Thirdly, the number of working days lost in any one year reflects, more than anything else, the contribution of a few large stoppages; for example, the figures for 1972 and 1974 were inflated by long disputes over pay in the coal industry. Approximately half the working days lost in 1979 were due to the series of one- and two-day stoppages in the engineering industry. Most significant of all, about three-quarters of the working days lost in 1980 were due to a single dispute in the steel industry. In fact, over the 20–year period from 1960–1979, just 64 stoppages accounted for nearly half the working days lost (*Employment Gazette*, September, 1980). Conversely, over half the stoppages recorded for 1979 resulted in a loss of less than 500 working days and a third of all stoppages lasted less than two days (*Employment Gazette*, August, 1980).

In other words, we can say with some confidence that Britain has two very different types of strike that account for the vast majority of our stoppage activity; firstly, there are the large industrial stoppages, usually official, generally over a pay agreement (annual) and mostly involving large numbers of workers. These either take the form of a long stoppage such as those by the firemen in 1978 (nine weeks) or Ford workers in the same year (nine weeks) or of a series of one- or two-day stoppages as illustrated by the engineering strike in 1979. The second kind of stoppage is totally different and reflects more of an *immediate protest* to some management action rather than the hard, long drawn-out slog of the other type. Most of these stoppages are short, usually unofficial and are generally over before the union even gets to know about them. For example, in 1979, Ford experienced a large number of these—many of which would be too small for inclusion in the statistics—over working practices on the Escort line at Halewood.

While these figures are instructive in telling us about the overall level of strike activity in Britain today, we also need to see if certain industries, sectors, or types of establishment are more likely to experience strikes than others. Since the war, we can identify four industries that have been particularly strike-prone; these are coal mining, docks, shipbuilding, and motor vehicle manufacture. More recently, we can add a fifth and that is the iron and steel trades. Over this period, for example, these industries have accounted for roughly a quarter of all recorded stoppages and a third of all working days lost while only employing 6 per cent of the working population. The coal industry is, however, considerably less strike-prone than it used to be; for example, in the latter half of the fifties, it accounted for nearly three-quarters of all stoppages whereas, by the late seventies, it was of the order of 20 per cent. Conversely, certain industries have been exceptionally 'quiet' in terms of stoppages; namely, agriculture and forestry, retail distribution, insurance, banking, and public houses to name but a few. As a sector, manufacturing tends to be predominant in stoppage activity with private services generally low. Local authority stoppages have been less regular than those in manufacturing but, when they occur, are often of a longer duration.

We can also detect differences between establishments on the basis of their size. It is not entirely unexpected to find that smaller plants experience fewer stoppages and lose less working days per employee than do larger ones. For example, for the period 1971–1973, working days lost per 1000 employees varied from an annual average of about fifteen for plants of 25 people or under to an average of over 2000 for those employing 1000 or more. Stoppages were also less likely in smaller establishments but these tended to stop rising once plant size exceeded 500 employees. However, Brown has queried this simple association by producing data on the *number of incidents* (rather than days lost) per 1000 employees in large and small plants. The likelihood of strike action is, *pro rata*, two to three times as high in plants employing less than 100 than it is in those employing more than 1000 (1981, pp. 91–92).

Again, as expected, there were also found to be regional variations although some of this is undoubtedly due to the differing industrial and occupational mixes in each area. However, in *Strikes in Britain*, the authors have made adjustments for factors such as this and still show certain areas to be more strike-prone than others; for example, Merseyside and Glasgow are much higher than the average, although Coventry, parts of South Wales, and Edinburgh also contribute more than their fair share. Conversely, the South East, parts of the South West, East Midlands, and East Anglia are relatively trouble-free (Smith *et al.*, 1978, pp. 117–122).

We have a situation, therefore, in which certain industries, regions, and generally larger establishments would seem to have an extra large effect upon stoppage activity; this would certainly conform with popular opinion on these matters. However, more recent analysis—at a further degree of disaggregation—has shown up even more interesting results. For example, taking Merseyside as an example, it has become apparent that, even there, some 95 per cent of all manufacturing plants are strike-free during an average year and approximately half of one per cent of manufacturing plants account for over four-fifths of the days lost in stoppages within the region (Smith *et al.*, 1978, p. 89). A similar finding has emerged in relation to the inter-industry analysis; again, quoting from Smith *et al.*, 'the stoppage activity in manufacturing industry is heavily concentrated in a small minority of plants in all subdivisions . . . the comparatively poor record of certain subdivisions in some years is due to *the much worse performance of a few plants* rather than the generally worse performance of most plants '(p. 28—my emphasis). Brown's figures also show that less than 10 per cent of manufacturing establishments account for more than two-thirds of incidents of action taken by manual workers; for non-manual, less than 1 per cent account for nearly one half (1981, p. 82).

Perhaps the most interesting of these detailed breakdowns relates to the size factor; in line with the other two factors dealt with, the vast majority (98 per cent) of establishments—and particularly the small ones—are strike-free in any one year. Over a three-year period examined in detail, only 5 per cent of establishments actually experienced a recorded stoppage, although they may well have experienced an incident other than a strike or one that lasted less than one day.

In other words, stoppage activity is highly concentrated and it has been estimated that just 150 plants accounted for two-thirds of all the days lost in recorded strikes during this period. This leads Smith *et al.* to suggest that it is now 'abundantly clear that Britain does not have a widespread strike problem but rather a problem of stoppages concentrated in a small minority of manufacturing plants and in certain non-manufacturing sectors' (1978, p. 63). Clearly, this has immense implications for the governmental and company attempts to control our so called 'strike problem'. Furthermore, since nearly half the large manufacturing establishments were strike-free over this three year period, 'large is not necessarily ugly' (p. 62).

The benefit of these recently available disaggregated data on strikes is crucial as can be seen from the above discussion. While not trying to underestimate the seriousness of strike action, and also the possibility that mere threats of action may be more effective in amending management decisions, it does at least enable us to consider conflict in a little more objective manner. To complete this section, four other points will briefly be made so as to put strikes into perspective; firstly, the average employee or union does not happily enter into strike action—after all, the consequences for them may be far more serious than they may for the employer. Secondly, and connected to this, is the role that supplementary benefits may play in financing strikers through payments to their families. Since payment is not due until after the second week of a strike, this immediately reduces the size of the issue and limits it primarily to official strikes. Moreover, two separate studies, one by the Engineering Employers' Federation and the other by Gennard, have both shown that the level of 'take-up' is generally low and contributes a fairly small amount to the average money received or used during a strike. During the seventies, for example, the proportion of those eligible for payments who actually received benefits was of the order of 20 per cent and the average total amount paid was about £35.00 (Gennard, 1977). Thirdly, in the international 'league table', the United Kingdom occupies a position mid-way between the more strike-prone countries (in terms of working days lost) such as Italy, Iceland, Canada, Ireland, and Australia and the less strike-prone such as Switzerland, Austria, the Netherlands, Norway, and Sweden. The USA occupied a fairly similar position (*Employment Gazette*, November, 1980). Finally, it is worth stating just how *little* time is actually lost through strike action; the average employee is on strike for a little less than half a day per year, and this is considerably less than that lost through accidents and a whole variety of illnesses. For the most part, Britain is strike-free—no matter what picture the media may present—and industrial relations difficulties are generally solved either at source or through constitutional machinery such as procedure agreements. Bearing this in mind, we can now turn to a closer examination of just what procedures have to offer.

The nature and extent of procedures
The need for procedural reform in industrial relations was repeatedly emphasized by the Donovan Commission; indeed, it was even suggested that procedural disarray was a major cause of industrial disputes. Reforms should produce 'procedures which are clear where the present procedures are vague, comprehensive where the present procedures are fragmentary, speedy where the present procedures are protracted, and effective where the present procedures are fruitless' (1968, p. 36).

That reform has been at least formally undertaken can be seen from

Brown's survey of manufacturing industry. For the sample as a whole, 92 per cent of establishments had some form of grievance procedure while 89 per cent made provision for a dismissal or discipline disputes procedures. The only industrial sector in which less than 80 per cent of establishments had grievance procedures was in textiles, and here it was 64 per cent; all chemical establishments, on the other hand, were covered. The likelihood of grievance procedures increased with size but, even so, 80 per cent of establishments employing less than 100 people still had a procedure (1981, pp. 45–46).

Whether these procedures are actually used, and are not merely 'paper' policies, is another matter. That not all of them may be used is reflected in a passage from the 1980 ACAS Annual Report in which employers and trade unions were urged 'to review their procedure at all levels and to seek a new relationship with each other which will be strong enough to survive the temptation for either side to ignore agreed arrangements when the balance of advantage moves temporarily in their favour' (1981, p. 10). Below, we shall examine some of the factors that might encourage management to use procedures, and of their value to industrial relations as a whole. Firstly, we shall briefly define a procedure agreement and outline the variety of forms that this can take.

In broad terms, a procedure agreement 'embodies a set of rules whose purpose is to influence the behaviour of management, employees, and trade union representatives in a defined situation. The rules are, in effect, an agreed code of voluntary restraints on the use of power' (Hawkins, 1979, p. 132). In addition, it provides a 'formal framework within which the day-to-day business of industrial relations is conducted' (Hunt, 1977, p. 86).

Procedures may be installed in a number of different areas; for example, there may be:

1. *Recognition* procedures specifying the rights of a trade union(s) to recruit, organize, and represent defined categories of employee in the workplace. Details may be included covering bargaining units, steward facilities, duties, and constituencies.
2. *Disputes* procedures indicating the route to be followed in the event of collective or departmental-type issues.
3. *Grievance* procedures indicating the route to be followed in the event of an individual issue or complaint. In effect, it is now a legal requirement under the Employment Protection (Consolidation) Act of 1978 that individuals be made aware of the person to whom they can complain, and this would normally be included in the statement of their terms and conditions of employment (given not later than 13 weeks after commencing employment).
4. *Disciplinary* procedures setting the standards of conduct expected from employees and specifying any acts that may be deemed serious enough to justify dismissal.

5. *Redundancy* procedures covering the company's policy on consultation, methods of selection, compensation, and assistance in finding alternative work.
6. *Equal opportunity* procedures outlining an organization's commitment to provision of equal opportunities irrespective of sex, race, and creed.
7. *Participation* procedures indicating a company's philosophy towards employee involvement and specifying the mechanisms for promoting this.
8. *New technology* procedures covering agreements of the introduction of new machinery.

This list is not meant to be exhaustive but merely indicative of the most common types of procedure in industry. The primary objective behind all these procedures is to devise a set of agreed rules so as to channel any discontent through the appropriate mechanism for its possible resolution. Procedures do not remove discontent; they merely provide a means for institutionalizing it.

The value of procedure
From this point onwards, we shall concentrate our attention on grievance and disputes procedures. Although procedural reform may have been taken on board quite adequately by the company as a whole, it may still present problems for the line manager who has to operate within this on a day-to-day basis. It may, as we saw in Chapter 6, during our discussion of the foremen, lead to by-passing of junior management by stewards intent on getting an issue resolved as quickly as possible. This may, of course, cause resentment as may the feeling of being increasingly constrained by rules that do not appear appropriate to a particular department. Hunt argues that, despite him being a crucial figure in industrial relations, the line manager is assumed to be able to handle grievances according to procedure without any help or training in the necessary skills for conflict resolution. In the author's experience, there is often considerable confusion as to what constitutes legal requirements and what are the interpretations of the personnel department. Moreover, there may seem to be little value in progressing grievances through procedure if this only appears to succeed in showing the junior manager in a poor light to his seniors. Perhaps the latter ought to be more concerned with a totally 'quiet' department than with its opposite since this may indicate suppression of discontent rather than its absence. Overall, line managers need to be aware of the value of procedures to the company in the hope that, in this awareness, they will be operated with speed and efficiency.

Quite a number of reasons have been put forward in favour of procedures and, even though the discussion will concentrate on advantages to management, many of these will be of benefit to trade union members and their representatives. The benefits are as follows:

1. The drawing-up of procedures involves both parties working together in

sorting out the agreed mechanism for resolving matters that arise. Joint 'ownership' of the procedure is likely to create a *willingness* to make the procedures work as effectively as possible, to the extent of using outside bodies—such as ACAS—to intervene in seemingly intractable problems.

2. Procedures help to *clarify* the relationship between the two parties and ensure that the right of the employee to discuss a grievance is explicitly recognized. This helps to focus conflict within agreed mechanisms, and allows for its resolution within these. In other words, hoping to create a framework for good industrial relations.

3. Procedures provide a mechanism for resolution by identifying the person to whom the issue should be taken initially and by specifying the *route* to be followed should there be a failure-to-agree at that level. Since it is estimated that most (say 75 per cent) issues are resolved in the first two stages of procedure, the likelihood is that procedures help to get solutions at the point where the conflict becomes overt.

4. Procedures act as a safety valve and provide *time* within which to assess, analyse and answer the complaint that has been made. It *should* enable the heat to be taken out of the situation as much as possible.

5. If complaints have to be written down, this helps the grievant to *clarify the issue* in his own mind. Moreover, by articulating the issue and considering it in more detail, this may help the employee to understand the nature of his problem; this may result in the grievance being dropped or, if not, at least pursued through the correct channels.

6. Procedures—of all kinds—help to ensure *consistency* across a site, factory, company, or whatever. They reduce reliance on word of mouth, rumour, custom, and practice, and minimize arbitrary or discriminatory treatment.

7. Procedures help to ensure that adequate *records* are kept by management and consequently improve management control and information systems. This can also lead to consistency in communication and planning across the organization.[1]

This list is of potential advantages to be gained from clear procedures and may not operate effectively in all situations and at all times. Furthermore, it is likely that junior managers, while appreciating the company need for consistency and record-keeping (points 6 and 7 above), may feel this constrains them to the detriment of company efficiency since it takes them off their 'primary' task—of production, for example—and directs them into the role of industrial relations managers instead. Presumably, if a company feels that procedures are important, then it is under an obligation to train line management accordingly and try to persuade it of the value of procedure. However, nothing is more frustrating than operating a procedure that seems inappro-

1. Other writers who produce lists of advantages for procedure agreements include Hyman (1972, p. 38), Hawkins (1979, p. 133), and Thomson and Murray (1976 pp. 42–43).

priate or unreasonable. What measures can be used, then, to assess the adequacy of a procedure?

Marsh and McCarthy have suggested that there are two main criteria for assessing procedural adequacy: *acceptability* and *appropriateness* (1968, p. 3). In order for a procedure to continue effectively, it has got to be broadly acceptable to all the parties involved. It can never be expected to operate to complete satisfaction since each party may have slightly differing expectations from it; for example, senior management may be more interested in the consistency of decisions emanating from procedure, and for the way in which it can filter out local matters and so allow major issues to be funnelled upwards without undue delay. Stewards and their members may value not only speedy resolutions to grievances but also opportunities for participation and guarantees against victimization. While junior managers may value the overall principle behind procedures, they may be more ambivalent about the success of its operation (Thomson and Murray, 1976, pp. 46–48). Perhaps it is easier to assess unacceptability since dissatisfaction will be voiced against the procedure by management if it feels that its rights are unduly restricted or by unions if they feel that their involvement is too limited (Marsh and McCarthy, 1968, p. 3).

Secondly, a procedure has to be appropriate to the structure of the industry or group within which it is to operate and it has to be closely related to the relevant levels of decision making within that group. Clearly, it makes little sense for a company to impose a uniform procedure upon subsidiaries in a wide variety of industrial contexts. Similarly, the disposal rate of issues at each stage may not be as high as the parties desire. Reference back to local levels may merely give employees the feeling that the procedures are little more than a stalling device on the part of employers and that nothing can be gained by taking an issue through procedure. Marsh and McCarthy illustrate this with reference to the old engineering procedure (pre-1971) that led to increasing disillusionment with it as an appropriate mechanism for settling matters arising in the workplace. The system came under increasing strain with a declining rate of effectiveness (1968, p. 86). To be successful, an agreement needs to be both broadly acceptable to the parties and appropriate to the needs of the units of production covered by it. The system would be in need of review if procedural disarray in itself led to conflict.

This is not to say, however, that the requirements of procedure must *always* override the commitment to a common-sense approach to grievance resolution. There may be occasions when it is eminently more sensible to break with procedure in order to sort out a pressing problem. In other words, the *process* of grievance resolution may not always accord with the formal *procedure*. Thomson and Murray, in their survey, discovered quite a number of deviations from the formal rules, although some of these may not be seen as deviations by the parties themselves. For example, there was some evidence of stages being missed out altogether or of stewards becoming involved before foremen were notified of a grievance. Similarly, procedure might be avoided altogether or 'outside' persons involved at an earlier stage. Issues that were proving difficult to resolve were sometimes referred to a works committee or consultative committee even though this was not prescribed in the constitution (1976, pp. 93–99). It may be sensible to tolerate a certain degree of informality. The key question, however, becomes one of achieving the right balance between seeing procedures as vehicles of convenience or as instruments of regulation (1976, p. 109).

One other assumption rests behind procedure agreements; namely, that both parties are generally willing to use them rather than settling their differences through other means such as industrial action before procedures have been exhausted, or unilateral and unconsulted management changes to working practices. If managers, for example, continually flout the *spirit* of a procedure, there should be little surprise if trade union representatives do the same. In order to be successful, procedures require some degree of normative agreement as to their functions and usefulness. Thomson and Murray refer to this as a 'collaborative' orientation in which grievants are equally willing to satisfy the others' concerns as they are to ensure that their own are satisfied; this leads, according to the authors, to a situation in which 'new approaches are sought which satisfy both parties' (1976, pp. 32–33).

Procedures have to be agreed, then, that reflect—to a large extent—current practice. If the *process* of grievance resolution is substantially at odds with the formal requirements, then the latter will soon fall into disrepute. Similarly, their acceptability and appropriateness may change over time, thus demanding some form of periodic review. If the procedure itself is seen as providing an effective framework for grievance resolution, which is generally observed but may not be used on occasion so as to benefit both parties, then it is likely to be operating effectively. We can now turn to an examination of procedural design.

The design of procedures

Altogether, 15 different procedures were examined in detail in order to assess both the differences and similarities in procedural design across a variety of workplaces; that is, between public and private sectors, large and small organizations, manual and non-manual employees, and for different industries within manufacturing. Despite the fact that procedures reflect circumstances appropriate to the relevant workplace, there is also remarkable similarity in terms of the basic facets. For example, while there may be variations in the number of stages in the procedure, the use of time limits at each stage, or the provision for external third-party intervention, the underlying managerial philosophy behind most of the agreements is one of generating commitment or structuring expectations to the use of procedure as a more appropriate mechanism for expressing discontent than taking industrial action. Rather than deal with each of the different basic facets of procedures, we shall concentrate on three areas:

1. The preamble and assumed 'spirit' behind agreements.
2. The role of the personnel department as custodians or guardians of procedure.
3. The role of external third-party involvement.

Most procedures contained some *preamble* or introduction outlining the principles behind the agreement and the spirit or intention in which it was to be operated. The detail of these varied considerably with some emphasizing the need for speedy resolution, others allowing the avoidance of time limits by mutual agreement, and yet others just referring to the framework of the procedure. Some also referred to the agreement being in the mutual interests of both parties. One or two went considerably further; for example, the electrical engineering agreement stated that 'in almost all situations, the problem can be resolved in a mature manner by the employees and their immediate supervisors or managers. However, where genuine disagreements occur which cannot be resolved in this way, the grievance procedure. . . .' Another, in the paper industry, referred to agreement that 'there will be no hostile or provocative action by either party whilst any issue is being progressed through procedure'. Overall, the idea behind the preamble is to highlight the spirit and the framework of the procedure, and to encourage this to be used in order to settle differences.

In certain cases, there is also specific reference to industrial action, and the stage at which this can be considered legitimate. Some procedures were fairly vague about this and merely referred to the fact that neither party should invoke sanctions prior to exhaustion of procedure. Others were more explicit in allowing for industrial action; the Health Service agreement (see the Appendix to this chapter), for example, specified five days written notice by a full-time union official to the area personnel officer. While such provisions are not (at the moment) legally binding, a clause was often inserted to bind them in *honour*.

Management, for its part, accepted a mutual obligation on itself to process issues through the relevant procedure as speedily as possible; time limits were used in a number of procedures so as to ensure that issues did not get bogged down although the length of these did vary considerably. In some of the manufacturing agreements, periods as short as one or two days were not uncommon whereas in local government—and particularly teaching—it was of the order of weeks rather than days. The primary purpose behind the inclusion of time limits would appear to be to articulate and demonstrate the company's commitment to speedy resolution after allowing for the heat to be taken out of the situation. However, there is danger that time limits may be used as a stalling device by management.

In other words, the underlying spirit or philosophy of procedures is often repeated in the actual agreement; both parties assume (and trust) that the other will be encouraged to use jointly agreed mechanisms for resolving conflict rather than any other unilateral sanction. A procedure agreement may therefore be part of an underlying process to operate under the same 'rules of the game'; as such, it may have more to offer management than employee representatives.

Since much of the impetus for procedural reform within companies has come from personnel departments, it is also important to examine their role within this process. The emphasis in quite a number of procedures is one of grievances and disputes being a line management responsibility with personnel available for advice and assistance should they be needed; for example, in the Health Service example, the services are offered at any stage and should be sought from the second stage onwards. In others, there is no mention of a personnel or industrial relations adviser until the third or fourth stage of procedure. But, since the personnel department will usually have been instrumental in drawing up the procedure originally, their influence over arrangements is considerable whether they are *formally* involved or not at each stage; moreover, it would be usual for there to be some discussion between them and line managers should a problem arise.

But, line managers often attribute a fairly restricted role to the personnel department, one which, according to Legge, is seen as little more than the provision of information or advice, or the interpretation of procedures. To enable them to do this, it is argued, personnel need to be closely in touch with the shop floor, the recent legislation, and the limits of company policy, as well as having long experience of the norms and customs of a particular plant. Too often, it is felt, they do not possess such characteristics and are consequently excluded from decision making, so being relegated to a back-seat role. Their only involvement in industrial relations issues is *after* rather than *before* the conflict has arisen; because of this, their contribution to organizational success is perceived as limited, and their services are not highly regarded. Thus, we get into a vicious circle in which the personnel department, due to its lack of power and authority within management, is continually down-graded (1977, pp. 50–59).

Indeed, a common criticism of personnel departments is that they 'always pass the buck', 'never make decisions', or are 'out of touch' with shop floor reality. This need not be so, and it is clear in certain companies that line and personnel management do work together effectively, particularly through their commitment to procedures.

The final area we shall examine is the use of provision of external agencies to resolve disputes should they exhaust in-company procedures. Some procedures automatically go to arbitration while others provide a role for conciliation. Some use the offices of ACAS whereas others are tied to an agreement between an employers' federation and a trade union. Yet others may make use of an independent but agreed arbitrator on an *ad hoc* basis. In order to get some idea of the extent of outside intervention, we can again turn to Brown's survey of manufacturing establishments. Just 21 per cent of these made provision for outside intervention in grievance procedures with food, drink, and tobacco (41 per cent) and chemicals (29 per cent) being well above average. For dismissal and discipline disputes, it was also 21 per cent with the same two industries well above average. Paper, printing, and publishing was well below—at 7 per cent. Interestingly enough, provision for external intervention was more likely the bigger the establishment (1981, pp. 45–46). Of those establishments who used outsiders, there was a high level of employer satisfaction with the results; indeed, 75 per cent were either fairly or very satisfied with the intervention, particularly in the case of conciliation rather than arbitration. ACAS certainly appears to satisfy the majority of employers when it becomes involved in an issue, and the service was the most important provider of third-party intervention (Brown, 1981, p. 49).

But, a warning note must also be sounded; ACAS should not, and probably would not itself want to, be seen as a substitute for the establishment of joint union–management procedures for resolving disputes at workplace level. To the extent that ACAS may be used habitually in order to 'pass the buck', this could damage industrial relations within the company since commitment to agreed procedures may wither away.

Conclusions

While we have argued to promote the usage of procedures by indicating their potential role as an aspect of good industrial relations, it should not be forgotten that—despite the expectations of the Donovan Commission—the reform of procedures has not resulted in a lowering of the level of recorded strike action. If anything, it has been associated with a massive increase in the number of working days lost. Does this imply, therefore, that greater formalization has exacerbated rather than reduced the likelihood of industrial action?

On one level, the answer might be yes in that formalized industrial relations procedures have provided more of a role for workplace representatives without any great change in the substantive outcomes of union–management discussion (Batstone, 1980). That is, stewards may have become frustrated by being incorporated into management decision making at workplace level while, at the same time, pay negotiations have become increasingly centralized within companies or been under the dictates of incomes policy. Alternatively, we would also suggest that, despite the much greater likelihood of procedures in workplace industrial relations, their introduction has not been implemented on the shop floor with the same rigour as intended by senior management. In other words, procedures are flouted *despite* their existence and a certain degree of informality has been inevitable (Terry, 1977).

Furthermore, it might be unfair to assess procedural success on the basis of the measure of working days lost. As we saw in the opening section of the chapter, a few large strikes have accounted for a considerable proportion of the total figure over the last 10 years. Since these are usually strikes over pay, they may cover a whole industry or company and not have their roots in any one workplace. That is, with or without procedures, these strikes would have taken place. If we focus attention upon the number of strikes, we see this has remained relatively stable around the 2500 mark; perhaps because of procedures, this has been a lower figure than it might otherwise have been. But, yet more important is the distribution of stoppage activity. This suggests that it is not procedures *per se* that have failed to institutionalize conflict but that it is certain plants and certain procedures. As we indicated above, procedural success requires both a willingness and commitment to use and abide by them. One needs to be aware of just what a procedure (for grievances and disputes) can and cannot do:

> It cannot solve the underlying causes of conflict. . . . It is very limited in the extent to which it can institutionalize conflict if there is not a basic consensus about the legitimacy of the roles of the parties. It cannot of itself make up for deficiencies in the structure of the relationship (Thomson and Murray, 1976, p. 84).

On the other hand, it is an absolute necessity in helping to resolve conflict when it does arise. This is an area in which the parties have been left very much up to themselves as to how they organize the employment relationship; the same is certainly not true of a number of other areas—dismissal, redundancy, equal rights legislation, and health and safety, for example—and we can move on to discuss the way in which legal intervention has influenced the approach of the line manager in relation to these.

Appendix to Chapter 8—Get better health authority
Procedure for settling grievances and disputes

If you have a grievance relating to your employment, either as an individual or as one of a group of employees with the same grievance, you have a right to express any such grievance. The intention must be to deal with every grievance as speedily as possible and every effort will be made to do so, in the first instance, informally by your superior.

A grievance not accepted as settled may become a dispute and the following procedure is designed to achieve settlements of both grievances and disputes.

The steps described are considered to be the most effective method of dealing with grievances and disputes. The stated time limits are regarded as the maximum for a reply to be given after discussion at each stage. However, it is recognized that there may be occasions, such as a need for referral to the appropriate Whitley Council or the DHSS for interpretation, when, by mutual agreement, it could be advisable to extend the time limit at some stage. It is expected that a major grievance or dispute will be passed quickly to an advanced stage in the procedure. Either the employee and his union or the appropriate level of management may take the grievance or dispute to the next stage and the other party will cooperate in its progression.

The services of an appropriate member of the personnel department will be available at any stage and should certainly be sought from stage 2 onwards. Employees not sure of how the various stages apply within their own departments should ask their immediate supervisors or union representatives for clarification.

Specific steps in the procedure

Any of these steps may be ommitted by mutual consent of the parties concerned.

Stage 1: an employee's grievance should first be discussed with the immediate supervisor. A shop steward may accompany the employee or may be authorized by the employee to take up the matter on his behalf. It is expected that the latter approach will be used when a group of employees is involved. The supervisor, will, as necessary, confer with the local departmental head and one or both will reply within three working days (Monday to Friday).

Stage 2: in the event that mutually satisfactory solution has not been found, the grievance may be referred to the next higher level of supervision, for example the sector administrator, functional head, or area manager. A meeting will be held as soon as possible, the date being notified within two working days of the request being received. A full-time union officer will be present at the request of either side. A reply will be given within three working days after discussion.

Stage 3: if the grievance is still not satisfactorily resolved, it may be considered by at least three members of the management team. A meeting will be held as soon as possible with a full-time union official present at the request of either side. A reply in writing will be given within five working days after the discussion to the union official concerned.

Stage 4: failing agreement, the matter may be referred to the health authority, who will set up a committee of three members to consider the matter, and to hear representations from the employee(s) and the full-time union representative, management and personnel officers previously involved will be asked to explain their decisions to the committee.

The committee will convey its decision to the employee(s), his union, and the administrator within two working days of the hearing. The decisions will be conveyed to the health authority at its next full meeting but no further representations may be made by either side at that meeting.

Stage 5: if, having passed the grievance or dispute through this procedure, or such shortened versions as may have been mutually agreed, the matter remains unresolved, it may be referred, subject to mutual agreement, to the Advisory Conciliation and Arbitration Service (ACAS), whose decision will be binding on both parties with immediate effect or from such date as decided by ACAS.

It will be a condition of the procedure that until it is exhausted the status quo will be maintained by management and staff, and that normal working will be maintained.

In the event of subsequent industrial action, five working days' notice will be given. Such notice will take the form of a written communication between the full-time official of the union(s) to the personnel officer.

Note in this context industrial action is defined as strike, lock-out, go-slow, work to rule, overtime ban, or any other similar restriction.

9. Law and the manager

Since the mid sixties, there has been a tremendous growth in the amount of law that affects the line manager's industrial relations responsibilities. Legal intervention now influences all aspects of the employment relationship; for example, in selection and recruitment, the employer has to be aware of employee rights against discrimination and on stating terms of employment. During the course of employment, discipline, health and safety, and discrimination are also covered by various statutes. Finally, on termination, the employer needs to take into account legislation on dismissal or redundancy.

But, despite the greater quantity of employment legislation, to what extent has this actually changed the *nature* of the employment relationship and the approach of the good manager in relation to his employees? What does the line manager need to do in order to remain within the law and promote good industrial relations? In attempting to answer these questions, we shall deal with two aspects of the law that are particularly pertinent to the line manager—dismissal and health and safety—and describe some basic ground-rules that may prove helpful in these areas. This chapter is not intended to be a guide to the *exact* provisions of the law nor is it intended to turn the line manager into a lawyer; rather, the objective is to promote a greater awareness of the law as it affects the employment relationship and to encourage a philosophy of being fair but firm in dealing with disciplinary issues. The manager is likely to gain much more by working to broad guidelines based on general principles than he is by searching for loopholes and then exploiting them. Moreover, he needs to be aware of disciplinary procedures operating in the workplace and of how these are applied in practice. Similarly, he needs to be aware of the limits of his authority and expertise in dealing with such issues, and be prepared to search for specialist expertise through a personnel department, the offices of ACAS, or a regularly updated employment law case book. In other words, he needs to ensure as far as possible that his activities *prevent* the possibility of going to a tribunal but that, if they do not, his prior actions have in no way jeopardized the chances of success. Before moving on to this, however, we shall briefly outline the general position of the law in British industrial relations.

The law and British industrial relations

Traditionally, the law has occupied a back seat in this country. Compared with other countries, there has been a minimum of legal intervention, and the character of our system has been moulded very much by the trade unions and employers themselves, and not by state regulation and interference. While the law is not categorically rejected by either side in all circumstances—and there are times when it is very much supported—most employers and trade unions see it as a mechanism of last resort to be used only after consultation and all other voluntary means have failed (Flanders, 1974, pp. 362–363). Legal intervention has to be assessed not only against its *desirability* but also against its likelihood of *attaining* the modifications expected from it; as such, it is viewed in an essentially pragmatic manner.

According to Kahn-Freund (1969), the law can play a part through three different roles; first of all, we have the *auxiliary* role, through which the state provides a statutory framework of organized persuasion. That is, providing benefits—financial or otherwise—for those who observe agreements and a number of pressures against those who do not (p. 304). For example, unions who have been granted a certificate of independence by the certification officer are entitled to certain benefits to which non-independent unions are not. Similarly, collective agreements are generally not legally enforceable although the parties can make them binding should they so desire. Probably, the most well-known illustration of this auxiliary role is provided by ACAS, which offers help and services to employers and unions should *they* ask for it.

Secondly, through its *restrictive* role, the law has provided a set of 'Queensberry rules' of what is allowed and forbidden in the conduct of industrial hostilities (p. 302). This relates to activities such as strike action, picketing, and emergency procedures, and has proved to be a very difficult and dubious area in which to apply the law. For example, despite the superficial attractiveness of restrictions on picketing, in practice this raises a series of problems for the role of the police, the willingness of employers to take legal action, and the long-term effect on industrial relations.

Thirdly, we have the *regulatory* role that sets out to provide a floor of employment rights for every employee—with a few exceptions—and a legal alternative for employees to express their discontent other than through collective industrial action. Rather than seeing recent provisions as 'an attempt by well-meaning legislators to impose an alien code of norms on employers and employees', they have merely brought us up to the level of other European countries and put the best existing practices in this country within a legal framework (Hawkins, 1978, p. 158).

Despite this, many managers still see the employment protection legislation of the seventies as shifting the 'balance' away from the employer and towards the employee. In certain circles, for example, the Employment Protection Act became known as the 'Employment Prevention Act' and it is still quite usual to hear managers talk of their being unable to dismiss someone, and to argue that they are not willing to take on new people due to their greater security of employment and the cost and difficulty of displacing them should the need arise.

However, a study by Daniel suggested that, for manufacturing companies employing between 50 and 500 people, the employment protection legislation had not inhibited management from taking on labour nor had it presented a major obstacle to the 'good' manager. It had led to changes, though, in the care with which people were selected, the formalization of disciplinary procedures, and the keeping of records (1978, pp. 658–660). In other words, the primary modification has been in the *nature* rather than the *degree* of management control. Whether the manager agrees with the provisions of the law or not, he still needs to be aware of them and take them into account when managing his industrial relations. We shall now look at these provisions as they affect dismissal.[1]

Dismissal
The concept of unfair dismissal, and the provision for industrial tribunals to hear cases in which this was alleged by an ex-employee, was introduced in the 1971 Industrial Relations Act. Prior to this, the only protection for an employee was in common law, against 'wrongful dismissal', and a claim under this would result in an employee going through the ordinary courts of law, often at considerable expense. For this reason alone, the idea to set up a speedy, cheap, and impartial tribunal was seen as a potential benefit to job security. There was another reason, however, that led to the Donovan Commission recommending a change in the law (its proposals were more or less totally adopted by the Act of 1971) and this related to employees taking industrial action in order to fight what they felt was an unfair dismissal of one of their colleagues. The Commission estimated that, for the period 1964–1966, an average of 276 strikes per year took place as a result of disputes about whether individuals should or should not have been employed, suspended, or dismissed; that is about 10 per cent of all stoppages (1968, p. 143). In other words, the introduction of the law could be seen as an effective way in which to formalize industrial relations, improve job security, and reduce strikes all at

1. We have chosen to deal with dismissal and health and safety as the two examples of the law because these appear to worry line managers more than most. It does not mean that these are the only two important areas. The basic principles that will be outlined below ought to pervade management approaches to race relations, sex discrimination, maternity rights, contracts of employment, and so on. Also, while many of these provisions might be dealt with mostly by personnel departments, dismissal (and discipline) and health and safety are fundamental aspects of managing on the shop floor.

the same time. As we saw in the last chapter, the link between the formalization of procedures and the level of strike action is not a simple one. Bearing in mind that the tribunal cannot, in the last resort, demand that an employer takes back an employee, who is found to have been unfairly dismissed, it is hardly surprising that unions may prefer industrial action as a strategy. The success of the law depends, to a large extent, on employers observing the rules.

As employers have become better at interpreting the law and operating through well-designed procedures, they have also been scoring a higher 'success rate' at the tribunals themselves. Table 9.1 shows the number of cases disposed of at each stage in the proceedings for the years of 1976 and 1979.

From this, it can be seen that approximately two-thirds of cases are settled out of court or withdrawn before reaching an industrial tribunal; many of

Table 9.1   Unfair dismissal disposals (1976 and 1979)

		Year	
		1976	*1979*
(*a*) Cases disposed of		33 701	33 383
(*b*) Cases withdrawn	(% of (*a*))	25	31
(*c*) Cases settled out			
of court	(% of (*a*))	37	34
(*d*) Cases heard	(% of (*a*))	38	35
(*e*) Cases dismissed	(% of (*d*))	67	73
(*f*) Reinstatement or			
re-engagement	(% of (*d*))	2	1
(*g*) Compensation	(% of (*d*))	31	26

these will have been sorted out after conciliation or advice from an ACAS officer. Some of these result in compensation and others in reinstatement although, as with the tribunals, the vast majority result in compensation. If a case actually reaches the tribunal, the employer wins in almost three-quarters of all the cases heard. Again, even if an employee were to win his case, the likelihood of getting his job back is small even though, originally, this was envisaged as the most appropriate remedy. For a number of reasons, compensation may appear a more attractive remedy to both parties, particularly after the case has been heard whereas, in others, it may no longer be feasible if the employer has filled the job or the employee has found work elsewhere. Again, as we mentioned above, the employer may still—if he prefers—'pay' to get rid of someone he does not want by refusing to comply with an order for reinstatement.

Compensation—despite the impression given by the media—is rarely very much. Moreover, as we can see from Table 9.2,[2] it is even cheaper to settle a case privately through conciliation. This table compares, for 1979, the amount agreed/ordered in compensation through conciliation or the tribunal. At the latter, the average settlement is about £500. Of course, we also need to allow for the time and effort the employer puts into fighting a case. Following the 1980 Act, it is now possible for the employer to be awarded costs if an applicant brings an 'unreasonable' claim.

Table 9.2   Compensation agreed/ordered after conciliation or tribunal (%)

	Conciliation	Tribunal
Less than £150	40.5	18.2
Less than £500	82.0	57.9
Less than £1000	91.8	79.3
More than £5000	0.7	1.1

Under Section 55 of the 1978 Employment Protection (Consolidation) Act, dismissal is covered by the following three categories of termination: an employee will be treated as dismissed by his employer if, but only if:

1. The contract is terminated by the employer, with or without notice.
2. At the end of a fixed-term contract not renewed on expiry.
3. The contract is terminated by the employee because of his employer's conduct.

It is important to be aware of these conditions since, if the dismissal is disputed (for example, the employer does not agree that he dismissed the employee), it is up to the employee to show that a dismissal did in fact take place. This is the case particularly in relation to point (3) above, which is commonly known as 'constructive dismissal', and this will be dealt with below.

The other two categories are usually more simple; category (1), for example, would normally involve the employer dismissing the employee either with notice or without it if his behaviour was such as to warrant summary/instant dismissal. If the dismissal is with notice, it is the *correct* notice, as laid down by the 1975 Act or by a collective agreement in excess of that, rather than the actual notice, which is taken into account when assessing an employee's period of employment. A failure to do this has caused more than one employer

2. Tables 9.1 and 9.2 are taken from Tables 3a and 3b in the *Employment Gazette*, February 1981, p. 82

to be required to face a claim of unfair dismissal at a tribunal when he believed that the employee did not have the requisite minimum period of employment in order to claim—currently 52 weeks. Also, it should be remembered that an employee only has to work, or be covered by notice, for a *part* of that week for it to count towards the period of employment. Other disputed cases of termination have arisen by virtue of swear words or similar 'angry language' that have caused an employee to consider himself dismissed. Probably, the best advice is not to swear at all!

Category (2)—end of a fixed term contract—has caused some problems particularly when employees have been taken on for a fixed time and then kept on after that contract has expired. In a case such as that, it would be reasonable to assume a continuation of the contract such that it is no longer fixed term in nature.

The final category—constructive dismissal—is one that has caused concern to many employers. Although there was a considerable amount of confusion up until 1978, much of this was clarified following a decision (*Western Excavating (ECC) Ltd* v. *Sharp*) in that year. Added to that, given the current economic climate and the fact that claiming constructive dismissal is a very risky route to take, it is unlikely that employees will be willing to resign in the hope of a fairly limited amount of compensation. The employer's conduct must be so serious that it shows he no longer intends to be bound by the contract such that this entitles the employee to quit without notice. Moreover, satisfying the test of constructive dismissal does not automatically result in a decision of unfair dismissal since the employer may provide a 'fair' reason for his action (*Industrial Rubber Products* v. *Gillon*, 1977). A list of factors that may be appropriate for constructive dismissal can be found in Kelway and would cover items such as:

1. Unilateral lowering of status/pay/conditions.
2. Steps taken to replace the employee unilaterally/force him to resign.
3. Discriminated against the employee/denigrated him in front of others/been deliberately unfair/showed contempt/ridicule/discourteous in relations with him.
4. Undermining of authority consistently.
5. Expected higher standard of work from the employee than from others (1977, p. 23).

Fair dismissal

Having agreed or established that a dismissal has actually taken place, one can next turn to the question of whether it was fair or unfair in the circumstances. Basically, under section 57 of the Employment Protection (Consolidation) Act 1978 (as amended by section 6 of the Employment Act 1980), dismissal *can* be fair if it relates to the following five reasons:

1. Capability or qualifications for performing work that he was employed to
   do.
2. Conduct.
3. Redundancy.
4. Could not continue work without breaking another law.
5. Some other substantial reason.

The onus of proof used to be on the employer until this was amended by the
1980 Act. Now, it is up to the tribunal to determine whether the dismissal was
fair or unfair; this, they will do, by taking into account the reasons shown by
the employer and his circumstances—including the size and administrative
resources of his undertaking. This will then put the tribunal in a position to
judge whether the reason for dismissal was reasonable in the circumstances.
Every case will be considered on its own merits. Many people agree that this
has merely made explicit what was previously implicit in this part of the
tribunal proceedings and its major impact will be of a psychological nature;
that is, that employers will no longer feel they have to prove themselves
innocent (Pitt, 1980, p. 234).

In other words there are two parts to every case; first of all, the reason has to
be a sufficient reason for dismissal—within the range of reasonable responses
to the nature of the offence. And, secondly, the employer has to go about it in
the right way. Below, we shall consider what would be an appropriate
managerial response under each of the headings identified above. Before that,
however, it might be worth noting a number of ground-rules that will be
applicable in every case[3]:

1. The needs of the business are of prime importance in dealing with any case.
   The tribunals are not designed to hinder efficiency provided that the
   employer has made reasonable attempts to communicate with and
   persuade employees of the situation in hand.
2. It is not the job of the tribunal to substitute its own judgement for that of
   the employer. Provided that the decision is within the range of reasonable
   responses in the circumstances, the decision to dismiss will be fair.
3. The facts that the employer had, or should have had, at the time of
   dismissal are the only ones that are relevant to this decision. If there has
   been a proper enquiry and management has collected all the evidence it can
   reasonably be expected to gather, this should be sufficient.
4. The employer does not need to prove his case; rather, all he needs is
   reasonable grounds for believing that an employee committed an offence
   and that belief is based upon a sufficient investigation of the facts. In other
   words, it depends upon the balance of probabilities (*BHS* v. *Burchell*, 1978).
5. A proper procedure must be followed in each case; the employee must be
   warned of his position, of the consequences of his behaviour, given a

3. See, for similar broad guidelines; Hawkins (1979, p. 110–112); Employment Case
Law Index (1980), Egan (1977, p. 19), and Upex (1980, pp. 39–40).

chance to present his side of the story, appeal, and so on. This is the area we shall deal with in more detail below.

In other words, provided the employer takes care over his investigation, keeps adequate records, and operates according to a reasonable or agreed procedure, he has much less to fear from the law than he might originally have envisaged. Certainly, as can be seen from a number of the points made above, the law is not intended to hinder his own business efficiency or lead to substitutions for his own practical and well-thought out ideas. We can now turn to examine each of the provisions in a little more detail bearing in mind that it is more important to spend time 'devising clear rules and procedures, and educating supervisory staff to secure uniform application rather than committing time and expense fighting cases at an Industrial Tribunal' (Egan, 1977, p. 3).

The objective of the next part of this chapter is to provide a checklist that can be followed in each case; managers will need, particularly if they are taken to a tribunal, to keep abreast of changes in the law or important decisions, and this should usually be provided by a specialist department or one of the reference books for employers updated every two or three months. Remember, this is not intended to be a law book for the simple reason that managers will gain more by working to broad guidelines based on general principles than attempting to become experts in the law. Remember that every case is judged on the facts of that particular case, and what is fair and reasonable in those particular circumstances bearing in mind the evidence that is presented to the tribunal.

Capability—incompetence

This category of capability is sub-divided into two sections for convenience; the first of these relates to the skill or aptitude of the individual whereas the second is conerned with ill-health and physical ability. The following are the points to bear in mind when dealing with a case of incompetence:

1. Get evidence of the alleged incompetence through production records if the job is one that has easily quantifiable results. If not, evidence needs to be gathered through performance appraisals, opinion of relevant supervisor, and so on. The basic questions that the employer should be asking are these: is this employee worse than others to the extent that he is actually below some specific standard? Have I got evidence to demonstrate this?'

2. If the employee is worse than others, put this to him. Explain what is wrong and ask him to say why this might be so. Give an opportunity to state his side of the story.

3. If it becomes clear that some outside-of-work factors may be affecting him, and this may have had an influence upon his ability, take these into account. This would be the case with a longer-serving employee who has suddenly gone off-the-boil.

4. Establish whether you have not done anything that you ought to have done so as to enable the employee to do the job. For example, has an adequate job description/specification been provided such that the employee knows what he is supposed to be doing? Does the employee know the level to which he is being expected to perform? Has adequate training and/or supervision been given? Are there sufficient facilities to enable the job to be done? In other words, could his poor performance have anything at all to do with you?

5. If all these things have been done, it may be appropriate to issue a warning to improve; if so, it must be made clear to the employee what is expected of him and it may be appropriate to specify a time limit. Overall, the employee must know exactly where he stands and what the consequences of non-achievement are likely to be. Remember, you must act reasonably in expecting an improvement.

6. If the employee does not appear likely to be able to do the job, consider him for another less arduous job; you are not obliged to actually *find* another job, say by creating one, but you ought to consider whether there are any alternatives. Again, pay special attention and consideration to longer-serving employees.

7. It is very rare that one event of incapability will be sufficient to justify dismissal; there has, however, been one case in which an airline pilot was sacked after a bad landing (*Taylor* v. *Alidair Ltd*, 1978), although this was particularly crucial because of the danger involved.

8. While warnings are generally necessary in such cases, the key question to ask is whether the warnings would have made any difference and whether the employee would have responded to them? In that case, a lack of warning does not *necessarily* make the dismissal unfair, just as going through the warning procedure does not *automatically* make the dismissal fair. If the employee suffers from irredeemable incompetence or rejects all criticism and denies incompetence, then dismissal without a formal warning may be fair. However, the reason given at a tribunal will generally be much more acceptable if the employee has been given warnings and a chance to improve (*Lowndes* v. *Specialist Heavy Engineering Ltd*, 1976; *Grant* v. *Ampex GB Ltd*, 1980).

Indeed, only when it is clear that the employee either could or would not improve would it be fair to dismiss him. The basic obligation on the employer is to discuss his shortcomings with the employee, and see if he can improve by giving him as much help as possible; the weapon of dismissal should be used very much as a last resort.

Capability—ill health

The key question to ask in cases such as this is 'can the employer reasonably be expected to wait any longer for the employee to return and, if so, how much longer?' The employer is, after a period of time—and, remember, there is no statutory figure in law—entitled to say 'enough is enough' and terminate the contract. The illness may be either one in which the employee is off work altogether or one in which a record of persistent and recurrent absence occurs over a period of time. In this case, we shall deal with the former, although a similar procedure may be adopted for recurrent absence. The points to bear in mind are the following:

1. Go and see the absent employee and consult with him. Find out the exact nature of the illness, the length of time he is likely to be absent, the likelihood of being able to return to his old job; in general, enquire into the likelihood of return.
2. If the employee occupies a key job, impress upon him the need for return and the amount of time you may be able to wait for his recovery. If appropriate, advise the employee of the consequences of non-return. This may be particularly important for the small company.
3. If you decide that you cannot wait for the employee to return, it would be in order to get at least one medical report. These must be independent and, as an employer, you will be expected to take this expert opinion into account in making your decision—you are probably not a medical expert yourself so you cannot be expected to substitute your judgement for that of the expert. Advise the employee again of your position. Consider alternative work but, again, there is no obligation to provide a job if one is not available. Take into account previous service.
4. If a decision is made to dismiss, check whether it is reasonable to do so in the circumstances; is it within the range of responses a reasonable employer might make under the circumstances?

The key cases in this area have sometimes appeared very harsh (for example, *Spencer* v. *Paragon Wallpapers Ltd* (1976)) and one would guess that most employers would be considerate and sympathetic to the person who is suffering from a genuine illness. However, as was made clear in that case, the interests of business efficiency must not be allowed to be overridden by other factors. Similarly, employers have been advised recently that it is better to consult with an employee and, if necessary, dismiss him for lack of capability rather than hoping that the contract will eventually become frustrated due to his illness. Selwyn suggests that 'perhaps the best way to express the employers' obligation is to say that he should treat the employee with sympathetic consideration and that he should hold the job open for as long as is possible' (1975, p. 120). Even though this may be in excess of the minimum required at law, it would be more in line with the objective of establishing good industrial relations.

Lack of qualifications
According to the 1978 Act, this covers 'any degree, diploma or other

academic, technical or professional qualification relevant to the position which the employee held'. Again, the following considerations are important:

1. The employer needs to assess exactly how essential the qualification is to the job itself and whether it forms a large part of the job if there are several parts to it. For example, a PhD in microelectronics would not be an essential qualification for a job as a gardener!
2. The employer has to discover whether the employee was taken on under the assumption that he would get it. If so, why has he not got it? Ask him about this and see why. Is there anything that you, as the employer, have not done which you should have? For example, has time been given to attend a course? Has he had a second chance to get the qualification?
3. Can this person be employed elsewhere where the qualification is not needed?
4. The above three points assume that the employee did not have the qualification when he started but that he was expected to have it within a certain period of time. It may also be that the employee has *lost* his qualification—for example, as an accountant—but that this is only a temporary measure. Again, enquire into the matter, ask how long it will be before he gets it back, consider a move for a short period of time, and so on. The major requirement for the employer is to find out the case from the employee so as to make a rational decision based on the evidence before him.
5. If, as an employer, you discover that an employee never had the qualification, despite saying so at the interview, and it is necessary for the job, you will be in a position to consider dismissal in these circumstances.

Conduct

Despite the fact that many disciplinary procedures make a distinction between ordinary and gross misconduct, it is a difficult process to delineate exactly where the one ends and the other begins. The major question to be asked in all misconduct cases is, therefore, 'is it reasonable in all the circumstances to dismiss the employee for that offence?' Employment Case Law Index notes that 'the first steps of disciplinary action will usually occur long before dismissal has even entered the employer's head. However, if matters should eventually come to a dismissal, the foundation of fairness will very often lie in the disciplinary action taken in the early stages' (1980, p. 225). Under this heading of 'conduct', we shall outline two different types of case, one of which is internal to the organization and would not involve any outside information; the second case—say, theft or criminal offences outside of employment— would have to be dealt with in a slightly different way.

First of all, taking a case such as recurrent lateness or minor acts of misconduct; this would usually proceed through a series of warnings and an example of a typical disciplinary procedure is to be found later in the chapter.

However, the procedure for dealing with a case such as fighting, breaking of works rule, sleeping on duty, or clocking someone else's card would also proceed under the approach outlined below but, in all probability, without the need for the full warnings procedure; the path to be followed would be:

1. Enquire into the matter and establish the facts promptly; this is included in the ACAS Code of Practice, para. 2. If the case is serious enough or if it is likely to take time to gather sufficient facts in order to proceed, suspend the employee on full pay. Clearly, this would not usually be necessary for a lateness offence since the groundwork ought to have been done already. Get evidence from other people if appropriate.
2. Interview the employee and give him a chance to explain his side of the story. Advise of rights to representation in accordance with procedure if this is appropriate. If necessary, counsel the employee in the hope that an informal warning may serve to improve the conduct. Very different behaviour may emerge from an employee who realizes and accepts the probable penalty for his misconduct. Examine past record.
3. If the offence is more serious, a more detailed interview may be appropriate. For example, in a case of fighting, take into account any provocation and ensure that you take into account your own biases of the fact that you may only have seen part of the incident. In other words, try to establish the full story (*Richards* v. *Bulpitt & Sons*, 1975).
4. Make a decision based upon the investigation: is it reasonable in the circumstances? If a works rule is broken, has that rule been well-publicized and consistently enforced? Is it likely that the employee knows the consequences of breaking that rule? How seriously was the rule broken? (*Meridian* v. *Gomersall*, 1977).
5. State clearly the action that is to be taken, having regard to the nature of the offence. State concisely the consequences of a further similar offence. Allow for an appeal if this is part of the procedure.

It is not always necessary to follow the procedure nor to give warnings if it can be demonstrated that they would have served no purpose nor led to a change in decision but, once again, it is always going to be harder to show that the handling was reasonable in the circumstances if the employee has been given no opportunity to improve. Perhaps it is best to use warnings automatically unless advised not to do so by a specialist department. However, a warning—if it is given—needs to be clear and more than a vague threat that 'leaves the employee with the impression that he was just being reprimanded and not warned of dismissal' (Employment Case Law Index, 1980, p. 262).

The other type of approach was amply demonstrated—in relation to theft—in *British Home Stores* v. *Burchell*, 1978 and the following points need to be borne in mind:

1. Enquire into the matter promptly. If there are fairly strong grounds for

suspicion, it is worth suspending the employee immediately while a brief time is spent collecting the facts. If there is delay in your allegation or allowance is made for an employee to continue working, this casts doubt upon the seriousness of the offence in the eyes of the employee.

2. A full investigation should be undertaken. The employee involved should be interviewed along with any witnesses. The allegations should be put to the employee and he should be given an opportunity of responding to them.

3. Although some employers automatically call in the police for matters such as this, their involvement and, in particular, their pressing of charges is not directly relevant to the case in hand. For example, the employee may be found not guilty and discharged. The case of thieving has to be divided into its criminal part—which is dealt with by the police—and that connected with the contract of employment—which is the job of the employer. The employer does not need to discuss the offence so much as the action he proposes to take. Egan, for example, suggests that 'there is no reason to suppose, and many reasons to doubt, that policemen know more about industrial relations and management than do managers' (1977, p. 160). The cases are most appropriately seen as separate matters.

4. Unlike the police, the employer does not actually have to *prove* guilt. All he needs is to believe that the employee is guilty, have reasonable grounds for that belief, and have carried out a reasonable investigation in the circumstances, ensuring that the employee has an opportunity to offer a full explanation. He has to, and indeed can only, base his decision on the information before him at the time he decides whether to dismiss or not.

5. The investigation should be undertaken by a senior member of management who needs to act with due formality in the circumstances.

6. For other criminal offences, the question the employer must ask himself is this, 'is the offence one that makes this employee unsuitable for work or unacceptable to other employees?' In order to make up his mind, he needs to take into account the nature of the work, that of the offence, the likely reaction of the employees, and so on. For example, a teacher convicted of molesting young children would be more likely to be found unsuitable for continued employment than would a docker found guilty of the same offence.

Misconduct cases, therefore, take a number of different forms and the *exact* procedure to be followed will vary from case to case. The basic principle, however, remains one of searching for the facts, giving the employee an opportunity to state his side of the incident(s), acting promptly and with due formality, acting reasonably in the circumstances, and making a decision on the basis of the evidence before the employer at the time. The employer who acts so as to set the standard of conduct in the first place will undoubtedly find himself better off than the one who tries to gain a grip over looser working practices and workplace behaviour.

Redundancy

Employees who are dismissed because of a redundancy situation will be in a position to claim unfair dismissal if it is shown that the reason for their being selected (in preference to others in the same unit of selection) was due to their union membership or activities on the one hand, or in circumvention of a customary arrangement or agreed procedure on the other, unless there were special reasons pertaining to this case. In order to ensure a fair selection for redundancy, the following points need to be borne in mind:

1. The industrial tribunal is not there to decide whether it would have called a redundancy situation or chosen the same method as the employer. All it is empowered to do—unless the method is hopelessly wrong—is to assess whether that method itself is reasonable and is consistently applied.
2. The procedure chosen needs to be worked out in advance and based upon facts that are appropriate in the circumstances. For example, this may be LIFO (Last In First Out), service in a department, skill, conduct, performance, or some well established and quantifiable method of selection.
3. The procedure must be reasonably applied and must be followed consistently.
4. If 10 or more employees are to be made redundant there needs to be consultation with an appropriate, recognized independent trade union at least 30 days before the first redundancy takes effect unless there are special circumstances that make this impossible. In practice, many employers would still consult even if there were less than 10 potential redundancies.
5. The employer needs to look at the possibility of offering suitable alternative work to the employees due to be made redundant although, in line with the commitment to business efficiency, he is not *obliged* to offer this.

The major factor to take into account is the consistent application of reasonable procedure; to be as humane as possible in the handling of the affair by providing as much notice as possible, and time off to look for alternative work. See the pamphlets produced by the DE for a much more detailed consideration of this situation.

Breaking another law

The vast majority of unfair dismissal cases come under the first three headings—those of capability, conduct, and redundancy—and we shall therefore only mention the other categories in passing. Probably the best known reason under this category relates to loss of driving licence by an employee who spends all or most of his time at work on a driving job. Clearly, an employer would not be able to continue to employ someone who had lost their licence since this would be breaking another law. However, the employer must still act fairly in these circumstances and the basic question would be 'can I afford to wait for the expiry of this disability?' Once it is established that a driving licence is a requirement for a substantial part of the job, the employer needs to consider the length of the disqualification, the needs of the business, whether the employee can do his job without driving a motor vehicle, whether alternative arrangements can be made, whether the employee could be given some other work to do until his licence is restored, and so on (Selwyn, 1975, p. 126). The disqualified driver may decide to employ a chauffeur at his own expense and, provided everything else is in order, the employee ought to be given an opportunity to see if an arrangement such as this would work. Once again, the employer would be expected to take greater care over an old and loyal servant.

Some other substantial reason

This potentially fair reason sounds rather like a bit of a catch-all, but, as Selwyn notes, 'it was never intended that the above four reasons for fair dismissal would constitute an exhaustive catalogue of the circumstances in which employers would be justified in terminating the services of an employee' (1975, p. 126). There have not been that many cases in the past although it is now becoming more popular; whatever the reason, it must be serious enough to warrant giving the employee the sack. For example, a clash of personalities creating an atmosphere of tension and disharmony may be sufficient reason for dismissal (*Treganowan* v. *Robert Knee & Company*, 1975). Pressure from an important customer who refuses to have work done by an employee who is no longer considered acceptable would also be covered by this (*Scott Packing and Warehousing Co. Ltd* v. *Patterson*, 1978). Again, the employer has to assess whether dismissal is the only realistic course of action open to him; it may be possible to offer an alternative job and the employer should not assume that the employee, faced with a choice between dismissal and a less than perfect job, would always go for the former (*Pillinger* v. *Manchester Area Health Authority*, 1979).

Other reasons

There are a number of categories that need mentioning even though there will be no detailed investigation of these cases. First of all, it will automatically be *unfair* if the reason (or principal reason) for dismissal relates to actual or proposed membership of an independent trade union or to taking part in activities of an independent union at an appropriate time; this is either outside working hours (which makes lunch and tea breaks an appropriate time) or during working hours, with the permission of management. Secondly, it is *unfair* to dismiss on the grounds of race or sex. Thirdly, it is *unfair* to dismiss an employee because of pregnancy or a reason connected with it unless the employee is either incapable of doing the work or, by so doing, automatically breaks another law. In this case, an employee should be given the chance of another job if there is a suitable alternative vacancy. Finally, the tribunals are not able to hear a case when strikers are dismissed unless one or more of the strikers has not been dismissed or has been offered re-engagement whereas the individual concerned has not. In other words, it is automatically *fair* (as we saw in Chapter 7) to dismiss strikers provided they are all dismissed during, and not after, the strike. Again, it should be borne in mind that these are merely *indicative* of the types of reasons that may result in unfair dismissal; in a complicated case, always make extra effort to check with a personnel or specialist department.

Exclusions

A number of classes of employee are excluded from these provisions and not protected by the dismissals and other employment protection legislation. These are subject to variation but at the present time (1982) they include the following:

1. Those employees not continuously employed for 52 weeks—remember that part of a week counts towards this figure—unless it is for an inadmissable reason such as trade union activities.
2. Above normal retiring age.
3. Husband or wife of the employer.
4. Those normally working outside Great Britain. Recently, however, an airline pilot who was found to be abroad 53 per cent of his time was still adjudged to be employed from his base within the country (*Todd* v. *British Midland Airways*, 1978).
5. Those working less than 16 hours per week unless employed for five years or more and employed for eight hours or more per week continuously. This is important as each week counts and employees who work nine hours one week and seven the next would not be covered even though they average eight hours per week.
6. Those employees working for an employer, employing 20 people or less, will require two years continuous service before they are eligible to claim. This number of 20 includes associated employers as well.
7. A series of other groups such as share fishermen and registered dock workers who have their own scheme.

Disciplinary procedures

One important factor that continually reappears in discussions about dismissal is the need for a well-defined and clear disciplinary procedure, and we shall conclude our examination of this aspect of the law by briefly considering procedures. Some general points will be made about their design and operation, and a typical example will be given in order to show up these points.

The best place to start is with the ACAS Code of Practice; this is only a short five-page booklet that was first issued in 1977. It is not binding in itself but, in the absence of other procedures or badly-designed ones, it can be admissable in evidence to a tribunal that is trying to determine a question of fairness of dismissal. Discipline is seen in a positive way in the code; that is, not just a method of dealing with offences but also, and most importantly, one trying to specify expected standards of conduct from employees. On the question of 'why have disciplinary rules and procedures?', the Code offers the following reasons: 'Rules set standards of conduct at work; procedure helps to ensure that the standards are adhered to and also provides a fair method of dealing with alleged failures to observe them' (para. 2). The responsibility for drawing up rules and procedures rests with management initially but, in order to be effective, these need to be operated with the agreement/acceptance of those covered by them (para 5). Rules should be readily available to employees, management should make every effort to ensure that employees know and understand them and are also aware of the consequences of breaking them. Although the exact nature of these aspects are bound to vary from one workplace to another, rules 'should not be so general as to be meaningless' (paras 6–8). In para. 10, 11 key points are made about procedure, specifying that, for example, they should be in writing, provide for matters to be dealt with quickly by specified authorized levels of management, allow representation for employees, appeals, and an opportunity to state their case. From then on, the Code deals with operating the procedure in very much the same way as we have done above—although, obviously, in less detail—and deals with some examples that would be deserving of special consideration (paras 11–15). The importance of appeals, records, and reviews are briefly mentioned in the last few paragraphs (paras 16–20).

Most companies will now have some form of disciplinary procedure, particularly if they are over a certain size, say 50 employees. Clearly, it would not really be either feasible or realistic to expect a small family butcher, for example, with one employee to have concisely-defined and well-formulated rules to deal with discipline; in a case such as this, the tribunal would take into account the amendments under the Employment Act relating to the size and administrative resources of the employer. However, there should now be a clause in every employee's statement of terms and conditions advising them of any disciplinary rules applicable to them and where to go in order to find a copy of relevant procedures. There is considerable variation, though, in the exact format of these procedures even for those organizations that have written them down. To illustrate some of the general points, a typical but fairly rudimentary example is given below. This also shows the way in which disciplinary procedures may be well within their legal 'limits'.

PAPERTHIN DISCIPLINARY PROCEDURES

1. It is the policy of Paperthin to apply these rules as reasonably as possible having regard to the particular circumstances. The rules are designed to ensure that an orderly and consistent manner of conduct is maintained throughout the company.

2. This disciplinary procedure will be used to deal with breaches of the rules (except where the offence is of a particularly serious nature and it is necessary to give an immediate final warning). However, only in cases of gross misconduct will summary dismissal result.

3. Gross misconduct is misconduct of such a nature that justifies the company in no longer tolerating the continued presence of the employee, at the place of work, who committed the offence. The following are examples of gross misconduct although this list is meant to be indicative rather than exhaustive:
   (a) Theft from another employee or the company.
   (b) Malicious damage to company property.
   (c) Physical assault on another employee.
   (d) Drunkenness or working under the influence of illegal drugs.
   (e) Leaving the site without permission.
   (f) Wilful disregard of health and safety rules.

4. *Procedure*:
   (a) The normal action in the first instance of a minor breach of discipline (this is to be taken to include poor performance in the job) is counselling or an informal warning or verbal reprimand from the employee's immediate manager. When a verbal warning is intended to be the first step in the disciplinary procedure, then it should be made clear to the employee concerned.
   (b) A further minor breach of discipline or the committing of a more serious offence will result in a formal written warning. This written warning will include details of the incident and the action to which the employee will be liable for any subsequent breach of discipline.
   (c) Any further misconduct will result in a final warning. This warning will be in writing and contain details of the incident and the action to which the employee will be liable for any subsequent breach of discipline.
   (d) If there is no improvement in the employee's conduct or a further recurrence of a breach of discipline, such action will result in disciplinary action that may be a suspension without pay or dismissal. In such cases dismissal with the appropriate period of notice will normally be given but in cases of gross misconduct, dismissal without a period of notice may be given. Dismissal without notice is only justified when the person cannot be allowed to remain at work in view of what has been done and when the offence is proven without doubt.

5. *Time limits*: warnings for breaches of discipline will be disregarded after six months if no further warning has been received during that time. In the case of a final warning it will remain effective for one year.

6. *Right of representation*: the appropriate union representative may, if the

employee so wishes, be present at any stage of the procedure detailed above.

7. *Right for appeal*: throughout all stages of the disciplinary procedure the employee will have the right of appeal to a level of management not previously involved in the incident. Unless the objection is lodged within five working days from the receipt of the written warning, it will be assumed that the employee accepts the decision.

8. *Records*: in all matters referred to in the foregoing that require a record to be made in writing, such record will include the following distribution:
   (a) To the individual concerned for his retention.
   (b) To the individual concerned for initialling as evidence of receipt after which it will be placed in his personal file held in the personnel/works office. Initialling does not imply acceptance.
   (c) To the appropriate union representative for information.

9. *General*: in all cases of disciplinary action the need to satisfy the test of reasonableness in all the circumstances should be borne in mind and mitigating factors taken into account.

   Periodically, rules and procedures will be reviewed centrally in the light of any developments in legislation or industrial relations practice and if necessary revised in order to ensure their continuing relevance and effectiveness. Any amendments and additional rules will be introduced only after reasonable notice and after union representatives have been informed.

   Each new employee will receive a copy of the company disciplinary rules that set out the standards of conduct that are expected, and it is in everyone's interest that these rules are read and understood.

Hopefully, we have been able to demonstrate throughout this chapter that, despite the increase in the amount of legislation concerning the floor of employment rights over the last 20 years or so, the good manager need have little to fear provided he operates in line with agreed procedures and acts reasonably in the circumstances. More than one chairman of an industrial tribunal has given this advice when asked what is the best way for managers to ensure that any dismissal satisfies the tribunal as fair. Since discipline and conduct are central to the job of managing people, we have concentrated on these aspects of legal intervention in workplace industrial relations. Since 1974, however, many managers have been confronted with another very important piece of legislation, one that operates to differing degrees in different workplaces but the basics of which now affect all of them; that is, health and safety at work, and we shall conclude the chapter by briefly examining the obligations that this places upon the line manager.

Health and safety at work

Prior to the Health and Safety at Work etc. Act (HASAWA), 1974, the law on health and safety reflected piecemeal development to deal with either public concern or union pressure over the course of nearly 200 years. By 1970, in fact, there were approximately 30 different statutes dealing either directly or indirectly with industrial safety, some 500 legal regulations and seven separate inspectorates. This led to a situation, according to the Robens Committee (which reported in 1972 and whose recommendations moulded the subsequent Act) in which there was too much law, that much of it was unsatisfactory and unintelligible, and there was overlapping jurisdiction between those bodies whose task it was to enforce the law. The result of this was that there was a general feeling of apathy in the day-to-day implementation of safety rules (Selwyn, 1975, p. 163). Moreover, the TUC estimated that about eight million people were not covered by any health and safety legislation at all prior to 1974, when they were brought under the umbrella of HASAWA. The 'new entrants' covered occupations such as teaching, medicine, prison workers, postmen, and some parts of the transport industry to name but a few. In addition, HASAWA could also apply to non-employees in certain circumstances as well as to employers in their capacity as manufacturers, suppliers, or importers of articles and substances.

The overall aim of HASAWA was 'to promote safety awareness and effective safety organization and performance, by schemes designed to suit the particular industry or organization (Health and Safety Commission (HSC), *The Act Outlined*, p. 2). This was to be done by a variety of means—as we shall see below—but there were at least three overriding intentions; namely, to prevent accidents happening in the first place, to make safety a matter of concern for *everybody* in the workplace, and to require management to take specific responsibility for the provision and maintenance of adequate safety standards. Specific obligations were thus placed upon an employer—or the person with the delegated responsibility for a particular matter. This was to be achieved through three mechanisms; a duty to every employee, a requirement to draw up a safety policy, and a willingness to operate with safety representatives through a safety committee if requested. Each of these will now be considered in turn.

Under HASAWA, it will be the duty of every employer to ensure, so far as is reasonably practicable, the health, safety, and welfare at work of all his employees. This is in relation to five areas:

1. Provision and maintenance of safe and risk–free *plant and systems of work*. This would cover all existing plant and any new introductions, provision for emergency plans, and monitoring of the environment for toxicity levels. Also, it would include, where appropriate, the need for protective clothing and training in its usage.
2. Ensuring the safety, etc., in *use, handling, storage, and transport of articles and substances*. The need here would be for an audit and correct labelling of

containers, particularly those likely to present a health and safety risk, and for the safe storage and transport of dangerous materials.

3. Provision of *information, training, instruction, and supervision*. This area is regarded as particularly important by the HSC. Everyone should be made fully aware of all potential hazards connected with a substance, piece of machinery, the environment, or whatever. Any training given must ensure that everyone is fully aware of the hazards and the potential consequences of hasty or thoughtless actions. Supervisors must also be trained properly since they are essential to the day-to-day observance of standards in the workplace.

4. Maintenance of a *safe workplace* and the provision of *means of entry and exit*. Incorporated in this duty would be the need to ensure buildings were up to standard and any special safety requirements were complied with. In addition, fire exits need to be accessible and clearly marked in line with other requirements of a fire certificate.

5. Provision of a *safe working environment* and adequate *facilities*. This would cover the need to observe regulations on heating, lighting, ventilation or noise, first aid arrangements, as well as adequate toilet and washroom facilities.

In addition to these duties, the employer also has a duty to non-employees whether they be visiting the site or are able to encounter risks due to unguarded machinery even when trespassing on the site; for example, the need to erect adequate fencing to prevent children from even entering a site where there are potential risks. Similarly, any noxious or offensive emissions that may affect the general public in the locality of the establishment need to be dealt with and removed or rendered harmless. Finally, the manufacturer of articles (plant and components such as machinery) and/or substances of any kind needs to take additional care to ensure that they are safe and without risks to health, have been adequately tested, and are accompanied by information or conditions necessary for safe usage.

The above list of duties and obligations is really quite comprehensive but all are modified slightly by the insertion of the phrase 'where this is reasonably practicable'. It may well be practicable to take action since this is 'able to be achieved in the current state of knowledge' but it may not be reasonable to expect an employer to do this. The time, trouble, and expense of taking safety precautions needs to be weighed against the foreseeable risk involved in this area. So, for example, if the risk is slight and the expense is great, the employer will probably not need to take precautions. Conversely, however, 'where the risk is a considerable one, say, one that could cause serious injury or death, it is no answer for an employer to say that his is a struggling company and the cost of putting matters right would be too great' (Rowe, 1980, p. 17). It would be reasonable for the employer to take such steps necessary to keep him in line with the great majority of similar employers and, provided this is done and proper steps have been taken to instruct employees, the employer would probably be seen to have discharged his duties (*Charlton* v. *Forrest Printing Ink*, 1980, IRLR, p. 331).

One way in which to ensure that employers do undertake a comprehensive analysis of their own undertakings is through the requirement to prepare and, as often as necessary, revise a written safety policy that brings matters to the attention of all employees. In their *Notes of Guidance*, the HSC stress that they attach the greatest importance to this requirement of the Act. For each employer it is the blueprint on which his entire health and safety at work policy, organization, and activity are based. It should therefore be drafted clearly so that the entire labour force, management and employed, understands it and knows what its responsibilities are' (Employers' Policy Statements, HSC 6). No explicit model or draft policy statement is given since it is the employer's duty to sit down and think about his own particular safety problems; the exact nature of this document will depend upon the specific circumstances prevailing at each place of work. However, the HSC do issue certain guidelines that are as follows:

1. The general policy statement should be a 'declaration of intent'; if appropriate, more than one formulation may be requested so that sub-groups can interpret policy realistically.
2. It should contain names and addresses of the executive responsible for fulfilling the policy and key individuals/appointments with specifically-defined responsibilities.
3. It should make it clear that the ultimate level of responsibility is that of each and every individual employee.
4. It should specify the organization for safety committees and include a list of people involved, including safety representatives.
5. It should specify the need for training and supervision. It is vital, for example, to spell out the key role of the supervisor and to consider how best to equip him for his responsibilities.
6. It should identify the main hazards and lay down procedures to deal with accidents or dangerous occurrences. These, should they occur, need to be recorded.

What is required is for the legislation to be complied with in the spirit as well as the letter of the law, for the policy to acknowledge that safety takes precedence over expediency, and for every effort to be made to involve all employees in the development and implementation of safe practice (Armstrong, 1977, p. 337).

Employees are to be represented in these matters by safety representatives, appointed by recognized, independent trade unions from among their number. Employers have a duty to consult with these representatives and, if asked for by two or more of them in writing, set up a safety committee. In practice, industries that have traditionally been high risk had such representatives (and sometimes committees) well before 1974; in coal mining, for example, there has been statutory provision for inspection by employees since 1872. The regulations give some guidance on these matters in relation to three areas. First of all, the appointment of safety representatives is the duty of trade unions and not employers. They should normally have at least two years service or experience in a similar industry or workplace, and the number to be appointed should vary in relation to factors such as the size of the workplace, variety of locations, numbers employed, and crucially, the degree and character of any inherent dangers in the workplace.

Secondly, safety representatives have a number of functions to perform that may require assistance from employers. These are as follows:

1. Receipt of information from employers and inspectors.
2. Representation of constituents in consultations with employers and inspectors.
3. Rights to investigate hazards and complaints and inspect the workplace on a regular—usually three-monthly—basis. This may also require reports to be written.
4. Attendance at safety committees.
5. Rights to facilities, such as a filing cabinet and telephone, and clerical assistance.
6. Time off with pay for basic training; it is to be hoped that employers would see this as being in their basic interests as well.

It must be remembered, also, that safety representatives are not liable except under their general duty as an employee.

Finally, we have guidance on the establishment and composition of safety committees. As mentioned above, the employer is obliged to set up a committee if requested, in writing, to do so by at least two safety representatives; this must be completed, after due consultation, not more than three months after the request was made. The guidance notes suggest that the committee should not be of an unwieldy size, should be chaired by a senior manager, should have a balance of managers from different functions and levels (including the safety officer), and should normally include less managers then representatives. It should have a separate entity and not be merged or interposed with other matters. The committee should be seen as a place where experience is 'pooled', and its effectiveness is best achieved by speedy management decisions, effective management action, effective publicity and propaganda, regular meetings, and the involvement of personnel in action items.

Indeed, committees have certainly been established in a large number of workplaces; a recent survey in *Industrial Relations Review and Report* indicated that over 80 per cent of workplaces had a safety committee. Although this varied slightly with size (60 per cent of those with 11 to 25 employees compared with 94 per cent of those with more than 1000) it was interesting to note that 83 per cent of workplaces with less than 10 employees actually had a committee. The very high percentage was not reflected in the number of workplaces where there were safety representatives appointed in accordance with the regulations; for the workplace of 10 or less, just 3 per cent had safety representatives. This percentage increased consistently such that those workplaces of 501 or more, had representatives in over 90 per cent of the cases. Similarly the average number of representatives varied in exactly the same way; for workplaces of 100 or more, we can estimate that there was one representative to approximately 40 or 50 employees. The survey concluded that, in the first year of the new regulations, the percentage of establishments that had safety committees rose from 50 per cent to 81 per cent (February 1981).

In line with the commitment to increasing health and safety *awareness*, HASAWA also places a duty on every employee to:

1. Take reasonable care for their own safety, and that of others, who may be affected by his acts or omissions.
2. Cooperate with other people (employer and inspectors) regarding any duty imposed under the Act.

In addition, no employee shall interfere intentionally or recklessly with any health and safety provisions, such as fire extinguishers, for example. Indeed, employees can be and have been dismissed for breaking safety rules, provided these are serious enough and they have foreknowledge of the likely consequences, or for being unwilling to learn about how to operate new equipment safely.

Conclusions

In this chapter, we have been intent on trying to persuade the manager to operate within a prescribed framewok utilizing a fairly simple approach. To be sure, the law has altered the job of the line manager inasmuch as it has caused him to be more careful in his dealings with employees. It would be wrong, however, to assume from this that the law has swung dramatically in favour of the employee. One has merely to consider the likely recourse of a dismissed employee who, despite being found unfairly dismissed and armed with a tribunal order for reinstatement, still fails to get his job back. Similarly, the employer who takes no notice of safety hazards may find himself outside the law, as may the employer who does not apply an equal opportunities policy. The obligation to take up the issue, though, generally falls upon the employee and it must be reckoned that many either do not know of, or do not wish to take up, their opportunity for independent hearing. However, good industrial relations are more likely to flow from a consistent and clear interpretation of legal enactments; one, that is, that sees the law as a mechanism of last resort, secondary to joint union–management agreements.

These matters, though, relate to cases where the employer and the employees are usually in conflict; what mechanisms have employers used in order to try and promote consensus in the workplace? The answer lies in some form of consultation, participation or involvement, and it is to an examination of this that we now turn.

10. Participation, consultation, and involvement

The involvement of employees in management decision making is a notion that has attracted a considerable amount of support during the seventies and early eighties. Companies have described their own schemes in glowing terms and a mass of publications have resulted from investigations into the topic; often, unfortunately, these have been based more on an anecdotal evidence and philosophizing rather than on detailed research and practical examples. More recently, however, the Institute of Personnel Management and the Department of Employment (DE) have sought to improve on this although, as we shall see below, these too may not explore the problems of participation in sufficient detail nor acknowledge any conflicting expectations from schemes in practice.

As with other chapters, we shall organize our discussion around a number of questions: first of all, why is there (and has there been) an interest in participation and what forms has this taken? Secondly, what do different interest groups expect from participation and to what extent do these conflict with each other? And, finally, what problems has participation (and particularly joint consultation) produced and what can the line manager do to minimize these? We shall begin by describing the various cycles of interest in participation and the current resurgence of joint consultation.

Cycles of interest

According to Ramsay, we are now in the midst of the fourth wave of interest in participation (1977, pp. 481–506). In the late nineteenth and early twentieth century, there was a considerable degree of interest in profit sharing, particularly in the coal and gas industries, by employers who were keen to foster some kind of longer-term employee commitment to their organizations. In a number of cases, there can be little doubt that the 'share' was offered as an inducement not to join unions, since quite a number of the schemes were started in anti-union firms. Interest was maintained in them only so long as the economic climate remained buoyant; at least 50 per cent of the schemes collapsed during a prolonged depression. It could be argued, of course, that such financial participation is, on its own and without any associated joint regulation of management decision making, a very dilute form of industrial democracy indeed.

The second surge of interest occurred during and just after the First World War in the period 1917–1920 with the development of Whitley councils. These were set up in a number of industries and were designed to operate at three different tiers—national, district, and workshop—to enable, among other things, workpeople to have a greater opportunity of participating in the discussion and adjustment of all those aspects of their employment conditions of most concern to them. Although 73 joint industrial councils had been set up by the end of 1921, most of these disappeared over the next 20 years, save for the exception of those in larger and more progressive companies/industries. For example, ICI's original scheme of consultation goes back to 1929 although, like many others of the time, it was partially independent of trade union machinery; it was not until 1973 that the consultative system became formally based upon the steward system.

During the Second World War, we find the beginning of the third wave of interest; joint production committees were set up voluntarily in a number of companies in an effort to stimulate production and reduce conflict. In 1942, following agreements between the TUC and the Ministry of Supply, and in the engineering industry, these received further backing. They continued beyond the war and throughout the rest of the decade; a survey at the end of the forties estimated that about three quarters of companies had maintained some form of joint consultation (Ramsay, 1977, p. 492). Once again, the next 20 years saw many of these fall into disrepute such that, in 1968, a little under one-third of all the companies surveyed by Clarke et al. still maintained a formally constituted consultative body. Larger firms were more likely to have kept them (over 60 per cent of those employing 2000 people or more) as were companies in the chemicals, shipbuilding and food, drink and tobacco sectors (1972, p. 73). The conventional wisdom of the time was that, due to their essentially limited powers, the decline of joint consultative committees would continue in direct proportion to the growth in the influence of shop stewards (McCarthy, 1966, pp. 32–36).

However, the converse has taken place over the past 10 years, not only with the 'revitalization' of consultation but also with broader and more radical developments in participation. Quite a number of reasons have been put forward for this increased interest:

1. The continuing economic and industrial decline of the UK still leads people to believe that participation may provide the answer to these problems.
2. The influence of the EEC either through the likelihood of directives promoting harmonization throughout the community, or through aware-

ness of 'good' economic performance elsewhere being associated with more developed forms of participation.

3. A more positive attitude to participation among senior and influential trade union officials, notably Jack Jones, thoughout the whole of the seventies.

4. The need to meet and harness the rising expectations of workpeople towards their employment prospects and the quality of working life.

5. The need to combat the increasing concentration of power and/or remoteness of senior management in industry, particularly with the growth of conglomerates.

6. An interest in democracy in general (Guest and Knight, 1979, pp. 5–9).

Even though the interest has ranged into a fairly diverse number of options—including job enrichment, briefing groups, value-added payment systems, profit sharing, worker directors, and, even, worker cooperatives and ownership—consultation, in one form or another, is now estimated to operate in a majority of organizations and seems likely to be the most appropriate mechanism used by management and unions over the next few years. A number of surveys towards the end of the seventies illustrate its revitalization, at least in arithmetic terms.

The DE found, in 1976, that approximately 75 per cent of all the companies they surveyed had some type of formally constituted joint consultative committee other than those designed specifically to deal with health and safety aspects of employment. Only a little over half of these, however, were either totally or partially based on union channels; that is, with shop stewards acting as the representatives on these. Of these, 46 per cent were not union-based committees (Hawes and Brookes, 1980, p. 356; Knight, 1979, pp. 35–39). A more recent survey, undertaken in Scotland and using a similar sampling technique, revealed similar levels of activity (Cressey et al., 1981, pp. 117–124).

In addition, part of the Warwick University survey, undertaken in 1978, and based on 970 establishments in the manufacturing sector, found 61.8 per cent of these companies to have some form of consultative committee. Certain industries had a high percentage of committees; namely, coal and petroleum products, vehicles, and shipbuilding to name a few. Conversely, those industries less likely to have committees were leather trades, textiles, clothing and footwear, and paper and printing; even so, there were still a sizeable minority of companies in these industries that did have committees. What is an even more significant finding from the survey, however, was that over half of these committees were introduced between 1973 and 1978 (Beaumont and Deaton, 1981, p. 51). Moreover, the authors suggested that joint consultative committees, as well as varying on an industrial basis, were also more likely to be found in circumstances where there was continuous or mass production technology, single employer bargaining, multi-unionism, a low level of industrial action, and in large establishments. They concluded by saying that 'overall, our results suggest that not only are JCCs on the increase in Britain, but they are becoming increasingly heterogeneous in nature, both in terms of the characteristics of the plants where they are established and in terms of their performance as viewed by management (1981, p. 68). Furthermore, consultation has tended to survive, irrespective of short-term trends, in those companies that have had a strong tradition of involvement.

Differing expectations

The concept of participation, however, means different things to different people even in situations where a strong tradition exists. Consultation, for example, may satisfy the expectations of differing groups and they may not even be aware of what the other parties really achieve from the system. Not surprisingly, managers, stewards, and 'ordinary' employees vary in terms of the *degree* of participation they want, the *subject matter* that they consider appropriate for discussion, or the *form* that participation should ideally take as well as in their assessment of the objectives for participation.

In order to illustrate these disparities, evidence will be drawn from a number of studies, several of which have been carried out by the author.[1] Management, as a group (and this would include foremen), tends to see the appropriate *degree* of participation as being little more than the passage of information or consultation over certain issues; the prerogative to make the decision, it is felt, should rest firmly with management. Shop stewards, on the other hand, see it as being more than this; consultation and information is a useful base from which to open the door to greater influence over decision making. Over most issues, they desire more joint regulation than management is prepared to accept. The shop floor, in general, tends to come in between its representatives on the one hand and its supervisors on the other. Greater involvement is wanted on a fairly limited range of issues particularly those 'close' to their own jobs. While they, themselves, are not particularly interested in a greater say at departmental or factory level, they do want their representatives to become more involved at higher levels in the organization, if for no other reason than to act as custodians of their interest and to ensure management accountability. They are not committed, in the present context, to any radical alternative system of decision making but to ensuring that management takes adequate notice of their views and worries. As we can see, even though there is broad agreement about the value of participation as a generally favourable approach to management, there are disparities over the *exact* meaning of such a concept to the different interest groups.

In a similar vein, there is some difference in the type of *subject matter* that the various groups see as relevant for participation; managers, for example,

1. See, for example, Holter (1965), Ramsay (1976), Wall and Lischeron (1977), Brannen *et al.* (1976), Clegg *et al.* (1979), Marchington and Loveridge (1979), Knight (1979), Marchington (1980, 1981), and Marchington and Armstrong (1981a).

seem to believe quite firmly that 'local' matters, ones over which the shop floor is likely to possess some specific expertise, are best for participation or consultation. However, along with this would often come the complaint of meetings dengenerating into discussions about trivia. Stewards, on the other hand, are often aware—once they have become used to attending meetings with management—that they are *denied* access to many more decisions or problems than to which they are actually allowed access. Consequently, they value meetings not only to deal with departmental issues but also those of a more strategic nature; the presentation of 'alternative' plans for company strategy have become more common over the last few years as stewards have fought to resist management plans by producing arguments to justify different solutions. The ordinary shop floor employee is also seen to be relatively disinterested in issues of a company-wide nature, preferring to leave this to his representative. However, when an issue 'explodes' on the shop floor, it is certainly not unusual to find employees questioning both management strategy and their stewards; this is one of the problems that stewards are always likely to face in maintaining a relationship with their constituents and one of which management needs to be aware—we shall return to this later.

Finally, there is some variation in the form that participation might most adequately take; as we mentioned above, joint consultation seems to be pretty-well liked by each of the different interest groups and, in the Kitchenco study undertaken by the author, this was the most acceptable form from a list including profit sharing, information disclosure, collective bargaining, worker directors, and worker ownership (1980, p. 106). Managers (including foremen) also favour the 'softer' forms of participation (direct participation, disclosure of information, and profit sharing), whereas stewards were keenest of all on committees with some joint decision making powers. None of the interest groups thought much about worker directors or worker ownership; perhaps these are seen as being so unlikely that they are not even considered as a possibility. Ursell *et al.* produce very similar results with regard to these more 'radical' forms of participation (1979).

We seem to have a situation, therefore, that is capable of interpretation at a number of levels. First of all, it is rare to find many absolute dissenters from the idea that participation is a good thing in principle. In a similar vein, there is broad agreement about the potential value of certain institutions for participation; this does not mean that they are uncritically valued but that, often, forms such as joint consultation are criticized in terms of *mechanics* rather than on *principle*. Thirdly, we can see that what managements appear to regard as the maximum acceptable to them (and would often prefer 'softer' forms of participation), the stewards seem to regard as the minimum basis upon which to build up their influence over a wider range of issues and with more joint decision making. Many stewards appear to accept consultation with fairly limited objectives provided that they know this is the case.

Information, for example, is gladly accepted but is seen to be of assistance for bargaining purposes in another arena. Finally, stewards may accept management-initiated forms of participation in a pragmatic manner, seeing them as the best possible compromise achievable in practice.

There is a danger that managements, drawing upon a broad consensus of opinion favourable to the concept of participation, may assume that *their* definitions and *their* solutions are acceptable to the different interest groups. While is is common to find stewards, for example, sharing certain broad management objectives—such as greater efficiency and productivity, improved cooperation, reduced conflict and a willingness to accept change—their methods for achieving these may be at odds with those of management. For example, efficiency and effectiveness look somewhat different from the shop floor than they do from the boardroom. Similarly, easing the process of change means quite a different thing if it is *your* job that is being changed. In other words, consensus may exist at one level while conflict is likely at another (Marchington, 1981, pp. 38–41).

We can see a similar process at work in relation to communicating information to the shop floor; Ostell and his colleagues were invited into a large chemical company, well known for its consultative structure, in order to help management put across some important business information to its employees. There were three objectives behind this communication; firstly, to *inform* employees of the basic facts. Secondly, to *educate* employees as to how the external environment actually affected the works, and, thirdly to motivate people to *change attitudes* and modify behaviour on the basis of this information. After following up the communication exercise some four to six weeks later, the authors concluded that, while the company had managed to get across the information, little else had been achieved. Their conclusion, which is just as relevant to consultation as to communication, was that management had failed to communicate successfully because it had not taken into account 'the interests and objectives of employees as well as their own objectives' (1980, p. 47).

The reason for reiterating this point about differing objectives is simple; it is unusual to find, either in interviews or in publications by managers or management bodies, that due account has been taken of alternative definitions of participation or objectives for its success. Consequently, there is a danger that managers become tied up with the *mechanics* of schemes without giving due consideration to the philosophy or assumptions behind them. Derek Williams (of Cadbury Schweppes) is clear on this issue when he states that 'a clear philosophical or thinking base for participation which has been talked through in the company is more important than any formal structure which may ultimately emerge' (1979, p. 193).

Because of this, it makes little sense to implant schemes from elsewhere without taking due account of current attitudes at a company or traditions in the field of employee relations. It may be impracticable to try to 'accelerate' the development of consultation (or whatever form of participation) without both sides learning to live with the structure and coming to terms with the problems it produces. We shall now devote the remainder of the chapter to an examination of the potential problems that may confront the line manager.

Problems and opportunities

This can be organized into three areas; first of all, we shall look at the problems facing managers themselves in terms of prerogatives, commitment, and skills. Secondly, we shall focus the problems that stewards face when trying to operate within consultative schemes and liaise with their constituents; clearly, these are tied in with the desire of management to achieve successful consultation. Finally, we shall examine the nature of the consultative meetings themselves.

Management

Perhaps one of the most pressing concerns influencing the line manager working in a 'participative' company is the way in which employee involvement will affect his decision making prerogatives. This can be seen in two different ways; firstly, management may reassert its own professional or technical ability to be the sole decider of an issue. This is often illustrated by reference to its 'objectivity' in decision making, something which, it is felt, stewards or their constituents would be unlikely to possess. Moreover, the linking of management with concepts of professionalism serves a particularly useful legitimatory function; indeed, as we saw in Chapter 3, managerial prerogatives can be well defended by persuading others of one's superiority in a specific situation. But, there is also a second strand to the reasoning, and this relates a defensive demonstration of the inability of stewards to make adequate or realistic decisions; this was a common complaint at Kitchenco, and elsewhere since then, when it was argued that the representatives were just not good enough to do the job, were out of touch with their constituents or lacked appropriate education or training to become intimately involved in decision making. Support for this feeling was drawn from experiences in consultative meetings in which the stewards had failed to immediately 'grasp' a point put across to them by management; on a number of occasions, however, the point had already been debated in management meetings for a period of time and, consequently, it was hardly surprising that the stewards—on their first exposure to the issue—would fail to comprehend its significance to the same degree as management. Furthermore, they were wary of committing themselves on an issue without thinking through its potential implications.

Overall, then, assuming that managements do actually *want* to participate, they need to be aware of a likely change in the nature of managerial authority; their approach to decision making may be amended without them automatically losing control. This is considerably harder for foremen or more junior levels of management who may see little advantage in working in an organization where, in their eyes, senior management continually appears to 'pamper' the stewards and forget about them (see Chapter 6). Despite the increased effort that a participative environment undoubtedly requires of line management, it is regularly argued that the latter must be prepared to act openly and not regard participation as 'another challenge to managerial rights that should be opposed, deflected, or met with minimum action. . . . The alternative is to identify the pressures for more participation and use them as sources of energy for change, to view them as opportunities to take a positive step to establish a new set of working relationships at all levels of the organization' (Guest and Knight, 1979, p. 313). Hopefully, according to Williams, 'the public examination and debate to which decisions are exposed increases the sharpness of decision making, and employees have greater faith in decisions if they feel that their representatives have had the opportunity to put their views' (1979, p. 201). In other words, participation may not only improve the quality of a decision but also its chances of successful implementation on the shop floor.

Leading on from this, an essential ingredient for success is the commitment of line management to the system; a commitment that it is not only positively felt but is also *seen* to be believed in by the stewards or other observers. In our recent research, it is apparent that, even within the same factory, different managers—using exactly the same mechanism for participation—have been responsible for very different forms of participation in practice. While a good committee structure is important, this is totally insufficient if individual managers are not committed to its success. Responding to this, it will hardly be surprising if stewards and their members treat the system with little more than indifference and define it as 'little more than a management farce'.

Even if managers are committed to the concept, they still require time to be trained in the skills elements of operating a system of joint consultation in an effective way; they need to be aware of the way in which to chair meetings so as to generate involvement yet also keep to the agenda, to draw out suggestions or explore fears while, at the same time, ensuring these contributions are relevant to the subject matter under discussion. They also need to be aware of the way in which to present information, either verbally or with the assistance of visual aids, so as to get their point across to the audience; written material may also be appropriate. One of the crucial advantages of consultation to both managers and stewards is the way in which it may enable them to convey information to the other party or to hear their ideas; in many ways, it may be a useful arena in which to structure the expectations of the other party before they have made up their mind about a particular issue (Marchington and Armstrong, 1981b, p. 13).

Conversely, management may, consciously or subconsciously, adopt a strategy for non-consultation. In an interesting and presumably satirical piece of work, Saunders has outlined a useful method for this, labelled I DOCTOR, that represents the seven basic means of appearing to consult without actually doing so. For example, there can be inappropriate documentation—too much, too little, or too late—or there can be confusion by an untamed expert. Similarly, meetings can be timed such that there is little opportunity to explore an issue—say, at 3.30 on a Friday afternoon (1977, p. 33). Once again, assuming that management actually does want the system to work, it needs to be aware of the way in which its approach may be perceived by employees and their representatives.

At Kitchenco, most of the managers (and stewards for that matter) characterized their approach as 'selling'; this may be important up to a point, but it depends upon the objective of the meeting as well; it is unlikely that much in the way of valuable contributions will emanate from the representatives/stewards if they feel that their opinion is not really wanted or is usually dismissed without what they feel to be a serious examination. Furthermore, commitment may be reduced, rather than increased, if representatives feel they are only being informed of changes or decisions *after* the event rather than before it. In the majority of the committees observed by the author, the personal power (charisma?) of the chairman has been such that he has usually succeeded in getting the decision he originally wanted; again, this may be a key facet of good chairmanship but it may also lead to alienated and uncommitted representatives who see little point in trying to put forward new ideas.

Managers need, therefore, to be aware of the effect that participation schemes may have upon their jobs and of the way in which their actions may be interpreted by others. Participation certainly requires a more 'open' style of management, one of operating by consent rather than coercion. To be successful, it also requires line management commitment; that this is lacking is a common criticism by stewards. And, above all else, it requires certain skills that may not be consistent with those required by managers in other areas of the business.

Stewards
Within this framework, managers also need to be aware of the potential problems that may confront shop stewards operating under participative arrangements; in addition to stewards feeling that management does not want or is unwilling to involve them realistically, they may also experience problems in relation to their own expertise or the expectations of their constituents.[2] Basically, we can examine this in relation to three different areas. Firstly, stewards may feel that they do not possess the necessary expertise or experience to enable them to contribute to consultative meetings while remaining firmly in line with their constituents; they may experience problems coping with the social situation of top-level meetings. Certainly, this was an oft-repeated fear from new representatives attending their first works council

2. These issues have been more fully explored in Marchington and Armstrong (1981a).

meeting at Kitchenco and, at a somewhat different level, for the British Steel worker directors observed by Brannen and his colleagues; the norms of boardroom or council behaviour needed to be learned by the representatives, and Brannen *et al*. even talk of them being socialized into the dominant norms of the boardroom (1976, pp. 176–177). Similarly, they may not feel they have the technical expertise to either understand or, if necessary, counter arguments put forward by management. Stewards attending courses run by Schuller and Henderson suggested that the most appropriate topics for inclusion in an advanced course were the following: how to interpret company reports, investment, or planning decisions; implications of industrial democracy for union organization and strategy *vis-à-vis* multi-national companies; manning levels and recruitment; economic democracy; and, crucially for the purpose of this section, communication skills (1980, p. 55). It was felt that the overall objective for the training of worker representatives should be the development of capacities and approaches that are 'critical though not necessarily hostile, independent though not necessarily conflictual; positive though not necessarily co-operative; and longer term but still related to the practical issues' (1980, p. 53). In this context, the role of the TUC in training shop stewards is clearly crucial.

Secondly, and particularly if they sit on top-level committees that involve them in travelling around different sites, stewards are concerned about losing touch with the membership and, because of this, representing them less effectively. The stewards' day-to-day job of resolving fairly minor and localized issues could become secondary to listening to company-wide proposals or sitting on specialized technical sub-committees. Moreover, there is the added danger that they and other similar stewards could begin to constitute an elite within the company and so create the potential for 'unofficial-unofficial' breakaway groups on the shop floor.

Finally, one of the most-quoted problems likely to confront stewards who sit on management committees of any kind is that of *role-conflict*. In other words, which hat to wear when sitting on bodies such as this; that of the members or of management? For many stewards, this problem has not been as great as might be expected since they feel that to avoid participation (and the information that this provides them with) would be to do more of a disservice to their constituents. The role of the steward, like many others, is bound to create a set of conflicting pressures and, rather than avoid them, these have to be confronted and coped with as best as possible.

Management can help the stewards overcome these problems by ensuring that they are given the necessary facilities to keep the channels open between themselves and their constituents, and by respecting their obligations to their members. It is no good to an organization committed to consultation to find that the stewards are unable to represent their members or report back to them, or that the stewards are resentful of perceived managerial opposition to their role. One problem area common to both managers and stewards is the level of shop floor interest in consultative machinery; a number of surveys have revealed a relatively limited desire, on the part of the 'ordinary' employee, for any great involvement in managerial decision making, particularly at establishment level. It would be realistic to expect the greatest interest for the average employee rests upon decisions of obvious relevance to his place of work and that it is preferable to leave any higher-level involvement to his representative. Consequently, it may be inappropriate to expect high interest in joint consultation—of an indirect nature and at higher levels in the company. If consultation serves to prevent dissatisfaction, or is correlated with low levels of industrial action, it may have served its purpose in relation to the rank and file. Moreover, informal consultation or briefing groups may be the best way to ensure involvement at shop floor level.

The mechanics of consultative meetings

We also need to mention the importance of organizing the work of consultative committees so as to reduce or remove some of the barriers that may inhibit their operation. Relevant in this context would be the skills training that was mentioned above. There are other important factors as well, however, and Nicholson has argued that attention needs to be given to eight different areas that can help committees undertake useful work. The following elements should be considered: constitution and powers of the committees; the setting, timing, and arrangements for operation; composition of the committee—who to include or exclude; chairmanship; agenda; controlling the quality of discussion; minutes; outcomes of the meeting and feedback (1978, pp. 42–46). In addition, consideration needs to be given to the provision of an 'action plan' to identify the appropriate manager who will deal with an issue, the possibility of setting jointly agreed agendas, and having a system of joint chairmanship with the senior steward taking the chair every alternate meeting. Also, a policy of allowing time and facilities for a joint shop stewards' pre-meeting can certainly affect not only the quantity of steward involvement in the consultative committee but also the quality of contributions. For example, in one company we have investigated in the plastics industry, the stewards have a well-organized multi-union pre-meeting that helps them to decide upon the key issues to be explored when they meet management and on the way in which they should do it. This appears to work to the satisfaction of both stewards and managers in this particular company.

It is important to consider the potential problems that participation may produce if only to cause managers to examine their own position and consider how this equates with those of other interest groups. It is unlikely that no problems exist, even in an organization with 'successful' participation, and an awareness of these potential sources of conflict may help the manager to confront them in a realistic manner.

Conclusions

Over the years, there have been a number of checklists produced so as to help companies introduce consultation or participation with a greater likelihood of success. For example, the Institute of Personnel Management's series referred to earlier rests upon a number of key considerations/principles that should form the basis of any carefully considered and comprehensive programme (Buckingham, 1980, pp. 38–39). However, there is a danger in becoming too obsessed with the *mechanics* of schemes to the neglect of the much more crucial *attitudinal* aspects of participation. That is, that management is prepared to adapt its style to make the system work, or that stewards do not feel they are constrained by a need to satisfy their members' traditional goals such that they find it impossible to sit on consultative bodies. The learning process of 'living with consultation' is a crucial element in success and it is arguable that other organizations can—or even should try to—pick up a good system from elsewhere and merely introduce this.

Furthermore, different companies operate under very different environmental circumstances and what is good for one may not necessarily be appropriate for another. Competing in different types of market may influence the potential for participation as too may different types of technology or different patterns of ownership. Because of these environmental characteristics, different methods of management decision making may be seen as more or less appropriate to the circumstances. In other words, with participation—as with industrial relations as a whole—we need to consider the external pressures that may confront managements and see the influence that these may have upon the system. This is the subject of the penultimate chapter.

11. A contingency framework for industrial relations

Industrial relations does not operate in a vacuum, regardless of factors external to the workplace, and it is important to assess the way in which these external factors—or contingencies—may influence the form and character of relationships on the shop floor. Despite the fact that many managers would argue that all plants or departments are different from each other, thus making any analysis unrealistic to their needs, it would appear that certain factors do exert a significant influence upon workplace industrial relations. In this chapter, we shall discuss those that have the greatest impact upon methods of management decision making and on employee attitudes to work. In other words, we shall outline a framework of factors and assess their effect upon the job of managing on the shop floor. In all, seven factors will be discussed:[1]

1. Product market.
2. Technological environment.
3. Institutional influences external to the plant.
4. Organization structure.
5. History and nature of unionism.
6. Labour context—markets, region, and sex.
7. Organization culture.

There is no assumption that any one factor *determines* the character of the industrial relations that emerges in an organization, nor is one factor to be accorded primacy over any other for an indefinite period of time. What does seem important is the way in which the different actors in the workplace

---

1. This chapter has benefited from a number of sources. Most important of these are Handy (1976), Legge (1977), and Anthony (1977). Also, the author has applied a similar but much shorter list to an analysis of participation in the furniture industry (Marchington, 1980, pp. 115–133).

actually *feel* that these factors influence their behaviour and may serve to use these to legitimize their actions. As mentioned above we shall concentrate particularly on the way in which these factors may influence the style and mode of management decision making that emerges in an organization—and, therefore, the opportunity for employee involvement—and also on the way in which employee attitudes to work may be affected by these.

The framework should enable the line manager to consider industrial relations in his own establishment from a wider perspective and, as such, assist him in carrying out his job. Moverover, it should cause the manager to question whether these environmental contingencies actually do *determine* management responses, or, conversely whether they are merely used to assist in legitimizing current methods of decision making. First, let us look at the nature of the product market.

The product market

The effect of the product market upon industrial relations is probably, along with the technological system, the factor most regularly quoted by practitioners and academics alike whatever the industry to which it refers. It is particularly important as a source of *potential* problems in cases where the situation is one of indeterminacy, although it need not necessarily lead to greater levels of conflict at work. Goodman *et al.* summarize the impact of the product market in the footwear industry in the following way:

> The major features of the product market are the relatively slow growth in total demand, the intensity of competition, the recent dramatic increase in import penetration of the home market, the enhanced importance of fashion, and marked seasonality in the nature and level of demand. All these factors have important implications for industrial relations, perhaps most notably in the frequent changes in both volume and type of production. ... Most firms 'make to order' and consequently flexibility and speed of response are at a premium, particularly in the fashion sectors (1977b, pp. 36–37).

Three factors would seem to be important when analysing the effect of the product market; firstly, one needs to consider the orientation of the market, whether the company is geared to the manufacture of components or parts to an industrial buyer or, conversely, to what extent the product is fashion orientated or not subject to repeat orders. Clearly, the lack of determinacy in a fashion-orientated market is likely to have an effect upon the way in which management feels is best to make decisions and the level at which this decision making takes place. If it is felt that quick responses are needed to the customer, this has implications for shop floor and even junior management involvement. On the other hand, appearance may not matter very much, and the primary influence on customer behaviour may be technical reliability or price. In cases such as this, decision making will probably be totally different with an emphasis, at shop floor level at least, on quality and cost savings. Secondly, companies—even within the same market—are going to vary in the degree of competition that they face from other sources either producing the same product or manufacturing suitable alternatives. Once again, the company that holds a monopoly or is able to dictate movements in the market is in a very different position from one that is susceptible to shifts in the market. The influence of competition on both preferred modes of management decision making and employee attitutdes has been illustrated on many occasions as we shall see below. Finally, it is feasible that the rate of change or variability of the market may have an impact upon workplace relations; for example, a market that is characterized by seasonal trends or one that is subject to unpredictable changes in demand may well have different problems from one that is fairly steady and/or predictable in advance. Indeed, many industries may experience extremely stable industrial relations even though there are strong cyclical or seasonal variations in demand precisely because these are predictable; consequently they may recruit a particular kind of employee, one who approaches employment from a casual perspective.

Two examples from very different industries—and with very different types of employee—show up both the influence of the product market on employee attitudes, and the way in which responses to insecurity reflect individual perceptions of employment. Most reports from the car industry illustrate the way in which the market sets very definite limits upon the extent to which security of employment may be guaranteed in such a competitive and fashion-orientated industry (Beynon, 1973, p. 158; Clack, 1967, p. 94). Consequently, this engenders feelings of insecurity—and an emphasis upon job security and collective reaction to managerial decisions—that have an enormous influence upon industrial relations.

Towards the end of the seventies, however, we saw more subdued responses to this insecurity as employees were more inclined to go along with management for fear of losing their jobs; in 1981, we witnessed a return to collective resistance. Lupton has reported a somewhat different reaction to insecurity by female workers in the garment industry due to their awareness of the 'seasonal deprivations which might throw them out of work altogether. Knowing that their work was highly specialised and that their skills were not easily transferrable, workers tried to make as much money as they could when work was plentiful' (1963, p. 145). In other words, the rational and subjective response to objectively similar product market conditions may be different depending upon the way in which employees assess their situation. Either way, the significance of the product market on employee attitudes cannot be overemphasized.

In a similar vein, managers may respond to the influence of the product market by preferring certain modes of decision making; in the highly competitive, fashion-orientated and relatively unpredictable furniture market of the mid seventies, opportunities for employee involvement were often felt to be inappropriate by line managers interviewed by the author due to the 'need' for quick responses to change. It was felt that, admirable though participation may be in principle, the pressures of the market just did not allow time for joint decision making. In essence, an inner cabinet of managers made decisions, without including the stewards, and these sometimes went against previously-agreed commitments to consultation. Participation *within* management— in certain departments and above a certain level—was of a very high order with little reliance on seniority or formal roles, whereas participation with the shop floor (through its stewards) was relatively low. Again, we can see the influence of the product market on the nature of decision making, and the level at which it takes place. To some extent, management may be powerless in the case of such changes in the economic environment; however, it can also be used as a powerful source of legitimation for non-participation (McCarthy and Ellis, 1973, p. 196; Marchington and Loveridge, 1979, pp. 171–184).

The technological environment

Perhaps one of the most common-place assertions in industrial relations relates to the way in which employee attitudes—and particularly alienation—may be affected by the impact of technology upon the organization of work. Writers and practitioners alike have grappled with the way in which alternative technical design may produce significantly different working conditions and employee attitudes to work; indeed, the attempts by a number of companies, such as United Biscuits or Volvo, in the field of job enrichment are well known. The idea that technology *determines* behaviour or management organization has been criticised on numerous occasions (see, for example, Rose, 1978, p. 201). Bearing this in mind, we can still say with some authority that, while technology does not necessarily determine behaviour, it is certainly an important influence upon employee attitudes—along with the others presented here—due to their reaction to technical organization of work, and on the most appropriate method of decision making chosen by management.

A number of aspects of the technological environment are worthy of mention; firstly, the rate of technical change is likely to have an impact on industrial relations in that worker resistance may be greater the more regular or dramatic the proposed change or the more likely it is to result in de-manning or de-skilling. As we saw in Chapter 2, trade union reaction to technical change varies depending on the industry and the type of change envisaged. Change may offer the opportunity for greater joint decision making if both parties are prepared to cooperate on this front whereas, conversely, it may increase the likelihood of conflict and increased opportunities for shop floor bargaining over piece-rates. Much depends on the management approach to change and the history of previous relations. Secondly, the degree of interdependence in the production system may influence industrial relations; as we saw in Chapter 7, the power capacity of individual groups or departments is affected by their position within the production flow. Moreover, it may well be that, while the technological system provides them with a source of power, it may also inhibit the development of group cohesiveness and identity, and reduce their willingness to take action. This aspect—the third—is evident in many descriptions of work on assembly lines or on individually operated machine-paced jobs. Conversely, the job of a craft worker, such as printing, may offer a considerable degree of variety and individual job control. Recent interviews undertaken by the author, in a variety of industries, have similarly noted the different way in which manual workers in craft occupations—such as fitters—perceive the production system as it influences them from the way in which semi-skilled process workers—often on assembly lines—see the technological environment as it affects them. The former refer to variety, control of quality and quantity, and flexibility; the latter talk in terms of boredom, monotony, and 'switching-off' while at work. Fourthly, the degree of technical complexity of operations has an influence on industrial relations and on preferred modes of management decision making; for example, many operations in the chemical industry are now routinized to the extent that process operators spend most of their time observing control panels. Their busiest times are likely to be when there is a fault on the plant or when they are required to undertake maintenance work. They are not regarded as possessing the available expertise to enable them to understand the complexities of chemical reactions, an attribute that may not be possessed by their foremen either. Finally, the technology—and particularly the need for expensive machinery—certainly has an effect upon the cost structure of an enterprise; capital-intensive industries, such as chemicals and oil, can find it easier to pay higher wages since, relatively speaking, they form a smallish part of the overall costs. On the other hand, local authorities pay out a much higher proportion in wages and salaries. This, too, can have an influence on industrial peace.

In other words, the technological system chosen by management will have an influence upon certain aspects of industrial relations. The exact nature of this influence depends again, of course, upon the way in which employees respond to the system and the expectations they have from work. It may well be that, as Goldthorpe and his colleagues discovered from the 'Affluent Luton Workers', seemingly objective deprivations are accepted while at work purely because central life-interests are elsewhere and work does little more than provide a means to that end. We shall return to this later.

Institutional influences external to the plant
There are certain factors that have an influence on all organizations in much the same way; for example, changes in the social and educational climate would be one while, at a different level, so would changes in labour law over the last 10 or 15 years. In this chapter, however, we are more interested in those factors that impinge differentially upon organizations and particularly upon their industrial relations activities. In particular, we are concerned to examine those factors that may limit or facilitate the opportunity for decision

making within individual plants or companies and consequently restrict or widen the scope of workplace industrial relations.

First of all, the scope for influencing industrial relations at workplace level may be limited by the degree of autonomy enjoyed by an individual plant. Most decisions of any significance may be made centrally and individual sub-units may have responsibility for *interpreting* policy alone. This has clear consequences for employee involvement if, for example, joint decision making is confined to relatively 'safe' or non-conflicting issues. Conversely, it may well be that each individual plant or company in a group operates as a separate profit centre and is under little direction from the centre—save for the fact that it must make money!

We can extend this concept, however, a stage further and consider the degree of autonomy that any individual company has within an industry by virtue, say, of being part of an employers' association. There are variations between industries in the extent to which the association tries to influence member companies; some, for example, such as the Engineering Employers' Federation, now exert a fairly loose influence over companies in terms of their industrial relations. The Federation and the Confederation of Ship-building and Engineering Unions (CSEU) negotiate over basic rates of pay, hours of work, holiday entitlements, and so on that, in the case of pay at least, are considerably superseded by those offered by individual com-panies. Some employers' associations may also offer a range of services to their members that may include, for example, representation at industrial tribunals.

Others, such as the system operating in the footwear industry, are considerably more influential. Goodman and his colleagues suggest that a major reason for the relatively dispute-free record of the industry—no postwar year in which more than 10 strikes have been recorded and no national strikes since 1895—has been the role of institutionalization that has remained since its establishment at the turn of the century. They note that 'formal rule-making at company level is infrequent, and is limited mainly to a few large multi-plant companies. The rule-making structure is thus character-ised by considerable reliance on multi-employer agreements, external to each firm, by a relatively clear articulation between levels . . . and a comparatively low level of development of shop floor bargaining within firms' (1977a, p. 189). Both employers and union officials have attempted to, and presumably succeeded in, ensuring that power resides with officials as opposed to lay representatives (1977, p. 198).

Finally, we can also see the way in which a complete industry may find its autonomy limited by virtue of government intervention, either in this country or elsewhere. It has been regularly argued, by trade union officials among others, that the government operates as a ghost at the bargaining table in negotiations over local authority pay; the climate of industrial relations may be significantly affected and the opportunities for joint decision making severely limited by such involvement. Similarly, foreign governments may put limitations on product design, for example, that affect managerial choice.

Organization structure

In this section, we are keen to examine the impact on industrial relations of the way in which management organizes its own activities; in particular, we shall look at two separate but not unrelated factors—size of establishment, and a variety of dimensions of organization structure (Pugh *et al.*, 1968, pp. 65–105).

The influence of size on employee attitudes is one that has intrigued social scientists for years; as we saw in Chapter 8, while it is true that small firms are considerably less likely to experience industrial action than are their counterparts in larger firms, there is still a sizeable majority of larger firms (over 100 employees in size) that are free from recorded strikes in any one year. Similarly, while it is generally suggested that communications tend to be better in smaller organizations—for fairly obvious reasons—this does not necessarily mean that they are automatically poor in large organizations. Indeed, the incentive to communicate and the traditions of a company may ensure that information gets through to the shop floor through a sophisticated network of representation. Moreover, as we shall see below when we examine organization culture, the small owner-manager may not want to disclose information to his employees due to his own ideological standpoint; furthermore he may believe that his employees do not *expect* to receive such information. Also, it would be wrong to see the influence of size on employee attitudes as a one-way linkage; it is likely that certain people *prefer* to work in either small or large organizations and, consequently, bring fairly strongly-held beliefs along with them into the workplace.

We can also discover some mutually reinforcing association between dimensions of organization structure, particularly as they relate to the personnel department, and the character of industrial relations within a company. Turner *et al.* set out to test the proposition that there may be some correlation between the level of industrial conflict and dimensions of structure such as standardization, formalization in the industrial relations role and the provision of facilities for stewards. They concluded by suggesting that, at the very least, there was nothing in their evidence that 'conclusively shows that an increased use of (labour relations) specialists favours industrial harmony' (1977, p. 43). Similarly, Batstone, in posing the question, 'what have personnel managers done for industrial relations?' suggested that their primary influence has been of a procedural nature; in essence, they have encouraged the growth of steward organization, formalized relations with them, and led to a greater centralization of management desision making, particularly in multi-plant companies. By concentrating on the procedural aspects, he argues, they may well have ignored the content or substance of those procedures and, consequently, exacerbated conflict (1980, pp. 36–39). It is always difficult to establish, for any correlation, the direction of causality; for example, it may well be that those organizations that were most prone to industrial action were keenest to appoint labour relations specialists rather than the converse as suggested by Batstone. Furthermore, it is likely that the economic climate changed so significantly over the seventies that an even worse result would have been produced had there been no reform at all. Finally, it could be suggested that all that the formalization and reform of procedures has done is to ensure that grievances and disputes are actually articulated rather than remaining latent or becoming manifest through other means. Whatever the answer, it seems inappropriate to put the blame primarily onto the personnel function.

History and nature of unionism

In earlier chapters, we have outlined the development of trade unionism in this country and examined some of the consequences of that development, particularly in its implications for management. Different unions vary in the amount of scope that they allow for workplace or lay representation; indeed, as we saw above in relation to the footwear industry, authority may be centralized within the union so leaving relatively little to be dealt with at workplace level. In the past, the situation in local government was broadly similar although this changed considerably over the seventies due to reaction against lack of flexibility at local level. In the engineering union, the district committees are particularly crucial in local affairs. Clearly therefore, the scope for steward involvement does vary although, with such a high ratio of members to full-time officers, there is only a limited amount the latter can do. Boraston *et al.* describe situations (in the engineering industry, for example) in which the full time official may only be able to visit a plant once every few years. In others the official may be called in to ratify agreements or regularly deal with issues arising within the plant (1975, pp. 191–192).

But also, as we mentioned above, the majority of large establishments are multi-union in character and this too will have an influence on workplace industrial relations. At one extreme, there may be a number of unions represented at plant or company level that have little or no contact between them. In some, moreover, they may actually refuse to sit down at the negotiating table with each other as sometimes occurs when blue collar or manual unions prefer to remain apart from their white collar counterparts. In others, as we saw in Chapter 5, steward organizations may have developed as a response to the structural problems of multi-union representation and have progressed to the point where most important decisions are taken by lay representatives on a formalized inter-union basis. But multi-unionism, even in well organized industries, may still cause problems for management and membership alike. The recent attempts by the general secretary of the TUC to speed up the merger process in the printing industry is a case in point here; managers need to be aware, however, of the different traditions of the various unions, of the key points in their internal decision making structure, and of their attitudes towards lay representation and inter-union cooperation.

The labour context

We have already laid some emphasis upon the way in which employees perceive their position at work and on their reaction to various factors external to the workplace. While it is clearly important to examine the way in which organizational factors—such as the nature of the product market, the technology, management structure, and so on—may affect employees while they are at work, it is also crucial to identify the expectations they bring with them from outside the workplace, or 'outside the factory gate'; to consider to what extent community traditions may have an impact upon people's behaviour at work, or on the salience of family networks to job expectations. In somewhat contrasting ways, tight close-knit communities are to be found in certain parts of the mining industry, in the docks, in printing, or in shipbuilding whereas, among car workers, it has been more usual to find that there is little contact outside work, and a much more privatized and instrumental attitude to work prevails. Clearly, this kind of experience would hold some significance for workplace industrial relations.

In addition to variations between different occupational groups, we might also expect to find expectations varying on a regional or rural-urban basis. It is common to conceive of Merseyside as an area of high industrial action but, as we saw in Chapter 8, this is not to say that all plants experience strike activity; on the contrary, strike activity tends to be highly concentrated in certain plants. In broad terms, though, attitudes to work and to one's employer vary between different parts of the country. Newby, for example, has examined in a particularly interesting way the position of the agricultural worker in East Anglia and argued that their oft-reported deference may be little more than some form of accommodation to, or quiescence with, their situation of powerlessness and dependence. It has been easier for them to keep themselves to themselves and ignore the possiblity of any overt rebelliousness primarily because their chances of succeeding are so slim (1977, pp. 414–416). With an increasing contact with non-agricultural workers, a growth in the size of farms, and a more significant lead from their union, their response may be somewhat different; it would be wrong to think of deference as some form of universal and enduring attitude but rather as a rational response to their current economic position (1977, pp. 436–437).

In a similar way, differences are often cited between men and women in their attitudes to work, or between different age groups. In general terms, there is much in the argument, for economic reasons, that work may receive a different priority or that attitudes to industrial action may vary between young women, old men, and parents with responsibilities for young children. Once again, however, it would be wrong to assume universal or all-enduring characteristics across any one of these groups.

Organization culture

It is not uncommon, on visiting a company, for people to refer to the culture or 'feel' of the organization and the way in which it pervades its interpersonal relations. In interviews with shop floor employees, for example, respondents often refer to an attachment to the company, to it being 'their' company or the fact that they have no intention of leaving. The length of service of a sizeable proportion of employees extends over a considerable period; in recent research, for example, the average length of service of respondents in one chemical company was almost seventeen years with one 'newcomer' only having eight years service! While these respondents may not have always liked the management line on a particular issue, they did react warmly to the overall philosophy or culture of the company. This seemed to have an important bearing upon their attitudes to work. In other organizations, a somewhat different culture may predominate.

Handy has made an attempt to categorize these different types of culture that may operate in an organization (1976, pp. 176–211); in all, he identifies four different types. First of all, there is the *power* culture that depends on a central power source radiating out from the centre. There is a predominance of individual decision making and a lack of committees, decisions being taken on a balance of influence rather than on procedural grounds. The web of influence emanating from the centre can break, however, if the organization becomes too large. Such a culture, it is suggested, is most likely to be found in small or family-founded firms, perhaps those with owner-managers still in charge. Secondly, he identifies the *role* culture that is characterized by functional specialization, predictability, and decision making governed by logic and rationality. Power depends upon one's position within the organization. The pillars leading to the top of the organization are strong and while this may be beneficial in stable or predictable stituations, it may be slow to react when confronted by change or disaster. This type of culture would be found in stable product market conditions, one in which the organization may be able to control its environment, since it is large and operates with a fairly routine or programmable technology. Similarly, it may attract people with a low tolerance for ambiguity. Thirdly, there is the *task* cuture that is open, based on expert power and geared to responding to the varying demands of the job-in-hand. The idea behind this culture—and the matrix organization is one form of this—is in achieving the best possible fit between the demands and the resources, in being flexible and sensitive to an indeterminate market environment or short product life technology. It may become inappropriate when resources are scarce or markets tighten up and priorities need to be accorded to different departments, groups or projects. While, as we noted above, it may encourage greater consultation and joint decision making *within* management, it may not be able to cope with demands for greater employee involvement. Finally, he describes the *person* culture and this is an unusual one; such a culture exists to serve the individuals within it and provide them with the opportunity of fulfilling their own personal needs. It is not particularly relevant to our discussion.

In addition, cultures may vary within a company, between different functions or establishments, as well as over time. Such shifts may cause problems in the industrial relations sphere especially if a particular method of decision making has become the norm or if employee expectations are not met. For example, the close-knit community spirit that may exist in a small firm can be upset as its size increases and it changes its culture from a power-based one to a role model. Conversely, consultation may be 'overlooked' as a role culture model tries to adapt to cope with increasing instability or indeterminacy by operating a more flexible task-based culture.

One organization that has remained relatively stable over the years, and probably operates according to a role culture, would be ICI. As Gill and his colleagues note, the traditions of the company are deeply embedded (1978, p. 121). It made reforms back in 1889 that were quite radical at the time in relation to hours of work and conditions. It established, through Mondism in 1929, a consultative structure that has survived to the present day, with certain changes, within a broadly comparable framework. After the Second World War, it strengthened its role in collective bargaining, undertook to accord certain representational rights to shop stewards, and clarified its stance to union membership by recommending appropriate unions to its employees (1978, pp. 82–88). In other words, the company established its relationship with manual trade unions at an early stage and incorporated them into the organizational culture that already existed. Its original stance in relation to white collar unions for managers was somewhat different however.

Other organizations have different traditions of course; the influence of the Quaker religion on companies such as Cadbury and Scott Bader have had an impact upon the character of labour relations that has emerged there. In the latter, despite the open structure of the company, the influence of the 'founding-father' is still very apparent in industrial relations terms. Conversely, the culture of the company may not always have been one that engenders good relations with the shop floor; employees may have little faith in the company or its management because of past events or treatment of labour during times of recession or conflict. History may be constantly resurrected and past events reinterpreted in such a way that two organizations, experiencing a very similar objective change, may get completely different reactions from employees by virtue of previous traditions. High trust may well be central to the processes of good industrial relations (Purcell, 1981).

Conclusions

This brief review of the factors likely to influence industrial relations, while helpful in distinguishing between them and in assessing their impact upon the workplace, raises a number of questions. For example, to what extent can managers influence the product market or the technology or, at department level, is there no realistic alternative to their present responses to these factors? Similarly, how is industrial relations likely to develop if different factors imply different managerial solutions? For example, what is likely to happen if the constraints of the product market lead management to put an emphasis on flexibility whereas the traditions of unionism or the regional context work against this? Unfortunately, the answers to such questions are beyond the scope of this book, and also, unlikely to be solved by the current state of knowledge in industrial relations research.

But, this is too negative in that the line manager can do certain things to increase the predictability of his situation. He can attempt to appreciate the way in which external factors influence not only his own perspective but also those of others in the workplace. He can try to achieve a better 'fit' between those factors he can influence and employee expectations from work. This will vary both between levels and between functions. The production engineer, for example, needs to be aware of the influence he can wield by virtue of system design or choice of machinery. Similarly the personnel manager, or line manager with responsibility for personnel matters, may need to give more thought to strategy towards unionization or specialization of the personnel function. Senior line management may like to assess the impact of organizational structure or culture upon employee attitudes and processes of decision making. Leading on from this, the line manager should be provoked, by this analysis, to take a much longer time-perspective with regard to industrial relations. Much of the energy in the subject is spent on fire-fighting, reacting to initiatives from the other party, and in consideration of short-term tactics rather than longer-term strategy. When seen from a military angle, which seems to underlie much industrial relations, tactics may enable the manager to win the battle but lose the war. Far better, it could be argued, to channel one's attention toward a longer-term conception of good industrial relations, one that enables both employers and employees to achieve their respective objectives from work within an agreed framework of joint decision making.

12. Conclusions

The mention of 'what the line manager can do' at the end of the last chapter brings us full circle to the question posed at the beginning of Chapter 1 and of the 'needs' of the line manager articulated towards the end of it. In this concluding chapter, the basic objective is to reassess the case study, described in Chapter 1, in the light of the subsequent analysis. First of all, we shall reiterate the 'needs':

1. To undertake advance planning in industrial relations.
2. To make use of integrative bargaining wherever appropriate.
3. To know more about the company, its objectives, and traditions in the field of employee relations.
4. To know more about the unions with whom the manager will be dealing.
5. To know where to look for information and advice.
6. To be willing to examine one's own attitudes to industrial relations.

It will be recalled that two separate incidents 'sparked-off' the walkout described in the case study; primarily, there was the issue of non-consultation about 'bought-in' parts and, attached to this, was the problem of breakdowns in heating equipment in one department. As we indicated, the line manager conceived of the issue very much in terms of personalities, and his whole approach to this—and other matters—could be characterized as one of a short-term fire-fighting response. While, on a fairly superficial level, he was willing to admit his own biases, he seemed unable to take these into account when dealing with industrial relations issues. Despite this (or perhaps because of it) he was still regarded as one of the more successful managers in the plant and one who made up part of the 'inner cabinet' of key decision takers. How would his approach have differed had he adopted a more proactive and searching approach to industrial relations?

First of all, he would have been more aware of the likelihood of a potential problem; by planning in advance, he may well have taken greater cognisance of the strength of feeling displayed by the stewards—or he would have been more willing to 'look' for potential conflict—at previous meetings, and the strength of their commitment to prior consultation. The steward–member link is a complex one and, as we saw in Chapter 5, it is far too simple to conceive of it in purely personal terms. Secondly, he would have been more aware of the 'integrative' aspects of the bargaining process; that is, been more willing to search for joint solutions in which both parties (management and stewards) were able to emerge from discussions with some 'success' to their credit. As we saw in the case study, the stewards put forward some useful ideas that were advantageous to the company as a whole. Similarly, the objective of the consultative structure was not so much to 'sell' company ideas as to search for potential employee fears and, by taking those into account, gain commitment and cooperation from the shop floor. Acts of 'bad faith' on the part of management are soon characterized as inefficiency and disloyalty on the shop floor. Thirdly, by undertaking some kind of contingency analysis of his own organization, he would have been more able to appreciate the constraints upon management decision making and the effect that variability in the product market and the technological system had upon employee attitudes. In particular, he would have been more sensitive to employee fears about job security and sought to explore these rather than exploit them. Fourthly, had he known more about union structure, he would have known that the response to the strike from 'trusted' employees may have reflected their own dislike of another department/group within the union rather than a realistic assessment of the strength of feeling on the shop floor. Similarly, he would have been able to operate more closely with the union officials or the senior steward, both of whom were keen on a return to work. Fifthly, and crucially, he would have been more aware of where to look for advice; it is a common complaint of personnel officers that they are rarely brought into an issue until after it has flared up. Through a strategy of involving them, and working within agreed procedures, industrial relations may be improved in the long term rather than coped with on an issue-to-issue basis. Finally, if nothing else, it would have enabled him to assess *why* he acted in a particular way. By being aware of his own attitudes and biases, and more aware of other people's, it may be possible to look at industrial relations from a new angle; that is, one that may reduce the likelihood of unpredictable industrial action or conflict on the shop floor. Furthermore, by undertaking an analysis of power, he would be more aware of where and when conflict was most likely to emerge. He may also appreciate the relatively limited formal role that is left for the foreman in modern industrial relations and, rather than blame the foreman for his incompetence or help in creating 'bad' industrial relations, consider what kind of role he may play in the future.

Throughout the book, we have also regularly referred to 'good' industrial relations; this is not necessarily equated with an absence of conflict nor does it imply a willingness always to agree with stewards. For management's part, good industrial relations is inevitably tied in with prior planning, full consideration of the implications of change, full recognition of the part that trade unions and shop stewards can play in management, and a willingness to consult and negotiate, though not necessarily agree, on substantive issues. If these factors help to promote successful, efficient, and productive companies, then they are worthy objectives in their own right. If this book has helped managers to look afresh at their industrial relations, it too will have succeeded.

Bibliography

ADVISORY CONCILIATION AND ARBITRATION SERVICE (1977) *Disciplinary Practice and Procedures in Employment*, HMSO.

ADVISORY CONCILIATION AND ARBITRATION SERVICE (1981) *Annual Report*, HMSO, London.

ANTHONY, P. (1977) *The Conduct of Industrial Relations*, Institute of Personnel Management, London.

ARMSTRONG, K. J., D. BOWERS, and B. BURKITT (1977) 'The measurement of trade union bargaining power', *British Journal of Industrial Relations*, Vol. **15**, no. 1, pp. 91–100.

ARMSTRONG, M. (1977) *A Handbook of Personnel Management Practice*, Kogan Page, London.

ARMSTRONG, P. AND J. GOODMAN (1979) 'Managerial and supervisory custom and practice', *Industrial Relations Journal*, Vol. **10** no. 3, pp. 12–24.

ARSCOTT, P. AND M. ARMSTRONG (1978) *An Employer's Guide to Health and Safety Management*, Kogan Page, London.

ATKINSON, G. (1977) *The Effective Negotiator*, Quest Publications, London.

BACHRACH, P. AND M. BARATZ (1962) 'The two faces of power', *American Political Science Review*, Vol. **56**, pp. 947–952.

BACHRACH, P. and M. BARATZ (1963) 'Decisions and non-decisions', *American Political Science Review*, Vol. **57**, pp. 641–651.

BAIN, G. S. (1972) *The Growth of White-Collar Unionism*, Clarendon Press, Oxford.

BATSTONE, E. (1980) What have personnel managers done for industrial relations?', *Personnel Management*, Vol. **12**, no. 6, pp. 36–39.

BATSTONE, E., I. BORASTON, and S. FRENKEL (1977) *Shop Stewards in Action*, Blackwell, Oxford.

BATSTONE, E., I. BORASTON, and S. FRENKEL (1978) *The Social Organisation of Strikes*, Blackwell, Oxford.

BEAUMONT, P. and D. R. DEATON (1981) 'The extent and determinants of joint consultative arrangements in Britain', *Journal of Management Studies*, Vol. **18**, no. 1, pp. 49–71.

BEYNON, H. (1973) *Working for Ford*, Penguin, Harmondsworth.

BEYNON, H. and H. WAINWRIGHT (1977) *The Workers' Report on Vickers*, Pluto, London.

BLAUNER, R. (1964) *Alienation and Freedom: The Factory Worker and his Industry*, University of Chicago, Chicago.

BORASTON, I., H. CLEGG, and M. RIMMER (1975) *Workplace and Union*, Heinemann, London.

BOWEY, A. (1973) 'The changing status of the supervisor', *British Journal of Industrial Relations*, Vol. **2**, no. 3, pp. 393–414.

BRANNEN, P., E. BATSTONE, D. FATCHETT, and P. WHITE (1976) *The Worker Directors: A Sociology of Participation*, Hutchinson, London.

BROWN, W. (1973) *Piecework Bargaining*, Heinemann, London.

BROWN, W. (1980) *The Structure of Pay Bargaining in Britain*, Industrial relations research unit discussion paper, University of Warwick.

BROWN, W. (ed.) (1981) *The Changing Contours of British Industrial Relations*, Blackwell, Oxford.

BROWN, W. and M. TERRY (23 March 1978) 'The future of collective bargaining', *New Society*.

BROWN, W., R. EBSWORTH, and M. TERRY (1978) 'Factors shaping shop steward organisation in Britain', *British Journal of Industrial Relations*, Vol. **16**, no. 2, pp. 139–159.

BUCHANAN, R. T. (1974) 'Merger waves in British Unionism', *Industrial Relations Journal*, Vol. **5**, no. 2, pp. 37–44.

BUCKINGHAM, G. (1980) 'Participation in practice: The emerging consensus and what to do about it', *Personnel Management*, Vol. **12**, no. 10, pp. 37–40.

CHILD, J. (1969) *British Management Thought*, Allen and Unwin, London.

CHILD, J. (ed.) (1973) *Man and Organisation*, Allen and Unwin, London.

CHILD, J. (1975) *The Industrial Supervisor*, University of Aston working paper series, no. 33.

CHILD, J., S. PEARCE, and L. KING (1980) 'Class perceptions and social identification of industrial supervisors', *Sociology*, Vol. **14**, no. 3, pp. 363–399.

CHINOY, E. (1965) 'Local Union Leadership', in *Studies in Leadership*, A. Gouldner (ed.), Russell & Russell, New York, pp. 157–173.

CLACK, G. (1967) *Industrial Relations in a British Car Factory*, Cambridge University Press.

CLARKE, R., D. FATCHETT, and B. ROBERTS (1972) *Workers Participation in Management in Britain*, Heinemann, London.

CLEGG, C., N. NICHOLSON, G. URSELL, P. BLYTON, and T. WALL (1979) 'Managers attitudes towards industrial democracy', *Industrial Relations Journal*, Vol. **9**, no. 3, pp. 4–17.

CLEGG, H. A. (1976) *Trade Unionism under Collective Bargaining*, Blackwell, Oxford.

CLEGG, H. A. (1979) *The Changing System of Industrial Relations in Great Britain*, Basil Blackwell, Oxford.

CLEGG, S. (1975) *Power, Rule and Domination*, Routledge and Kegan Paul, London.

COMMISSION ON INDUSTRIAL RELATIONS (1973) *The Role of Management in Industrial Relations*, HMSO, London.

COOPER, B. and A. BARTLETT (1976) *Industrial Relations; A Study in Conflict*, Heinemann, London.

CRESSEY, P., J. ELDRIDGE, J. MACINNES, and G. NORRIS (1981) 'Participation prospects: some Scottish evidence, *Employment Gazette,* pp. 117–124, March.

CROZIER, M. (1964) *The Bureaucratic Phenomenon*, Tavistock, London.

CUTHBERT, N. and A. WHITTAKER (1977) 'The rehabilitation of joint consultation: a recent trend in the participation debate', *Personnel Review*, Vol. **6**, no. 2, pp. 31–36.

DAHL, R. E. (1957) 'The concept of power', *Behavioural Science*, Vol. **2**, pp. 201–215.

DANIEL, W. W. (June 1978) 'The effects of the employment protection laws in manufacturing industry', *Employment Gazette*, pp. 658–661.

DEPARTMENT OF EMPLOYMENT (September 1980) 'Large industrial stoppages 1960–79', *Employment Gazette*.

DONOVAN (1968) *Royal Commission on Trade Unions and Employers Associations 1965–1968*, HMSO, London.

DUNKERLEY, D. (1975) *The Foreman: Aspects of Task and Structure*, Routledge and Kegan Paul, London.

EGAN, B. (1977) *Dismissals*, The New Commercial Publishing Co, Ltd, London.

ELLIOT, J. (1978) *Conflict or cooperation: The Growth of Industrial Democracy*, Kogan Page, London.

ENGINEERING EMPLOYERS FEDERATION (May 1979) *Financial Support of Strikers*.

ENGLAND, J. (1979) 'How UCATT revised its rules: an anatomy of organisational change', *British Journal of Industrial Relations*, Vol. **17**, pp. 1–18.

FARNHAM, D. and J. PIMLOTT (1979) *Understanding Industrial Relations*, Cassell, London.

FLANDERS, A. (1970) *Management and Unions*, Faber and Faber, London.

FLANDERS, A. (1974) 'The tradition of voluntarism', *British Journal of Industrial Relations*, Vol. **12**, pp. 352–370.

FLETCHER, C. (1969) 'Men-in-the-middle: a reformulation of the thesis', *Sociological Review*, Vol. **17**, pp. 341–354.

FORES, M., A. SORGE, and P. LAWRENCE (March 1978) 'Germany's front line force', *Management Today*.

Fox, A. (1966) *Industrial Sociology and Industrial Relations*, Royal Commission on Trade Unions and Employers Associations, research paper no. 3, HMSO.

Fox, A. (1973) 'Industrial Relations: A Social Critique of Pluralist Ideology', in *Man and Organisation*, J. Child, (ed.). Allen and Unwin, London, pp. 185–233.

Fox, A. (1974) *Man Mismanagement*, Hutchinson, London.

Friedman, H. and S. Meredeen (1980) *The Dynamics of Industrial Conflict*, Croom Helm, London.

Gallie, D. (1978) *In Search of the New Working Class*, Cambridge University Press.

Gennard, J. (1977) *Financing Strikers*, Macmillan, London.

Gennard, J., S. Dunn and M. Wright (1980) 'The extent of closed shop arrangements in British Industry', *Employment Gazette*, Vol. **88**, pp. 16–22.

Gill, C. (1974) 'Industrial relations in a multi-plant system: some considerations', *Industrial Relations Journal*, Vol. **4**, no. 4, pp. 22–35.

Gill, C. and H. Concannon (1977) 'Developing an explanatory framework for industrial relations policy within the firm', *Industrial Relations Journal*, Vol. **7**, pp. 13–20.

Gill, C., R. Morris, and J. Eaton (1978) *Industrial Relations in the Chemical Industry*, Saxon House, Farnborough.

Goldthorpe, J. H., D. Lockwood, F. Bechofer, and J. Platt (1968) *The Affluent Worker: Industrial Attitudes and Behaviour*, Cambridge University Press.

Goodman, J. and T. G. Whittingham (1976) *Shop Stewards*, Pan.

Goodman, J., E. Armstrong, J. Davies, and A. Wagner (1977a) *Rule-making and Industrial Peace: Industrial Relations in the Footwear Industry*, Croom Helm, London.

Goodman, J., E. Armstrong, J. Davies, and A. Wagner (1977b) 'Focus on footwear: a formula for conflict but a pattern of peace', *Personnel Management*, Vol. **9**, no. 6, pp. 23–27.

Gouldner, A. (1955) *Wildcat Strike*, Routledge and Kegan Paul, London.

Guest, D. and D. Fatchett (1974) *Worker Participation: Individual Control and Performance*, Institute of Personnel Management, London.

Guest, D. and K. Knight (1979) *Putting Participation into Practice*, Gower, Farnborough.

HMSO (1974) *Workplace Industrial Relations Survey*, London.

Handy, C. B. (1976) *Understanding Organizations,* Penguin, Harmondsworth.

Hart, M. (1979) 'Why bosses love the closed shop', *New Society*, 23 February.

Hawes, W. R. and C. C. Brookes (April 1980) 'Change and renew: joint consultation in industry', *Employment Gazette*, pp. 353–360.

HAWKINS, K. (1978) *The Management of Industrial Relations*, Penguin, Harmondsworth.

HAWKINS, K. (1979) *A Handbook of Industrial Relations Practice*, Kogan Page, London.

HEBDEN, J. and G. SHAW (1977) *Pathways to Participation*, Associated Business Press, London.

HEMINGWAY, J. (1979) *Conflict and Democracy: Studies in Trade Union Government*, Oxford University Press.

HICKSON, D. J., C. R. HININGS, C. A. LEE, R. E. SCHNECK, and J. M. PENNINGS, (1971) 'A strategic contingencies theory of intraorganisational power', *Administrative Science Quarterly*, Vol. **16**, pp. 216–229.

HILL, S. (1974) 'Norms, groups and power: The sociology of workplace relations', *British Journal of Industrial Relations*, Vol. **12**, pp. 213–35.

HININGS, C. R., D. J. HICKSON, J. M. PENNINGS, and R. E. SCHNECK (1974) 'Structural conditions of intraorganisational power', *Administrative Science Quarterly*, Vol. **19**, pp. 22–44.

HOLTER, H. (1965) 'Attitudes towards employee participation in company decision making processes', *Human Relations*, Vol. **18**, pp. 297–321.

HUGHES, J. (1967) *Trade Union Structure and Government*, Royal Commission research paper no. 5, part 1, HMSO, London.

HUNT, D. (1977) *Common Sense Industrial Relations*, David and Charles, Newton Abbott.

HUNTER, L. (1980) 'Dispute trends and the shape of strikes to come', *Personnel Management*, Vol. **12**, no. 10.

HYMAN, R. (1972) *Disputes Procedures in Action*, Heinemann, London.

HYMAN, R. (1975) *Industrial Relations: A Marxist Introduction*, Macmillan, London.

HYMAN, R. (1978) 'Pluralism, procedural consensus and industrial relations', *British Journal of Industrial Relations*, Vol. **16**, pp. 16–40.

INGHAM, G. K. (1970) *Size of Industrial Organisation and Worker Behaviour*, Cambridge University Press.

INSTITUTE OF PERSONNEL MANAGEMENT (1976) *Closed Shop Agreements*, IPM, London.

JACKSON, M.P. (1977) *Industrial Relations*, Croom Helm, London.

JENKINS, D. (May 1979) 'The supervisor solution', *Management Today*.

KAHN-FREUND, O. (1969) 'Industrial relations and the law: retrospect and prospect', *British Journal of Industrial Relations*, Vol. **7**, pp. 301–316.

KALIS, P. J. (1978) 'The effectiveness and utility of the disputes committee of the TUC', *British Journal of Industrial Relations*, Vol. **16**, pp. 41–51.

KELLY, J. and N. NICHOLSON (1980) 'Strikes and other forms of industrial action', *Industrial Relations Journal*, Vol. **11**, no. 5, pp. 20–31.

KELWAY, J. (1977) *An Employer's Guide to Fair Dismissal and the Maternity Provisions*, Kogan Page, London.

KNIGHT, I. B. (1979) *Company Organisation and Worker Participation*, HMSO, London.

KUHN, J. (1961) *Bargaining in Grievance Settlement*, Columbia University Press, New York.

LANE, T. and K. ROBERTS (1971) *Strike at Pilkingtons*, Fontana, London.

LEE, D. J. (1979) 'Craft unions and the force of tradition: the case of apprenticeship', *British Journal of Industrial Relations*, Vol. **17**, pp. 34–49.

LEGGE, K. (1977) *Power, Innovation and Problem Solving*, McGraw-Hill, London.

LOVELL, J. (1977) *British Trade Unions, 1875–1933*, Macmillan, London.

LUKES, S. (1974) *Power: A Radical View*, Macmillan, London.

LUPTON, T. (1963) *On the Shop Floor*, Pergamon, London.

MCCARTHY, W. E. J. (1966) *The Role of the Shop Steward in British Industrial Relations*, Royal Commission research paper no. 1, HMSO, London.

MCCARTHY, W. E. J. (ed.) (1972) *Trade Unions*, Penguin, Harmondsworth.

MCCARTHY, W. E. J. and N. ELLIS (1973) *Management by Agreement*, Hutchinson, London.

MCMULLEN, J. (1979) *Rights at Work*, Pluto, London.

MANSFIELD, B. (1980) 'The supervisor's share of job enrichment', *Supervisory Management*, Vol. **31**, no. 3.

MARCHINGTON, M. (1979) 'The issue of union power', *Employee Relations*, Vol. **1**, no. 4, pp. 3–7.

MARCHINGTON, M. (1980) *Responses to Participation at Work*, Gower, Farnborough.

MARCHINGTON, M. (1981) 'Participation: consensus or confusion?', *Personnel Management*, Vol. **13**, no. 4, pp. 38–41.

MARCHINGTON, M. and R. LOVERIDGE (1979) 'Non-participation—the management view?', *Journal of Management Studies*, Vol. **16**, no. 2, pp. 171–184.

MARCHINGTON, M. and R. ARMSTRONG (1981a) 'Employee participation: problems for the Shop Steward?', *Industrial Relations Journal*, Vol. **12**, no. 1, pp. 46–61.

MARCHINGTON, M. and R. ARMSTRONG (1981b) 'A case for consultation', *Employee Relations*, Vol. **3**, no. 2, pp. 10–16.

MARPLES, D. L. (1967) 'Studies of managers—a fresh start', *Journal of Management Studies*, Vol. **4**, pp. 282–299.

MARSH, A. (1966) *Disputes Procedures in British Industry*, Royal Commission research paper no. 2, part 1, HMSO, London.

MARSH, A. (1981) 'Employee relations from Donovan to today', *Personnel Management*, Vol. **13**, no. 6.

MARSH, A.I. and W. E. J. MCCARTHY (1968) *Disputes Procedures in Britain*, Royal Commission research paper, no. 2, part 2, HMSO, London.

MARTIN, R. (1977) *The Sociology of Power*, Routledge and Kegan Paul, London.

MAUDE, B. (1977) 'Why Christie-Tyler lost its foreman', *Supervisory Management*, Vol. **28**, no. 4.

MECHANIC, D. (1962) 'Sources of power of lower participants in complex organisations', *Administrative Science Quarterly*, Vol. **7**, pp. 349–364.

MINTZBERG, H. (1973) *The Nature of Managerial Work*, Harper and Row, New York.

MORTIMER, J. (1981) 'ACAS in a changing climate: a force for good industrial relations?', *Personnel Management*, Vol. **13**, no. 2,

MUSSON, A. E. (1972) *British Trade Unions, 1800–1875*, Macmillan, London.

NAPIER, B. (1980) *Law at Work: Discipline*, Sweet and Maxwell, London.

NEWBY, H. (1977) *The Deferential Worker*, Penguin, Harmondsworth.

NICHOLS, T. and P. ARMSTRONG (1976) *Workers Divided*, Fontana, London.

NICHOLS, T. and H. BEYNON (1977) *Living with Capitalism*, Routledge and Kegan Paul, London.

NICHOLSON, N. (1976) 'The role of the shop steward: an empirical case study', *Industrial Relations Journal*, Vol. **7**, pp. 15–25.

NICHOLSON, N. (November 1978) 'Can consultation work?', *Personnel Management*, Vol. **10**, no. 11.

NICHOLSON, N., G. URSELL, and P. BLYTON (1980) 'Social background, attitudes and behaviour of white collar stewards', *British Journal of Industrial Relations*, Vol. **18**, pp. 231–239.

OSTELL, A., I. MACFARLANE, and A. JACKSON (1980) 'Evaluating the impact of a communication exercise in an industrial works', *Industrial Relations Journal*, Vol. **11**, no. 2, pp. 37–48.

OWEN, T. (1979) *The Manager and Industrial Relations*, Pergamon, London.

PARKIN, F. (1972) *Class Inequality and Political Order*, Paladin, London.

PARTRIDGE, B. (1978) 'The process of leadership on the shop floor', in *Managerial Control and Organisation Democracy*, B. King *et al.* (ed.), Wiley, New York.

PEDLER, M. (1973–4) 'Shop stewards as leaders', *Industrial Relations Journal*, Vol. **4**, no. 4, pp. 43–60.

PELLING, H. (1971) *A History of British Trade Unionism*, Penguin, Harmondsworth.

PITT, G. (1980) 'Individual rights under the new legislation', *Industrial Law Journal*, Vol. **9**, no. 4, pp. 233–242.

POOLE, M. (1975) *Workers Participation in Industry*, Routledge and Kegan Paul, London.

PUGH, D. (ed.) (1971) *Organisation Theory*, Penguin, Harmondsworth.

PUGH, D. S., D. J. HICKSON, C. R. HININGS, and C. TURNER (1968) 'Dimensions of organisation structure', *Administrative Science Quarterly*, Vol. **13**, no. 1, pp. 65–105.

PURCELL, J. (1979) 'Applying control systems to industrial relations', *Journal of Operational Research Society*, Vol. **30**, pp. 1037–1046.

PURCELL, J. (1981) *Good Industrial Relations: Theory and Practice*, Macmillan, London.

PURCELL, J. and R. SMITH (ed.) (1979) *The Control of Work*, Macmillan, London.

PURCELL, J., L. DALGLEISH, J. HARRISON, I. LONSDALE, I. MCCONAGHY, and A. ROBERTSON (1978) 'Power from technology: computer staff and industrial relations', *Personnel Review* Vol. **7**, no. 1, pp. 31–39.

RAMSAY, H. (1975) 'Firms and football teams', *British Journal of Industrial Relations*, Vol. **13**, pp. 396–400.

RAMSAY, H. (1976) 'Participation: the shopfloor view', *British Journal of Industrial Relations*, Vol. **14**, no. 2, pp. 128–141.

RAMSAY, H. (1977) 'Cycles of control: worker participation in sociological and historical perspective', *Sociology*, Vol. **11**, pp. 481–506.

ROBINSON, D. (1979) 'Trade union recognition and the case for goliath', *Personnel Management*, Vol. **11**, no. 8.

ROSE, M. (1978) *Industrial Behaviour*, Penguin, Harmondsworth.

ROWE, P. (1980) *Law at Work: Health and Safety*, Sweet and Maxwell, London.

SAUNDERS, J. (May 1977) 'The non-consulting manager', *Management Today*.

SAYLES, L. R. (1958) *Behaviour of Industrial Work Groups*, Wiley, New York.

SCHEIN, E. H. (1965) *Organisational Psychology*, Prentice-hall, New Jersey.

SCHULLER, T. and S. HENDERSON (1980) 'Worker representation and the articulation of training needs', *Industrial Relations Journal* Vol. **11**, no. 2, pp. 49–57.

SELWYN, H. (1975) *The law of employment*, Butterworth, London.

SHIELDS, P. (1979) 'Putting the future in industrial relations', *Employee Relations*, Vol. **1**, no. 4, pp. 13–16.

SMITH, C., R. CLIFTON, P. MAKEHAM, S. CREIGH, and R. BURN (1978) *Strikes in Britain*, Department of Employment manpower paper no. 15, HMSO.

STEWART, R. (1965) 'The use of diaries to study managers jobs', *Journal of Management Studies*, Vol. **2**, pp. 228–235.

STEWART, R. (1967a) *Managers and Their Jobs*, MacMillan, London.

STEWART, R. (1967b) *The Reality of Management*, Pan, London.

STEWART, R. (1976) *Contrasts in Management*, McGraw-Hill, London.

TAYLOR, R. (1980) *The Fifth Estate*, Pan, London.

TERRY, M. (1977) 'The inevitable growth of informality', *British Journal of Industrial Relations*, Vol. **15**, no. 1, pp. 76–90.

TERRY, M. (1978) *The Emergence of a Lay Elite? Some Recent Changes in Shop Steward Organisation*, Industrial relations research unit discussion paper no. 15, University of Warwick.

THOMSON, A. W. J. and V. V. MURRAY (1976) *Grievance Procedures*, Saxon House, Farnborough.

THURLEY, K. AND H. WIRDENIUS (1975) *Supervision: A Reappraisal*, Heinemann, London.

TRADES UNION CONGRESS (1979) *Employment and Technology*, TUC, London.

TURNER, H. A. (1962) *Trade Union Growth, Structure and Policy*, Allen and Unwin, London.

TURNER, H. A., D. ROBERTS, and G. ROBERTS (1977) *Management Characteristics and Labour Conflict*, Cambridge University Press.

UPEX, R. (1980) *Law at Work: Dismissal*, Sweet and Maxwell, London.

URSELL, G., T. WALL, C. CLEGG, J. LUBBOCK, P. BLYTON, and N. NICHOLSON (1979) *Shop Stewards Attitudes Towards Industrial Democracy*, Medical Research Council, social and applied psychology unit, memo no. 233.

WALL, T. D., and J. A. LISCHERON (1977) *Worker Participation*, McGraw-Hill, London.

WALTON, R. and R. MCKERSIE (1965) *A Behavioural Theory of Labour Negotiations,* McGraw-Hill, New York.

WEDDERBURN, D. and R. CROMPTON (1972) *Workers' attitudes to technical change*, Cambridge University Press.

WEIR, M. and S. MILLS (1975) 'The supervisor as a change catalyst, *Industrial Relations Journal*, Vol. **4,** no. 4, pp. 61–69.

WHITE, C. F. (1981) 'Why won't managers cooperate? Innovation and productivity in engineering', *Industrial Relations Journal*, Vol. **12,** no. 2, pp. 61–71.

WHITE, J. (1975) *Successful Supervision*, McGraw-Hill, London.

WHITEHEAD, K. (1977) *Industrial Relations*, Hodder and Stoughton, London.

WILLIAMS, D. (1979) 'Multi-level participation at Cadbury Schweppes', in *Putting Participation into Practice*, D. Guest and K. Knight (eds), Gower Press, Farnborough.

WILLMAN, P. (1980) Leadership and trade union principles: some problems of management sponsorship and independence', *Industrial Relations Journal*, Vol. **11,** no. 4, pp. 39–49.

WINCH, G. (1980) 'Shop steward tenure and workplace organisation', *Industrial Relations Journal*, Vol. **11,** no. 4, pp. 50–62.

WINKLER, J. T. (1974) 'The ghost at the bargaining table: directors and industrial relations', *British Journal of Industrial Relations,* Vol. **12,** pp. 191–212.

WOOD, S. and K. THURLEY (1977) *An Overview of the Study of Management in British Industrial Relations*, SSRC Conference, Windsor.

WOODWARD, J. (1958) *Management and Technology*, HMSO, London.

WOODWARD, J. (1965) *Industrial Organisation: Theory and Practice*, Oxford University Press.

WOODWARD, J. (1970) *Industrial Organisation: Behaviour and Control,* Oxford University Press.

WORKPLACE INDUSTRIAL RELATIONS (1974) HMSO, London.

Index